P9-CQG-732

late-
life
love

ALSO BY SUSAN GUBAR

Reading and Writing Cancer: How Words Heal

Memoir of a Debulked Woman: Enduring Ovarian Cancer

Judas: A Biography

Lo largo y lo corto del verso Holocausto

Rooms of Our Own

Poetry After Auschwitz: Remembering What One Never Knew

Critical Condition: Feminism at the Turn of the Century

Racechanges: White Skin, Black Face in American Culture

Masterpiece Theatre: An Academic Melodrama
(with Sandra M. Gilbert)

No Man's Land: The Place of the Woman Writer in the Twentieth Century
(with Sandra M. Gilbert)

Volume 1: The War of the Words

Volume 2: Sexchanges

Volume 3: Letters from the Front

The Madwoman in the Attic: The Woman Writer and the Nineteenth-Century Literary Imagination (with Sandra M. Gilbert)

EDITOR:

True Confessions: Feminist Professors Tell Stories Out of School

Feminist Literary Theory and Criticism: A Norton Reader
(with Sandra M. Gilbert)

MotherSongs: Poems for, by, and about Mothers
(with Sandra M. Gilbert and Diana O'Hehir)

English Inside and Out: The Places of Literary Criticism
(with Jonathan Kamholtz)

For Adult Users Only: The Dilemma of Violent Pornography
(with Joan Hoff)

The Norton Anthology of Literature by Women:
The Traditions in English (with Sandra M. Gilbert)

Shakespeare's Sisters: Feminist Essays on Women Poets
(with Sandra M. Gilbert)

SUSAN GUBAR

late-
life
love

A Memoir

W. W. NORTON & COMPANY

Independent Publishers Since 1923

NEW YORK | LONDON

Late-Life Love is a work of nonfiction. Some names
and potentially identifying details have been changed.

Copyright © 2019 by Susan Gubar

All rights reserved
Printed in the United States of America
First Edition

For information about permission to reproduce selections from this book,
write to Permissions, W. W. Norton & Company, Inc.,
500 Fifth Avenue, New York, NY 10110

For information about special discounts for bulk purchases,
please contact W. W. Norton Special Sales
at specialsales@wwnorton.com or 800-233-4830

Manufacturing by Lake Book Manufacturing
Book design by Ellen Cipriano
Production manager: Lauren Abbate

ISBN: 978-0-393-60957-8

W. W. Norton & Company, Inc., 500 Fifth Avenue, New York, N.Y. 10110
www.wwnorton.com

W. W. Norton & Company Ltd., 15 Carlisle Street, London W1D 3BS

1 2 3 4 5 6 7 8 9 0

For other aging lovers,
And with veneration for mine

Why would they want one another,
those two old crocks of habit
up heavy from the stale bed?

—JOHN CIARDI,
"THE AGING LOVERS"

Contents

Part I Fellow Travelers

Part II Grounded

Part III   Vacating the Premises

late-
life
love

PART I

fellow travelers

Thanksgiving

I AM SICK and he is old, but a fierce affection binds us to each other and to this country house, which we will have to leave. When twenty-one years ago we first made our way down its sloping driveway alongside a meadow with massive trees, I called it Pemberley, but Don thought its brick façade and long windows looked more like the cottage in which Jane Austen herself resided. Eventually, because of its address, it became simply the Inverness.

At that time, Don lived in a subdivision, I in town. Both places were saturated with histories we had no wish to escape or negate, but we wanted a home of our own. Neither of us could have afforded the Inverness alone. With enough space to accommodate his two grown daughters and my younger two as well, it represented our new life together. We marveled at our luck when we found it in the spring of 1994. All the peonies were blooming in a side garden near a small red barn, really more of a shed. Built in the sixties, the house had been gutted and redesigned by a businesswoman who never moved in, because she was called away by a job in California. She had been much more competent than we could have been about restoring or constructing the gleaming hardwood floors, the white kitchen cabinets, and the nut-brown screened-in back porch with its skylight.

But now it seems too large for just the two of us. The steps from the second-floor bedroom to the basement hurt Don's knees. I worry that arthritis or his swollen left foot will cause him to stumble while he labors to bring a laundry basket down or up. My weekly job hauling the garbage bin up the driveway all the way to the road gets progressively more taxing, especially in bad weather. Recycling means loading the car with heavy boxes of glass bottles and plastic containers and a long trip to the dump. The rusty garage door creaks; the exterior trim needs painting; the noisy dishwasher should be replaced.

Except for some tall grasses I planted a decade ago, the side garden has gone to ruin. Clogged by weeds, the sliding door of the red shed jammed shut long ago. Given all the trees, a windy day can produce electrical outages, knocking out the furnace, phones, water heater, oven, lights, and (worst of all) the Internet. We feel daunted by leaf-cluttered drains, a rutted driveway, rattling storm windows, successive infestations of mice or ladybugs or wasps.

The house, positioned between a wooded ravine and a rolling field, remains a pastoral retreat from strip malls, grocery and drug stores, restaurants and the noisy hangouts of the students at the university. The only sounds we hear are birds tapping on feeders in the winter, their songs in summer. But Don's driving has recently become erratic—in the pauses that punctuate switching lanes or pulling out onto the highway, the weirdly wide turns, the jerky reverses and forwards needed to repark between the lines. Since being driven by me distresses him, we know we should move into town. Yet we shudder at the thought of a unit in a retirement community, a condo apartment, or a 1950s ranch house in what is euphemistically called a "heritage" neighborhood of unsightly bungalows.

On Thanksgiving in 2014, the Inverness lived up to its promise by hosting family members also arriving to celebrate my seventieth birthday. Three of our daughters, two of their husbands, the brother of one of the husbands, and three of our grandsons stayed at the house. None of us had thought I would make it to the biblical span of three score and ten, since my ovarian cancer diagnosis back in 2008 came with a three- to five-year prognosis. Unexpectedly, an experimental drug in a clinical trial was keeping the disease at bay, and we hoped it would continue working at least for a while. Despite all the treatments, I did not feel seventy—maybe because the current regimen has eased up considerably. When I can ignore physical disabilities and fatigue, my psychic age hovers, as it did before diagnosis, around fifteen.

The commotion turned out to overwhelm Don. Seventeen years older than I, he seemed dazed by the noise, the constant cooking and serving and clearing and cleaning, the antics of the infant, the toddler, and the second-grader. During the party the girls organized for my birthday, I found him sitting by a window in a corner of his study, probably counting the days until peace would descend. His withdrawal contrasted with his usual courtesy to guests. So as the house started to empty out, I went to sleep glad that I had boiled the turkey carcass for the soup I knew he would enjoy after the last stragglers left.

The next morning, I woke to find in the bathroom, next to vials of the trial pills, a little tote from Argentum, a local jewelry store. How like him, I thought: not wanting to make a public display of his gift. Touched, I peeked into the velvet case in the box inside and saw the most beautiful ring. Tiny blue gems glittered within a channel setting. Never before had I received such a lovely present. The modest engagement ring I wore before my first marriage had been financed by my grandmother. Don and I had picked out a thin gold band for our wedding—just one, since he would never wear jewelry. How very unlike him, I thought, to buy something so extravagant and apparently without any consultation. What if it doesn't fit, and how much time would I have to wear it?

I took the small shopping bag down to the kitchen where Don was having breakfast and opened the box more ceremonially: exclaiming over the sapphires, worrying that it might slip from my finger, listening to him admit that he had been unable to sleep after such an audacious purchase, and realizing that the price made him anxious about its falling off and getting lost. I put it back in its velvet case, kissed the white thatch on the darker hair at the back of his head, and took the turkey stock out of the refrigerator, as I considered the sense of an ending that saturates the powerful affections of love in later life.

Are there stories or novels, movies or poems, plays or memoirs about antique lovers, I wondered. Nothing came to mind except images of dirty old men and lewd widows, as if the real lovers throughout the ages were all as youthful as Paris and Helen, Achilles and Patroclus, Romeo and Juliet, or Elizabeth and Darcy. Dorothea's marriage to the dried-up pedant Casaubon becomes a nightmare from which the plot of *Middlemarch* happily delivers her.

Decades of teaching and writing about literature prompted me to riffle through the Rolodex in my brain. Yes, the Wife of Bath lustily seeks a sixth husband in Chaucer's *Canterbury Tales*, but she tells a tale about a young man horrified at being forced to bed a gross hag. Congreve's appropriately named Lady Wishfort personifies the narcissistic delusions of a lascivious has-been. A ghastly amalgam of the expectant bride and decrepitude, Miss Havisham in Dickens's *Great Expectations*—a grotesque caricature of a young lover preserved into old age—presides over a moldering feast in her withered wedding dress, a waxwork skeleton.

Nor are amorous older men exempt from derision. The lecherous old debaucher or repulsive *senex amans* is scorned from antiquity onward or unmasked as impotent. For better or for worse, in mass-market books today the aging couple remains an absence. Despite its title, the best-selling erotic romance *Fifty Shades of Grey* does not depict a bunch of randy retirees.

From classical times onward, Eros was thought to be the youngest of the gods, and his mortal companions were also in the flower of youth. In Plato's *Symposium*, in a conversation about the youthfulness of Eros's cohorts, one speaker argues that "it is the nature of Love to hate old age, and not to come even within range of it." Cupid with his bow and arrow always looks like a cherub, a baby or boy, sometimes with and sometimes without a diaper. He generally takes aim at adolescents and young adults. Seniors are not his presumed targets. So-called senile sexuality—sex beyond the period of procreation—has generally been considered abnormal and sickening. Deemed revolting, it has also been supposed to cause degenerative diseases.

According to the tradition established by Socrates and Plato, the old are viewed as wise and philosophical. According to the tradition handed down by Aristotle, the old remain self-absorbed, caring only about enfeeblement or the past. Both of these antithetical lines of thought typecast seniors as unsexed: they are alleged to have transcended desire or sadly to have lost it. This terrible and terribly influential belief that Eros hates old age seems to be intensified by a lens of ageism that presents people beyond their prime as fearful, garrulous, foolish, solipsistic, or doddering; as useless, isolated, or exploitable—characteristics that crowd out the idea of older people as loving or longing for love. From fifth-century Athens onward, authors have cursed "abhorrent old age, powerless, unsociable, friendless, in which all the worst evils cohabit."

Of course, adoring and adored grandparents abound in literature, as in life, but their love fosters a younger generation. In literature, as in life, curmudgeonly bachelors and eccentric spinsters gain our admiration by disentangling themselves from the messy confusions of sexual longing, though maybe the esteem is for bachelors more than spinsters. (It does continue to seem sinister to me that the Latin word for old woman is *anus*.) But if the desires of the antiquated persist, they are mocked. The first-century poet Martial's verse to "Miss Oldlady" catalogues her "three hairs," "four teeth," "breasts that sag like spiderwebs," and "bony cunt" to conclude in outrage: "you have the gall to want to marry, and madly seek a man / to cuddle up to your ashes. It's as if a piece of marble / suddenly started itching."

Do I seem to be rushing through all this material? Yes, I am. Its message is way too familiar. I'm looking for newfound territory, searching for trail markings on an uncleared path.

Given the mental foibles and physical frailties of older people—"senescence" is the term for the condition of deterioration during aging—later life is generally considered a time when desire for others and sometimes for life itself erodes or should erode. "Love," in the opinion of Montaigne, "is not properly and naturally in its season except in the age nearest to childhood": "The shorter the possession we give to Love," he decides, "the better off we are."

If adolescence presages maturity, senescence portends its end as we, like the solitary King Lear, are told to unburden ourselves to crawl toward death. Even in the nightly TV commercials for Cialis, a drug for erectile dysfunction, older lovers are presented in two equal but separate bathtubs—"'Cuz," my friend Jonathan says, "as you get older, you realize everyone is marooned in their own bathtub"—though the couples in the ads don't look old, we agree.

Yet Don and I cannot be the first or the last partners cherishing each other while all too aware that death will soon us part. Certainly many, if not most, of our contemporaries live alone; and many want to live alone, relish living alone, savoring their solitude. More power to them, I say. However, the desires of older people for love and companionship have been consistently ridiculed or insistently disregarded in painting, drama, poetry, and fiction. "Literature has neglected the old and their emotions," the storyteller Isaac Bashevis Singer believed. "The novelists never told us that in love, as in other matters, the young are just beginners and that the art of loving matures with age and experience."

Is it true that all the novelists have neglected elderly lovers? Singer himself did not, and surely there are other artists aware that the number of older readers must be increasing. The aging couples I know, entranced by the companionability of their relationships, seem freed from the manifold inhibitions challenging the younger lovers I know: fear of pregnancy (or of not getting pregnant), the heavy burdens of responsibility for babies or young children, financial insecurity, and the inexorable demands of taxing professions. If I could track down the poets and novelists, dramatists and filmmakers who neither ignored nor satirized senior couples, what emotions and negotiations would distinguish their characters' lives?

For the past few years, my writing has focused on sickness in literature, but now I would procrastinate over the logistics of moving by seeking old lovers: characters either cultivating their relationships despite the ordeals of aging or finding an exhilarating second chance after a confused or lonely midlife. This endeavor to collect imaginative accounts of the longevity of desire would be my holiday from reading about cancer, the subject of the manuscript I had just completed and sent to my editor. There must be literature about Cupid beaming on or cavorting around maturing or aging couples. If such a tradition exists, what does it tell us about the physical and psychological, the sexual and familial challenges of later-life love?

One myth from Ovid immediately sprang to mind, though I only dimly recalled its outlines. Baucis and Philemon, an elderly couple, welcome two disguised gods into their rustic cottage and are rewarded for their hospitality by being transformed into intertwined trees. There are two such braided trees at the Inverness, down in a gully outside the kitchen door. And at the front door we had planted a dogwood of white flowering and pink flowering branches, grafts growing from a shared trunk. Studying the myth would reveal its deeper significance, I trusted. But I also realized that myths with their luminous metamorphoses provide a different version of reality from novels and testimonies or, for that matter, lyric poems.

Then I managed to lay my hands on a book memorable for an explicit sex scene staged by a sixty-eight-year-old character who had earlier obtained hormonal cream to aid with lubrication since she had not engaged in intercourse for twenty-five years. Daphne Drummond ties up the object of her dreams, a revolted but inebriated middle-aged man, in Jenny Diski's comedy of bad manners *Happily Ever After*. Daphne wants "to reacquaint herself with her desire." Smelling, touching, and tasting his throat, chest, and abdomen reactivate in her "an old channel": "desire ran its familiar route from out-there to in-here."

At the same time, her partner's disgust at her age and his captivity does "a *pas de deux* with desire": "He strained against the bonds that held him in place, no longer in an attempt to escape, but wanting to explore the loose flesh around the neck, to weigh the drooping breasts in the prickling, sweaty palms of his hands, to caress the fallen buttocks and the hanging folds of her belly with his mouth." The thought that "Daphne's body was a time machine" arouses him, for "He didn't fear decay in Daphne when he looked at her and saw what she had been and would be; he was excited by the workings of time that took fresh-faced prettiness as nothing more than raw material for the real face it would become."

Significantly, Daphne Drummond is "the mad woman in the attic" of *Happily Ever After*, which is probably why I recalled her. Ever since Sandra Gilbert and I embarked on our first collaborative project, *The Madwoman in the Attic*, I have been on the lookout for these sorts of figures. Traumatized by horrific childhood abuse—this is a novel obsessed with horrific abuse, let me warn you—Daphne Drummond had withdrawn from the pain of the world to spend two and a half decades engaging in dialogues with God, practicing to become a bag lady at the ripe age of seventy, and plotting to obtain happiness in the "late-flowering love" of a "geriatric courtship," a "whirlwind autumnal romance." She never takes off a black velvet hat, trusting that it will season with dust, damp, and spots of grease from her breakfast, because she deems it an "essential part" of the bag lady "equipment" needed in "her very old age."

That Daphne Drummond's future will include a motor home of her own and the dumping of her lover for the lure of the open road suggests how influential the feminist goal of autonomy has been for creative writers at the end of the twentieth century. Before that ending, though, Daphne thrums with erotic desire. The sadistic sex scene she stages somewhat demoralized me, but wanting to have, hold, and keep another can and often does involve aggression. And surely we are programmed to find the idea of late-life sex unseemly. It is "non-normative"—that's the current academic term.

Instead of setting out with preconceived notions, I want to follow the books and movies wherever they lead so they can surprise me with new insights into the different sorts of loving in which older people like me and Don engage. Jenny Diski's novel gave me hope that I could find earlier and later portrayals of aging women and men less damaged than her madwoman and her madwoman's alcoholic lover, more satisfied with the geriatric courtships of autumnal romance.

Simone de Beauvoir, a real person but also a character, composed a pioneering book on aging that made the idea of later-life love inconceivable. Yet she had a passionate affair in her forties with a man seventeen years younger, and in the last years of her life an intimate relationship with a much younger woman. In later life, Georgia O'Keeffe sustained a close relationship with Juan Hamilton, who was fifty-eight years her junior. Against the objections of his adult children, Frederick Douglass embarked on a late-life second marriage with a white woman some twenty years younger than he. I thought of the interviews of aging couples spliced into *When Harry Met Sally*, their fond pats and reminiscences of how they met, though they remain at the margins of the movie. I considered the growing number of people over fifty who cohabit with an unmarried partner.

In *Love, Again*, the journalist Eve Pell interweaves interviews of fifteen gay and straight couples—who met and mated after they were sixty or older—with her own experience; she argues that "the process of coupling is as intoxicating at 70 as it was at 16." Pell calls late-in-life romances "a lagniappe," a bonus or extra gift. Such romances have played a prominent role in a number of television shows, such as *Last Tango in Halifax*, *River*, *Transparent*, *Grace and Frankie*, and *Downton Abbey*. Millions of viewers trusted that Mrs. Hughes and Carson might make a lasting match. Hope springs eternal for older people trying to find partners.

A dating site called Our Time, serving fifty-plus men and women, is "the third largest paid dating site in America." Roger Angell, a longtime editor at the *New Yorker*, believes that seniors "throng Match.com and OKCupid" because "We oldies yearn daily and hourly for conversation and a renewed domesticity, for company at the movies or while visiting a museum, for someone close by in the car when coming home at night." However, "these feelings in old folks are widely treated like a raunchy secret." Angell clings to few life precepts in his old age, "except perhaps to Walter Cronkite's rules for old men, which he did not deliver over the air: Never trust a fart. Never pass up a drink. Never ignore an erection."

Like Angell's essay, literature and film will provide me not an idealized view but a multifaceted series of perspectives: a sense not of what late-life love should be, but of what it actually entails in a host of quite different circumstances—and a vocabulary to comprehend its distinctive features. Books and movies may establish a tradition that is minor, but living in the slower tempo of later life often evokes a muted, minor key.

Literature has always served me as a guide; however, I do not want to assemble an exhaustive or exhausting archive. Instead,

I will look for honest portraits that clarify the tensions, tussles, and triumphs of my own later-life love affair. And since I am unwilling to limit myself to contemporary fiction and film, I will need to consider the fact that life expectancy varies over historical epochs. At the start of the twentieth century, average life expectancy in the West was not quite fifty years, while at the start of the twenty-first century it reached the late seventies. Stories and novels, poems and plays, memoirs and movies will help guide my efforts to nurture and cherish a partnership that has enriched my existence, and illuminate it as well.

This, then, would become my quest as Don and I decided whether, when, where, or how to move from the Inverness: to see if I could locate works of art that help me draw a multidimensional picture of later-life love—with all its blemishes and disabilities, loyalties and glories. Bibliomemoir: that's the coinage Joyce Carol Oates created to describe the genre I have in mind, the sort of book that combines "criticism and biography and the intimately confessional tone of autobiography." I revere Joyce Carol Oates for her wonderful words, but also because she and her late husband, Raymond Smith, were two of the few people who invited Don and me out to dinner during a lonely year we spent at Princeton. Still, her term does not sound euphonious to my ears, so I am thinking about stories—Don's stories and mine and those spun by creative writers and filmmakers about imagined characters.

The eminent literary historian Harold Bloom, often a curmudgeon about newfangled approaches, believes that the best interpretive reading always involves personal confession: "True criticism recognizes itself as a mode of memoir." He never invited me to dinner when I lectured in New York or New Haven, but then again I never invited him either—though he did come to Indiana half a century ago. Don met him at the tiny airport then in service and Harold said, "They left me alone in Iowa. Don't leave me alone."

When we sat down to eat the turkey noodle soup, I gave Don one end of the wishbone. I cannot remember who cracked the longer prong, but I will never forget the words that followed my request that we reveal our silent wishes to each other.

"I always wish that I will die before you," I confessed.

After a pause Don said, "I always wish that you will get your wish." That made us both laugh.

The next day we went to Argentum, where the jeweler explained that the ring could not be exchanged. It was one of a kind. She would attach a tiny bead on the inside of the band to keep it secure on my finger. But surely we ourselves are not one of a kind.

A Second Chance

PERHAPS I SHOULD have hired a driver to negotiate the snowstorm that beset us on our monthly trip to my oncologist in Indianapolis. With or without glasses, Don and I found our vision blurry and the trip perilous. We chanced it so as not to be inhibited by a stranger, so as to enjoy the quiet intimacy of five hours alone with each other: one and a half hours there, two hours in the hospital, then the return. "Heroic driving," I said, as I always do, when he returned us safely, and then "East west, home's best." After the research nurse emailed to say the blood marker had gone up two points—not a good sign, but it was still well within the normal range—I determined not to tell the kids and instead to use the miserably cold weeks as an excuse to expedite Project Divest. Too much stuff had piled up and much of it had to be discarded, if we wanted to move.

Three or four cartons of books stood stacked on my study floor, filled with sundry novels and Holocaust studies material, but more categories had to be created to cull the huge number of volumes that had accumulated. I would be ruthless and box three shelves devoted to African American studies and four full of the history and literary criticism of feminism. Been there, done that, I thought as I determined to donate them to various centers at Indiana University, for we were still ensconced in the community of the English department from which we had both retired quite a while ago. I would leave some shelves beautifully bare—maybe decorated with photos of grandchildren—and others would house the books accumulating on late-life love.

At one end of a newly emptied shelf, I found *Major Pettigrew's Last Stand*, a library paperback since I was determined not to keep the physical form of what I read, but I still craved the heft of a real book in my hands, type on a page, not pixels on a screen. As in any new venture, I needed to make my way tentatively with whatever was at hand, while I searched for more ambitious and perhaps transcendent works on later-life love. Did they exist . . . would I discover them? I hoped so, but the conventionality of Helen Simonson's novel would be a boon, providing me a glimpse of the traits of the later-life love tradition.

My friend Fran had recommended *Major Pettigrew's Last Stand* and for good reason. Not likely to become a classic, Helen Simonson's light and bright and sparkling comedy of manners nevertheless charms by sounding all the expected chords on a late-life romance involving two or three families in a country village. Because her novel visits many of the issues older couples confront, the interaction of her characters—less abused and abusive than Jenny Diski's—can supply a blueprint of the impediments facing aging lovers as well as some of the tactics they have devised to overcome them.

From the moment Mrs. Ali arrives for the newspaper money and offers the fainting Major Pettigrew a glass of water in a tumbler he had used to soak his partial bridgework, awkward tenderness characterizes their evolving relationship. The sixty-eight-year-old Major—a starchy Englishman devoted to maintaining his dignity and the two Churchill hunting guns handed down by his father— has been weakened by recent news of his brother's death, which reminds him of his wife's death six years earlier. His embarrassment at being seen by Mrs. Ali in his deceased wife's housecoat leads to her confession that she used to wear her dead husband's tweed jacket.

Later-life relationships are born of loss, *Major Pettigrew's Last Stand* suggests: grief at being home alone for both the central characters as well as the added isolation of retirement for him. Mrs. Ali continues in her fifties to keep the grocery shop her husband owned, where she mixes the Major special blends of tea. Widower and widow commiserate over each other's losses at their second meeting outside the shop when, again faint, the Major accepts Mrs. Ali's offer of ginger ale and a lift to his brother's funeral, despite his aversion to being driven by a woman.

Their budding relationship reminds me that it was amid a smog of grief over the dissolution of first marriages that my decades-long friendship with Don blossomed into something else. I periodically ground up meats in a Cuisinart to make a pâté for his ailing wife that I would deliver to his front door. When he had to pick up one of his daughters at the airport, I stayed at his house with Mary-Alice, who looked tiny in her hospital bed and never awakened from what appeared to be more a coma than a sleep. At this same time, in the late 1980s, I had engaged the services of a kindly therapist to help me puzzle over the sorrowful breakup of my marriage. In the midst of one tearful session, she had asked me with some exasperation, "Can't you imagine being with anyone else?" Blowing my nose and wiping my eyes, I paused for a second. "Yes," I admitted, "but he's married."

For this reason, I kept my distance from Don as Mary-Alice began dying. I attended the funeral, but ducked out of the reception afterward as quickly as possible, using the intense heat as an excuse. The thought of the funeral meats furnishing a wedding feast sickened me. Then I concealed our deepening relationship, ashamed that it started so soon after Mary-Alice's death, though she had been incapacitated for years.

Both the Major and Mrs. Ali exhibit the hesitation and embarrassment that Don and I began to feel as we sensed that we might—could it really be happening at our advanced ages?—be wanting to become more than colleagues and friends. The Major especially finds himself tongue-tied. Mrs. Ali relies on their common love of the classics to ask if she could consult him about an author they both admire. When the two manage a tea at his cottage, their affection for Kipling is filtered through very different perspectives: his nostalgia for the patriotic ideals of England and Empire, her wistfulness that her immigrant father's belief in British inclusiveness would not earn him an invitation to the local pub. Coming from such different backgrounds, they nevertheless share an esteem of literature and of Sussex—its gardens, flowers, herbs, and unchanging views.

The stops and starts of cautious late-life lovers distinguish the beginning of such relationships from the opening of the customary story of young lovers who fall for each other instantly. In *A Lover's Discourse*, the French thinker Roland Barthes discusses impulsive young lovers: the "suddenness" of "love at first sight," he explains, "makes me irresponsible, subject to fatality, swept away, ravished." The tempo of later-life love seems less ferocious, more measured. Even in the warmth of conversations assuring the Major and Mrs. Ali that they are becoming more than friends, he stops himself from uttering the word *intimacy*, and instead expresses his satisfaction at their progressing to a "level above mere pleasant acquaintance."

Similarly, when Don was driving me home from a dinner party months after Mary-Alice's death—we were invited together because we were known to be widowed (him), divorced (me), and also good friends—I searched one night for a way to express my delight in his company. It helped to be staring straight ahead into the darkness when I came up with a lame remark—"I like being with you"—which, once spoken, felt astonishingly bold. And it must have been heard that way, too, because it emboldened Don to propose that instead of dropping me off at my house, we stop at a bar off the highway for an after-dinner drink. In the grungy Office Lounge—dark, seedy, empty—I quickened with excitement. He, leaning forward over a sticky table, dapper, alight in the neon signs with soft-spoken interest, but never prying; me, determined not to put coins in the cigarette machine. We talked and talked into the night—about Dickens's best novels, where to get a good bagel, our griefs. The rest is not history but an often derailed romance as we shied away from disclosures that might presume more than they ought.

Fearing ridicule, we guarded ourselves from becoming figures of fun in each other's eyes and in the eyes of our kids or community. The constitutionally decorous Major in Helen Simonson's novel also avoids speaking about personal matters to protect his dignity. Yet he finds himself blurting out words of help to Mrs. Ali in potentially embarrassing circumstances. When a group of church women organize an annual dance around the theme of the Mughal Empire, for example, they snub Mrs. Ali by asking her to stand as "a welcoming goddess" because she is "so quintessentially Indian, or at least quintessentially Pakistani." The Major intervenes by saying that she cannot serve in this capacity since he has asked her to be his guest. It's news to her.

At this point in *Major Pettigrew's Last Stand*, the particular impediments to late-life love pertain to the long history that trails behind each one of us as we age, drawing me into a world unlike my own, which is precisely what we want from fiction. Of course Don and I come from quite different backgrounds. He was raised Catholic in Chicago, I Jewish in New York; he was drafted into the Army just after World War II, whereas I was born at the war's close. But the Major and Mrs. Ali have to deal with nasty cultural stereotypes as well as uncongenial offspring who oppose their alliance when they have the wit to imagine it: the Major's social-climbing son and Mrs. Ali's orthodox nephew.

The effrontery of these young men backfires, persuading the

Major and Mrs. Ali not to be pushed around by relatives. Here resides another distinction between early and later-life love stories. While young lovers must often contend with antagonistic parents, later-life lovers may have to deal with hostile or incredulous adult children who see the match as an outrage, a joke, a threat to prospects of inheritance, or an act of disloyalty to a biological parent. Oldsters look obstinate in stories of young love, but youngsters appear clueless in stories of later-life love. Alongside the officious interventions of relatives, the couple must continue to deal with their own inhibitions. When the Major escorts Mrs. Ali to the annual golf club dance, his kindled desire is dampened by consciousness of his age: "A boy could be forgiven a clumsy attempt to launch a kiss but not, he feared, a man of thinning hair and faded vigor."

Cultural differences come to a crisis at the dance organized around a pageant that disastrously mixes the Mughal Empire (a dynasty that ended in the middle of the eighteenth century) with the service of the Major's father during the genocidal period of Partition in 1947. At this crowded costume party, a circus of outlandish stereotypes greets the couple, to which Mrs. Ali responds first with amusement, then with sarcasm, and finally with a sort of dazed stupor at the inanity of British orientalism. The Major gets a taste of the racism of his neighbors when Mrs. Ali in a Western gown is not recognized by people who have frequented her convenience store for years.

Late-life lovers, according to *Major Pettigrew's Last Stand*, carry the baggage of deeply entrenched loyalties rooted in family histories that can impede a new union. In Simonson's novel, such family histories reflect national hostilities that continue to inflect the ways those conflicts are represented. The party's grotesque travesty of history reaches its peak with a dramatization: a skit about the Major's father, who held off a train of thugs to rescue the wife of a local maharajah. At its climax, the Major's son, playing his grandfather, receives the maharajah's gift of the two Churchill guns. Outraged, the elderly father of the Pakistani caterers begins denouncing the theatrical as an insult to the suffering of his people. In the free-for-all that follows, Mrs. Ali knows that the grievous atrocities of Partition should not be reduced to a dinner show. However, she also sympathizes with the Major's pride in his father's past.

It seems to me that Simonson's lovers are thwarted not only by conflicting national allegiances but also by the absence of intimate friends. My best friend, Fran, had encouraged me during my secret love affair with Don, as did colleagues when they found out about it. We would need a new vocabulary for all the younger people who now install Spotify for one of us or join the other in a walk or escort us to a concert. And by phone, I could always count on my lifelong collaborator Sandra in California: a vital force through thick and thin, more like a sister than a friend. The Major and Mrs. Ali do not benefit from a comparable group, for which Don and I credit our decades spent teaching in the same department and my decades of friendship with the parents of my children's friends.

Though we had decided not to go through the hassles of having a Christmas tree, our friends Judith and Aidan made our Chanukah get-together the occasion for a tree trimming. They encouraged us to pick out a tree, hauled it into the house and onto its stand, brought the broken boxes of decorations up from the basement, and strung the lights while I celebrated by composing four dinner plates of three circles: potato pancakes, sliced roasted beets, rounds of broiled eggplant.

After supper, we played *The Messiah* and put on the ornaments: tiny wooden ducks painted by my girls as a tribute to Donald, Mexican straw figures from his sister, Tweedle Dee and Tweedle Dum as well as Alice herself, red velvet musical instruments, birds with wires on their claws to twist around branches. The little teddy bear wearing a sweater with a Jewish star was placed on the mantle; the menorah already stood on the kitchen counter along with Latke Larry—a chubby cook who sings a doleful song when his foot is squeezed. Plush Santa dogs and penguins that could sing and dance at the push of a paw or a flipper sat in front of the big fireplace in the family room, treasures acquired on Don's trips to the drugstore.

The tree was magical for me, since neither my kids nor I grew up with a living tree in the house. I pleaded to keep it up, but Don had his traditions, one of which was to take it down on New Year's Day. Throughout the subsequent weeks, the place it had occupied looked so empty that I resisted the lure of the blue couch and went upstairs, where a space heater under my desk and a blanket from Fran kept my numb feet from freezing. The comforter and the heater made the study feel like a cozy haven, as did Simonson's novel, for even in its analysis of racism *Major Pettigrew's Last Stand* holds out hope.

What ultimately divides the couple in the novel is the Major's inability to defend Mrs. Ali's difficult position at a club that would never offer membership to her or people like her. She leaves the party alone, determined that the Major should stay to receive his award and that she should relinquish the relationship by leaving town and giving her shop to her nephew, a sacrifice that will require her moving in with her husband's uncongenial family. Apprehensions about retirement, bequest, and inheritance worry later-life lovers more than they do young lovers, for obvious reasons. And in a racist environment, uncongenial family ties can trump elective affinities.

Advice from a friend with the appropriate name of Grace motivates the Major to ride out and rescue Mrs. Ali from her relatives. They consummate their late-life love in a cottage by a lake. Before he gratefully accepts her invitation to make love, the thought of sex predictably produces anxiety, but then it is accompanied by relief and joy. What follows when they return home, where they expect to be reviled by English and Pakistani neighbors, is an unexpected gun fight. I need to consider the significance of that ending, but now I am mulling over the impulses that overcome the couple's long-held loyalties to conflicting national and family ties. People who meet late in their lives have had time to solidify such allegiances: the baggage, or armor, weighs heavily on them.

Part of what pries us loose from the binding allegiances of the past, what lightens the load, is the unexpected and exhilarating sense of getting a second chance. Friendship encourages late-life lovers to put some of those bags, some of that armor, down. Physical attraction, a common awareness of the vulnerabilities and sorrows of aging, the wish to be released from loneliness, a devotion to books and landscapes and conversations about books and landscapes, and a shared sense of alienation from the vulgarities and deluded values of youth: both the Major and Mrs. Ali relish the sort of Old World courtesy I enjoyed when, to my surprise, Don would open the passenger car door so I could get in.

However, not every late-life affair evolves out of friendship, I quickly reminded myself as I plucked another book off a shelf. And not every older person wants a second chance at love and marriage. Some, like Jane Juska back in the 1990s, want a second chance at sexual pleasure. After a bad marriage, divorce, single parenthood, and retirement, Jane Juska put an ad in the *New York Review of Books*: "Before I turn 67—next March—I would like to have a lot of sex with a man I like. If you want to talk first, Trollope works for me." (Quite a few of her correspondents thought that "Trollope" was a code word for "trollop" and meant talking dirty.) Sex for this senior woman involved a number of partners, some of whom became good friends and many of whom star in her popular memoir about the enterprise, *A Round-Heeled Woman*.

Jane Juska did not begin her adventure seeking a husband, but she got the idea of placing the advertisement from a romantic comedy, Eric Rohmer's beautiful movie *Autumn Tale*. Its widowed heroine, Magdali (Marie Rivière), fears that she will never get a second chance at love. At her age, she believes, it is easier to find buried treasure than an available man. Her friend puts an ad in the newspaper and then auditions candidates, while her prospective daughter-in-law decides an older philosopher would be an ideal prospect. All kinds of misunderstandings result as Rohmer enlists our affection for the frizzy-haired Magdali, so we are delighted when the vaguely sleazy philosopher loses out to the quiet man who answered the ad.

That Magdali looks so fetching with her uncontrollable hair makes me reassess the decades I spent straightening mine—with rollers, with all sorts of pastes and potions, with a blow-dryer—and how happy I would be to have any sort of pelt now. Like Simonson's novel, Rohmer's movie offers an autumnal happy ending without denying or diluting the difficulties and uncertainties of later love affairs.

Did Don open the car door for me when we went to look at two prospective houses in town the other day? A house in town would mean nearby neighbors as well as street-side garbage and recycling removal. With a master bedroom and bathroom on the ground floor, both sounded promising. The first, a yellow bungalow built in the 1920s, sported a lovely front porch with a swing, but the rooms that would have been our studies were up a perilous, narrow staircase. The second, on a run-down block of student rentals, was as dark as a crypt inside.

No, I don't think he does open the door for me these days, and yet I feel as if we both continue to show our courtesy to each other on countless occasions in small ways—especially by not forcing each other to do what feels uncongenial. The second chance of a later-life love affair affords an opportunity not to make all the mistakes made in the first love affairs of youth. When it became clear that a very sick grandchild needed help in New York—more precisely, that my younger daughter needed help helping her very sick baby—Don and I immediately made plans for me to travel alone so he would not have to endure the miseries of air travel.

His tendency to be a stick-in-the-mud only intensified through-out his eighties, whereas my propensity to be a gadabout and flib-bertigibbet abated after cancer. In this case, though, I was wanted and had to go.

Agitated about the grandbaby, I welcomed a weekend visit from my friend Dyan, who drove down from Chicago with her guitar. Dyan's presence felt like a godsend. Years ago, I had taught her hand quilting and now, to take my mind off my wor-ries, she encouraged me to start a quilt for the baby, helped select fabrics from my stash, and sang folksongs of her own devising, some about her own late-life love affair with folk music: "But this could be / Last chance that I get / Reinvent me / With a new mind-set. . . ."

The baby's story is not mine to tell, nor is his mother's, but it fueled my urgent need to be with them. In the polar extremity of the worst February I could remember, the giant firs drooped motionless, weighted down by their white mantle. I watched scarlet cardinals, backgrounded by heaps of snow fleecing and flocking and limning every branch of every tree at the Inverness, and prayed that LaGuardia would not shut down and that I could get the monthly blood tests and pills in the Indianapo-lis hospital before boarding the plane. Don knew I had to go; I knew he had to stay.

Signs of Decline

DESPITE FRIGID STORMS, the ten days spent shuttling between my daughter's apartment and the hospital in which her darling baby received care, followed by the trip back home, had taken less of a toll on me than on my husband. Or perhaps I was seeing him through the clear pane of time spent apart. Don's gait was slower and more tentative, but what distressed me was a startled look when I addressed him, a loss of hearing or comprehension that he attributed to massive congestion in his sinuses and then a band of pain around his forehead.

In the midst of my worries about the baby, my fears about Don spiked when he tried to explain why he was packing up magazines and newspapers in the family room.

"They might come," he said.

"Who?"

"You know, the ones who come but maybe not with the snow."

We looked at each other—fast friends since 1973, loving mates since 1990—and knew something was wrong. Could it have been a stroke? Don has always been a master of words, spoken and written. We once attended a small dinner party for Seamus Heaney, who was in town to give a reading. When the name Louis Mac-Neice came up, I asked if anyone knew his verse. Don chanted, "Though you may break the bloody glass" and was thrilled when Seamus Heaney joined in on the next line: "you can't hold up the weather." I quickly realized that Don could not remember the names of the cleaners who arrive twice a month and who probably would not be able to negotiate the icy roads. The same sort of word loss occurred again in the early afternoon. He tried to nap, but the headache worsened. Finally, at 3 p.m. I Googled "Should I go to the ER with a headache and word loss?" and was told that I definitely should and we did.

Ushered at 4 p.m. into an ER room with a big clock on the wall, we made a bet about when we would get out, in part to mask my dread that Don would be admitted. He guessed 7 p.m. and I guessed midnight. Then the scans began: blood and urine tests, cognitive and motion and balance tests, an EKG and a chest X-ray and a brain CT. As the drug administered through an IV eased his headache, he knew the day, the date, and the name of the president, and could touch the tip of his finger to the tip of the finger of the nurse practitioner. But his skin looked papery in the fluorescent light and his bulk—he was six feet tall and about 180 pounds—somehow contracted in the hospital bed.

Don's high blood pressure—which might have been raised by the ER itself—subsided and around 8 p.m. we were discharged, with orders to contact a neurologist the next day. He had won the bet, but had to submit to my driving us home on the dark, snowy roads. And we both had to acquiesce to a subtle recalibration of our relationship. He had taken care of me, especially during the past seven years of cancer-related surgeries, radiological interventions, and chemotherapies; now I would be taking care of him.

That would be harder on him, because he prided himself on his independence and also on his caregiving. That night in bed, with this acknowledgment of an altered future, we embraced throughout intermittent periods of wakefulness. Intermittent wakefulness during the night accompanies our aging, along with tender pats and reassuring caresses that remind us that, yes, the other is here: he on my right, me on his left. At the start of sleep, Don always curls away from me, but by the morning he's always curled toward me.

The next day we would have to make an appointment with the recommended neurologist. The next few weeks would be taken up with more tests, I suspected. I nudged aside my worries about a stroke—paralysis, memory lapses, speech loss—by planning the orange meal I would prepare for supper: red pepper soup, grilled salmon, spicy sweet potato wedges. But I was also thinking that ripe love—in life and in Helen Simonson's novel—involves a diminution in masculine privilege.

When men age, after all, they get less bristly around the chin, softer in their muscles, shorter, aware of their own possibly waning sexual desires and of frailties and failures as they retreat from the public sphere. Sigmund Freud and his followers, who always upped the linguistic ante, consistently associated loss of teeth and hair with castration. A more diffident proposition teases me. Can it be that aging equalizes the sexes, that it produces men and women able to see each other as similarly challenged by the physical signs of decline?

Positing just such a proposal, the ending of *Major Pettigrew's Last Stand* contains breathtaking scenery, a shootout, and the start of a wedding that will unite the aging couple as well as the town they love. In Simonson's bracing conclusion, the Major must save Mrs. Ali's nephew from throwing himself over a cliff favored by the suicidal: Abdul Wahid's religious orthodoxy has flooded him with shame. The Major realizes that if he fails to save the young man's life, he will lose the love of his life. His "last stand" also involves saving himself from the bankrupt ideals of Empire and England that have threatened to divide him from Mrs. Ali.

The Major addresses the issue that consumes Abdul Wahid by displaying his Churchill guns and talking about his own shame— that at the golf club party he valued them more than he had Jasmina Ali: "For the sake of these guns, I let down the woman I love in front of a whole community of people, most of whom I can barely tolerate. I let her leave, and I will never get rid of that sense of shame." After his efforts fail, the Major loads his gun, situates himself between the distraught man and the cliff, and pushes the weapon into Abdul Wahid's hands. He will have to shoot the Major, if he wants to die. As Abdul Wahid throws the gun away, the discharge hits the Major, whose legs slip over the chalky edge.

Every aspect of Simonson's ending emphasizes a decline in the wounded Major's power. The novel closes right before a May wedding on the ancestral grounds of Lord Dagenham, which have been rented by the Pakistani caterers as a country house hotel. We are given a capsule history of the future of great aristocratic estates and also a tidy image—through the lost gun—of patriarchal power's fortunate fall. As the Major morphs into—of course!—Ernest Pettigrew, he does not feel as upset as he believes he should be at relinquishing the symbol of his preeminence.

When I consider the process of aging as an equalizer, I realize that Mrs. Ali takes the initiative in many of the smaller and larger steps that lead to the couple's betrothal. Though she is younger than the Major—no, *because* she is younger—she understands the insecurity that hounds him: the fear that he may be too old to attract her, or that his future may be compromised by physical disabilities or, worse yet, might be too brief.

Helen Simonson inherits this theme of male anxiety about aging from nineteenth-century fiction. In two of Anthony Trollope's novels, *The Way We Live Now* and *An Old Man's Love*, forty- and fifty-year-old male characters find themselves brooding that younger men would be more eligible grooms for the women they love. Both therefore relinquish their attempts to marry and turn themselves into kindly guardians. They have lost more than the cultural capital of masculinity, as the last name of one of these characters makes clear: William Whittlestaff.

In some contexts, however, acknowledgment of male insufficiency need not signify impotence or castration, as one of my favorite of Don's stories makes abundantly clear. He was chosen by the nuns in his high school to enter a citywide competition. He had to write an essay and then give a speech on what to do about Germany—it was April 1945—after the war. He did his best, but a girl won the All-American Catholic Boy contest that year; Don came in second or (he cannot remember) maybe third. At the time, he did not mind. He was worried that he would be going to war. But I have always believed it was the beginning of his magnanimity about competing with and maybe losing to smart girls. Our friend Judith calls this story "The Girl Who Became Best Boy, or How I Came in Third." It never harmed Don's confident sense of adequacy in adulthood, as far as I could tell.

The anxiety of an aging man about his chances at love percolates throughout a wonderful film directed by Ritesh Batra and edited by one of my sons-in-law. In a haunting scene of *The Lunchbox*, the aging hero shaves before a mirror, worrying that the woman with whom he has fallen in love does not deserve to marry a man who looks and smells like his own grandfather. A mistaken series of deliveries in Mumbai's ingenious lunchbox delivery system sparked this romance. The widower begins relishing the food he receives from an unhappily married woman and then warms to the epistolary friendship that evolves, though he must consistently battle his insecurities that he is too old to be an eligible suitor. At one point, he feels so handicapped by his age that he arrives at a planned meeting in a café, notes how attractive she looks, and withdraws without revealing himself.

This same dynamic surfaces in a novel by Fay Weldon that centers on the love affair of the eighty-something grandmother Felicity and her seventy-something suitor William in the hilariously spoofed Golden Bowl Complex for Creative Retirement. *Rhode Island Blues* depicts William's hesitancy about lying down in bed with Felicity during a series of conversations in which they disclose parts of their quite different but complicated pasts: "You don't know how anxious I am," William says when Felicity proposes that they talk in bed. "I'll only disappoint you. I think I'd better go now."

Felicity realizes that falling in love with William—an idea that her relatives scorn as "an indignity and an absurdity"—might be "compulsive, a strategy for postponing thoughts of death and the physical and mental decline that led up to it." However, she overcomes her own and William's doubts because the other people at the retirement home "only have pasts," whereas she and William "have a present." Indeed, they hurry their courtship because "there was so little time left." More financially secure than the many seniors who must take on part-time jobs to survive, Felicity and William—like most characters in fiction and like me and Don—have been freed by economic security from having to retool themselves for the workforce.

While Don and I began meeting for a lunch or a walk as more than friends, I feared that his seventeen-year seniority would inhibit him. But I had been so obnoxiously pushy in my first marriage that I determined not to take more initiatives—after, that is, the bold sentence "I like being with you." The word for late learning, I just discovered, is *opsimathy*: the process of acquiring a later-life education. My father used to say, "A wise man learns from experience, a wiser man still from the experience of others." Embarking on a second chance, some of us have to learn from experience, being unable to learn from the experience of others, though until now I could not conceive of using the word *opsimathy* in a sentence, and probably never will again.

My father looked depleted in the photographs taken a few weeks before his death, though he was fourteen years younger than I am now. When older men become sick, I thought, remembering a novel I read a while ago, they can become petulant about their dependency. In Jane Smiley's novel *At Paradise Gate*, a bedridden seventy-seven-year-old husband keeps calling for "Mother" when he wants his wife to help him to the bathroom. Although throughout fifty-two years of marriage she chaffed at her submission to his demands, as his heart gives out she is struck by her strength, his weakness: "When had she gotten so much bigger than he? Was there a moment that passed unnoticed, when she could have ceased feeling overtopped, surrounded, invaded, muscled here and there, when the balance changed and she could have stepped back, sat down, eased away?"

The idea of Don having to relinquish his privilege and strength upsets me, since throughout his professional life he used both judiciously. His career in academia had been based on tireless activism for diversity and the democratization of higher education: to connect white with black colleges, to link high school teachers with university faculty, to join the local community to the college, to promote faculty governance and represent faculty grievances. This sort of service was rare back then and unthinkable now, when research alone counts for promotion.

There were countless stories about his international students. "Freddie Wahba," I would say—to prompt a retelling of the Egyptian graduate student who had arrived at Don's office, brandishing a fistful of ties: "There are sporty ties and you are a sporty man." Don had asked how Freddie got his first name. Apparently his father had named his kids after his bosses working on the railroads.

"Do you have brothers or sisters?" Don had asked.

"Yes, I have a sister."

"What's her name?"

"Schwartz," Freddie said.

In his retirement, Don often goes to Emeriti House, where he leads poetry discussions or works on projects to preserve the past. As the university necrologist, he tries to ensure that every faculty death issues in a memorial resolution. As a collector of oral histories, he oversees the videotaping of retiring faculty, who are interviewed as they consider the trajectories of their careers. These activities slowed down and then came to a halt during the aftermath of the aphasia incident. Or maybe they were nudged aside by the new critical edition of *Pride and Prejudice* that he was completing with our friend Mary. He had produced earlier editions on his own, but invited Mary to collaborate so that she could oversee its future republications.

At the neurology appointment set up by the ER physician, Don told me, he concluded the session by reciting the three words—*table*, *pencil*, *apple*—that the doctor had asked him to remember at the start of their session. He had been able to subtract 7 from 90, then 7 from 83, then 7 from . . . but at any age I would have failed that test. (I am the sort of person who does not rise to the challenge of the eighth-grade Common Core math test.) He had tried to draw two shapes like home base, but failed to make them overlap. While I waited in the Inverness during the afternoon of Don's consultation, which issued only in an order for more tests in the hospital, my levels of nervousness crested. I would have to begin accompanying him to scans and doctor appointments, which—I reminded my friend Fran—I had never done before.

Fran had given me such an imaginative and touching gift for my birthday. On one sheet of paper, she had typed a numbered list of the names of people or places. On another sheet of paper, she had typed an alphabetized list of events or snatches of conversation. While I matched the numbers to the letters, the people or places to the events or conversations, I marveled at the extensive past we shared: activities with my kids at their every stage of development and with her parents, siblings, nephews, and nieces; intense exchanges over our writing projects—hers historical, mine literary; and rowdy derision of academic bloviating.

The antique magnolia was putting out sparse pink and white blossoms on its spindly branches when I went with Don to the hospital for various scans and then back to the neurologist's office, but thankfully the results led her to conclude there was no need for more procedures.

"You are in good health," she declared. "You look great, decades younger than your age. It was maybe a mini-stroke or an instance of TGA, just episodic. Transient global amnesia. Try an aspirin every day."

Don did seem better. He often woke with a tune in his head, and the day after seeing the neurologist the words were a ditty his Uncle Don used to sing to him when he was little: "Picky, picky porcupine / I see you under the northern pine, / I take my shoot gun and shoot you dead / Picky, picky porcupine." It was time to resume the activities that take up my retirement—reading, writing, and eating neatly—the goals so devoutly wished for by Leo the Late Bloomer, an inept young lion in a vibrantly illustrated picture book that entranced my girls at bedtime. With Don sitting in the parked car so we wouldn't get a ticket, I could run up and gather the books and DVDs my graduate assistants were collecting in my office.

Neither of my daughters could travel to us this Passover, and therefore with some misgivings I accepted an invitation to attend a seder at friends of our friends Jonathan and Alexandra. Ever since the girls were young and every year before this one, I had enlisted family or friends to haul up from the basement a long table to accommodate our many guests at the seder. We would position it to form a T with the dining room table. Fran had produced an ecumenical Haggadah that we always used.

Even though she had stopped attending years ago, Fran's spirit presided in the spiral booklets with their uplifting prayers for peace and justice. But this year instead of spilling wine on our plates, as we had at my seders to commemorate the suffering of the plagues, our hosts distributed plastic animals. Even more upsetting was their use of a 1950s children's book for the Haggadah. "What to make of a diminished thing?" Maybe I should not relinquish my own traditions, exhausting though they were, I thought.

In the past, putting on a face to meet the faces at Passovers had always buoyed up Don's spirits, even though he insisted on loading the dishwasher afterward, washing all the pots, laundering the linen, and grousing about it. At all of our twenty or so seders, when we dedicated the first glass of wine to family or friends who had died, Don had raised his glass and spoken Mary-Alice's name. It often triggered stories about her wit. When a doctor suspected she had lost her eyesight and asked her about the color of his shirt, she had said, "It's very becoming, suits you perfectly." And that memory invariably brought to my mind a later moment when Don and I were becoming more than friends—I had inadvertently left a book in his car—and he bounded up the stairs to my house, backlit by the sun and full of vitality, much more vitality than his sixty-odd years would suggest, in his usual outfit: dark pants, a laundered shirt, a sports jacket, and a tie. That was the instant when the embers sparked and I realized why so much food remained on our plates at our lunches together.

He soon became my sartorial model. What a relief to abandon skirt suits in the classroom or lecture hall (Sandra dubbed me Esther Polyester in one of those outfits) and Laura Ashley dresses (we called ourselves the Milkmaids), to have an easy uniform always at reach. For his laundered shirt, I substituted a T-shirt, for his tie a scarf, for his trousers leggings. Late-life dressing has its own logic. When my mentor, the feminist critic and detective novelist Carolyn Heilbrun, entered her seventies, she favored loose pants, billowy tunics, and sturdy old lady shoes, precisely the attire I had to adopt during all the cancer surgeries.

After Carolyn's death, I brooded about her decision to relinquish life: was it a rational one or a sign of depression at not finding another writing project? A year or so before her suicide, Carolyn had packed up all the hoods she had been given with her honorary degrees and mailed them to me so I could use them for a quilt. There was no way I could get a needle through the thick satin and velvet linings, I explained, but she did not want them returned. As Fran and I traveled back from Carolyn's funeral, Fran confided that she thought Carolyn was afraid of the loss of control associated with aging.

The picture on the cover of *Major Pettigrew's Last Stand* features the main characters' coats and hats on a coat stand, as if locked in an embrace. Although Simonson's characters find the clothing of their deceased spouses comforting, the image disturbs me: coats hung upon a stick, their wearers gone. But the news about Don was good, I tried to assure myself. I should confine my worries to the sick baby and to my traveling back to New York. It would be easier now that the most fearsome late winter I could remember had finally ended.

Falling in Love

WITH LAGUARDIA SHUT down for the day, reading was the only way to calm my taut nerves; and who better expresses the awkward hesitancy, astonishment, and delight of the second chance of later-life love than the poet I had taken with me? I was too agitated about Don to help out with the baby, so I stayed alone in the empty apartment of my stepdaughter Susannah.

The phone call from the ER the night before had shocked me: Don had stumbled on the first two steps leading up from the basement. He had torn a knee tendon—but it would be impossible to fly back today. In Bloomington, his other daughter, Julie, would email updates on the surgery and I had a seat on the first flight out tomorrow. Turbulence, the airport reported, but the day looked picture-perfect: sunny and warm with all the bulbs in Central Park blooming. Just two days ago, Don had phoned to describe the glowing forsythia and apple tree. How could this have possibly happened, and what would anesthesia and an operation on his already arthritic knee mean at his advanced age? I had always considered February the cruelest month, but maybe T. S. Eliot was right.

Still, I had to calm myself, for there was nothing to do but wait and hope that Don's physical strength would see him through. All those decades of running may have hurt his knees, but surely they also built resilience. So many people, like my collaborator Sandra, recover quickly from hip replacements, and this would be an easier recuperation. Since the surgery required only a one-night stay in the hospital, I had to be resolute and with luck I would arrive in time tomorrow to pick him up when he was discharged. He would need me more out of the hospital than in. I should change the ostomy apparatus, email Fran to inform her of the situation, and rest for what would be a challenging day. Julie, deft and tenacious, would never leave his side and would keep me informed of his condition, I knew.

Images of Don dragging himself up the basement steps, of his hauling his body across the family room to call 911, of his being taken on a stretcher to the ambulance, of his long wait in the ER, of Jan and Jon staying with him until he got a room at 3 a.m., of Julie suffering heightened anxieties before the operation: I needed to quiet myself with a book he had given me, a 1946 reprint of a very slim, very small 1936 edition of *Sonnets from the Portuguese* that he had purchased from a used-book barrow when he was a college student and that had easily fit in my handbag.

The name of the poet does not appear on the cover, which is composed of a diminutive orange grid, forming squares like

a miniature quilt in which a green bird on a branch alternates
with a stylized pink flower sprouting a few leaves. The slight book
looks delicate, old-fashioned, and feminine. The author's name,
apparently again assumed to be either trivial or self-evident, is
also absent from the frontispiece: a languishing, white-gowned
lady holding a red rose and swooning (from illness, fright, desire?)
before the looming figure of her manly lover as they stand in front
of an open door. The woman is blond, not brunette like Elizabeth Barrett Browning, her hair in a bun, not in ringlets. She
reaches over to clutch the doorknob: will she lock the phantom
lover out, simply faint on the spot, or let him swoop down and
carry her away beyond the threshold? On the title page, a drawing of a bronze cast of two clasped hands—one hand cradles the
other—tells me that the little volume is a meditation on the cradling clasp.

"How do I love you?" forty-year-old Elizabeth Barrett
Browning famously asked in her once admired and later dis-
missed poems, and then she answered, as quite a few schoolchil-
dren of my generation could repeat, "Let me count the ways."
In her historical period, when the life expectancy of women
was about fifty years of age, she must have considered herself
over-the-hill. As I pondered the different ways she loved Robert
Browning and the surgery scheduled for 11 a.m., I whispered,
"*Baruch*, my darling: blessed you are, blessed you will always be
to me," and opened the book to the startling first encounter of
the lovers.

In the melancholy years of her life, a mystic presence moves
and draws Elizabeth "backward by the hair":

And a voice said in mastery, while I strove.—
"Guess now who holds thee?"—"Death," I said. But, there,
The silver answer rang,—"Not Death, but Love." (I)

Surely Robert Browning did not have the audacity at one of their early meetings to yank Elizabeth Barrett's hair! Perhaps Elizabeth feels flung back by Robert's presence, expecting not love but death in what she considered her stunted later life. Given Elizabeth Barrett's years of illness, tragedy, and confinement in her father's house, she must have felt frail and vulnerable. Paradoxically, the union with Robert Browning *would* mean death—the death of her incapacitation and misery.

Throughout the sonnet sequence, hesitancies about love ripening in later life plague the speaker. "What has *thou* to do / With looking from the lattice-light at me," Elizabeth asks her lover, for she is a "poor, tired, wandering" person (III). The problem of feeling undesirable—which Barrett Browning transposes from the sonnet tradition of the lover-poet's unworthiness—relates to embarrassment about not only the aging body but also the worn-down spirit: "For I have grieved so I am hard to love" (XXXV). How could Elizabeth confide her misery and sense of guilt over the drowning of her brother, her discontent with her controlling father, her dismay at her physical disabilities? She feels faded: "frequent tears have run / The colours" from her life (VIII). Her cheeks are pale or wet with tears, her hands and knees trembling. To herself, she appears "not one / For such man's love!—more like an out-of-tune / Worn viol" that would "spoil his song" (XXXII). Elizabeth's outbreaks of inadequacy are interrupted by the ping! of the iPhone—Julie telling me the surgery has been delayed—so I skip to the poem that always reminds me of Don at Lake Ogle. One of Robert's first kisses "sought the forehead, and half-missed / Half falling on the hair" (XXXVIII). Awkward, it misses its mark, as did Don's and my first kiss when we were walking a trail in Brown County State Park, adrift in yellow and orange leaves. We had stopped to wonder at the golden light when drawn together and then we were more amused than mortified by a mistimed bumping into each other.

How long ago that first embrace seems today, and how very long this morning, though numerous email messages from Julie assure me that Don is pain-free, confident, and they expect the surgery around 2 p.m. Of course I shouldn't be here, so far away when he is in such dire straits. Wasn't he always the one who in the past had said, "Whither," meaning that he would accompany me on trips he had no wish to make? It was a mistake to leave him, for I shared Elizabeth Barrett Browning's amazement at her extraordinary luck in encountering later in life the sense of two-being-one or one-being-two. Once acknowledged, love dissolves Elizabeth's lonely singularity. Robert's touch means her heart pulses with "a beat double" and her eyes shed "the tears of two" (VI).

At a climactic point in the sequence, Elizabeth imagines the commonality and reciprocity of "our two souls":

> *When our two souls stand up erect and strong,*
> *Face to face, silent, drawing nigh and nigher,*
> *Until the lengthening wings break into fire*

At either curved point,—what bitter wrong
Can the earth do to us, that we should not long
Be here contented? (XXII)

What a resplendent portrait of passion both spiritual (souls standing erect) and erotic (drawing nearer until breaking into fire).
Touched by winged Eros, the lovers sprout wings. The image of
flight leads Elizabeth to the surmise that a transcendent world
elsewhere might encapsulate their love, keeping two intact as one,
protected from the "bitter wrongs" visited upon those embodied
and embedded in quotidian existence.

But she rejects a flight from materiality in a reversal that would
ground Barrett Browning and her poetry in earthly realities:

Think. In mounting higher
The angels would press on us and aspire
To drop some golden orb of perfect song
Into our deep, dear silence. Let us stay
Rather on earth, Belovèd,—where the unfit
Contrarious moods of men recoil away
And isolate pure spirits and permit
A place to stand and love in for a day,
With darkness and the death-hour rounding it. (XXII)

Whereas in heaven the lovers would be surrounded by throngs of
angels pressing perfection on them, on earth contrary creatures
will lend them a private space to experience the poignant tran-

sience of love in a daily life that will surely end with death, but with an hour of death that curiously encapsulates life.

Perfection can wait, the ripe lover decides, since aging informs us daily that death will come soon enough. Better alone together on imperfect earth than crowded in a perfect heaven. Ripe love converts Elizabeth Barrett Browning from faith in the hereafter to allegiance to the here and now, from divine to human love.

A succession of pings. An email from Sandra, laid low by a tumultuous scene with her partner, but the anesthesia has begun. Unnerved, I try to take heart by turning to the most exultant and erotic sonnet in the sequence, which imagines the subtraction of two beings into one. Here "our two souls" do not stand face to face or pulse with "a double beat," but instead become one, as Elizabeth meditates on her own orgasmic obliteration. The poet presumed to be the epitome of Victorian propriety first seems to tap a discouragingly conventional image of herself as a parasitical plant dependent upon its strong male host, for she thinks of herself as the scraggling vines obscuring the woody trunk of Robert, envisioned as a palm tree. Do the clinging vines reflect her dread that her infirmities and resultant dependency would thwart his flourishing?

Perhaps, but the rest of the sonnet revels in the ecstasies of her lover's potency and her own ecstatic desire:

> *Renew thy presence; as a strong tree should,*
> *Rustle thy boughs and set thy trunk all bare,*
> *And let these bands of greenery which insphere thee:*

Drop heavily down,—burst, shattered everywhere!
Because, in this deep joy to see and hear thee
And breathe within thy shadow a new air,
I do not think of thee—I am too near thee. (XXIX)

As she falls, splitting open the fruit or flower of herself, their intimacy annihilates individuation. Hers is not a clingy femininity, though she has known disability. Perhaps because he may have to become her stalwart shelter, she needs to comprehend—and needs him to comprehend—her capacity for self-obliterating union.

That rush of pleasure at the strength of another: what drew me to Don in the first place was his rootedness, for he could be depended on to be exactly where he was supposed to be when he was supposed to be there. The "new air" of being too intimate to think of the other while merging with the other: even before Don and I hid our affair from our kids and colleagues, I had thrilled at the awkward length of his splayed fingers in relation to his palms. The word *tryst* came to mind when we arranged our secret early meetings at night in his house or mine. Like Elizabeth, I wanted us to say over and over again that we loved each other, although on two awkward occasions, when my girls unexpectedly returned home, I hustled downstairs in a bathrobe as he quickly dressed upstairs.

Before Julie sends glad tidings—the operation has gone well, Don will be moved from recovery to a room, he will be released tomorrow—I have determined never to leave him again. Each separation has had damaging repercussions, I realize as I send consolatory emails to Sandra, urging her to rest, to take comfort in her kids, to persevere. Maybe the bruised relationship with her partner can be patched up. She needs to be strong; I count on it.

A jolt of adrenaline gets me through the airport surveillance lines (and my dread that the ostomy bag will lead to a body search), the turbulence (in a smaller than usual plane), the longer than usual limo ride (because of highway construction), the sight of wan Don in a wheelchair at the hospital entrance (with a black brace from his thigh to his calf, requiring him to lie on the back seat of my car), and the trip home (where Julie and I quickly roll up scatter rugs so he can use the supplied walker). Our friend Andrew, Mary's husband, has already installed a riser on the ground-floor toilet to elevate the seat. I will be given an opportunity to care for the man who has so generously and thoughtfully cared for me.

We are greatly relieved to be reunited, despite a scare the first night home. Don was standing in the bathroom holding on to his walker and then to the counter when he toppled. I could not pick him up. He had to brace his arms to push himself on his bottom all the way to the steps leading to the second floor. Gripping the banister, he hauled himself up one step and then upright and then we fell asleep exhausted, he flat on his back in the guest bedroom on the ground floor: me on his right, he now on my left, to be closer to the bathroom.

In a dream that night, Don walks before me toward the big sliding doors of Kroger's supermarket and I see him fall. As I run to help, his detached knee joint jerks and inches over to his calf. Then he manages to slide down, leaning back against the brick façade of the market with his reassembled leg outstretched before him. I notice how handsome he looks as he instructs me to phone 911. I gaze at my iPhone, willing myself to push the tab that will get me the phone number keyboard. After puzzling over this dream, I realized that I must get Don a cellphone he can keep with him at all times.

Because of the fall in the bathroom, the next day we went to the ER, where a physician assistant outfitted Don with a longer brace: black Velcro fasteners now snap from his upper thigh to his ankle. In two weeks, we will see the surgeon, and so we settle down to a recuperative routine. For the first time in our relationship, I unload the dishwasher, make him breakfast, give him sponge baths, help him put on his clothes, do the laundry, load the dishwasher, and revel in the fact that I am strong enough to take on these tasks. Since I cannot leave him home alone, Jayne—my neighbor when I lived in town—brings in groceries. It is a struggle getting the bright yellow, nonskid hospital socks over his swollen feet and orange toes. He looks like an antique camper in his shorts, but the usual long pants do not fit over the black brace.

Hunched on a chair in our kitchen, he glares at me, a wild thing trapped. It's like seeing an eagle shot down. "Don't fuss," Don says, trying to lift himself up. Medications proliferate on the counter, as they did when I was at my weakest after surgeries. Then I could not open the childproof vials; now he cannot. Then I could not walk on my own; now he cannot. Then I dozed through pain; now he does.

"This isn't a disease, but it takes as much attention as a disease," he says.

"One, two, three," I recite, pulling with one hand under his armpit and holding the walker steady with my other hand.

"Give me a minute," he says.

I leave the room so he can garner the strength he will need to move into a standing position. There are aspects of Don's care he does not want discussed. We do not discuss them. A proud and fastidious man, he finds his dependency humiliating. The less said the better, I think as I Google "how to use a bed urinal" and "what to do about swollen feet." There are lists of chores: scheduling appointments with his GP and kidney doctor, doing lots of laundry, making the ground floor habitable since he cannot go upstairs to our bedroom or downstairs to his basement study.

"How do you feel, Bear?" I whisper.

"I'll take the pain pills now, and the cyanide later," he deadpans.

In the midst of all these tasks, my cancer, my ostomy, my medications, and my port have dwindled into irrelevance. That I am well enough to be here seems a miracle. In his crumpled state, Don helps me more than I help him. We are still together, even more closely together through these two weeks of convalescence than ever before, and I rejoice that soon the surgeon will see how much stronger Don has become, how well he gets around with the walker, how few pain pills he needs.

I think of Elizabeth Barrett Browning's most famous sonnet, which focuses with bravado neither on her emotional reactions nor on Robert's physical characteristics, but on the capacity and magnitude of love itself. In a sequence that contrasts the before and after of ripe love—a before that is quite a bit longer than the before of young love and an after that might, alas, be briefer—she reminds herself that her love derives from "the passion put to use / In my old griefs" and the "Smiles, tears, of all my life" (XLIII). The past definitely infiltrates her future. Indeed, past sorrows intensify the joys of the second part of her life, which would stand in sharp contrast to the "old griefs" of the first part.

During the two weeks of recuperation from the operation, poor Don hates his dependency: relying on the walker, being unable to stand without my help, peeing in a plastic urinal, getting his hair washed at the kitchen sink, having to ask for his eyeglasses or a pencil or the iPad. He drowses in his chair, while I ponder a ranch house being built on a quiet street in town. Should we move or stay put? A move would be hugely disruptive, but we would be forced to get rid of half of the stuff we have accumulated. I don't want our possessions to become the sort of quagmire for our children that Roz Chast had to confront in her funny but wrenching graphic memoir about dealing with her aged parents' crammed apartment. It would be easier in town—a one-level apartment. I can't figure out what would be best for us.

In the past, I would have discussed this sort of problem with Fran, who has always been more practical than I. Every single move I have made was based on lengthy discussions with her. In fact, she found the last house I lived in; she even stripped the paint off the wood around the dining room windows. Decades ago, when I spent a year in Boston, she loaded the truck. Unlike me, she is sturdy, palpably grounded, a source of strength.

But I am upset—no, I am deeply wounded—that she has not made one effort to help out. The only way I can keep myself from reiterating irate tirades in my head is by gazing at the blazing prairie fire crab apple, the pink and white flowers floating above the dogwood's greenery, the unfurling copper scrolls of the stately beech, its thick trunk like an elephant's leg. We are surrounded by the clemency of great beauty. During the nights, I find it easier to shelve Fran. Since she has always gone to sleep hours before I do, we never talked on the phone at night, only in the afternoons— every or every other afternoon, sometimes for an hour, for exactly forty years; how many hours does that add up to? Our common past, so long and thick, has shattered. I had informed her of Don's surgery and she has not offered any assistance. She called once or twice, but seemed oblivious, chatting on about some event she had attended.

To distract myself, I would put in a CD, pour a glass of wine, and consider Elizabeth Barrett Browning's lineage. For Anne Bradstreet, America's first published poet, as for Barrett Browning, the married couple constitutes a doubled creature. More than one of Bradstreet's poems repeats the point: "If ever two were one, than surely we." Similarly, Katherine Philips, now enshrined in the lesbian literary tradition, celebrated a dear companion in "To Mrs. M.A. at Parting": "Thus our twin souls in one shall grow, / And teach the world new love."

Barrett Browning's contemporary, Harriet Taylor, was in her twenties, married with two children, when she met John Stuart Mill. Soon she separated from her husband and engaged with Mill in twenty-one years of intimacy and collaboration. He began to view her as the coauthor of his greatest works of philosophy. Two years after her husband's death, Harriet Taylor and John

Stuart Mill finally embarked on a marriage—they were in their midforties—that concluded seven years later with her death. It was a late-life marriage, but not a late-life passion. When Mill explained that happiness can be attained not by making it a direct goal but rather by fixing the mind on the happiness of others, he described one foundation of late-life love.

While Don slept in a hydrocodone daze, I started stepping around the living room to the stately strains of a Mendelssohn octet. It was a prayerful dance, asking the powers that be for the physical strength to continue doing this good work. On previous nights, last year or the year before, had he done the same? No, it would have been Charlie Parker or Ella—"Let's fall in love" was one of Don's first hidden notes, tucked in my bathrobe's pocket— and he would never have danced. He would have had his head- phones on, listening to Ellington with a beatific smile. Getting into the wrong side of the bed, I think: a supreme privilege that I can care for this resolute man who has cared for me. I awake to his hand in mine, our fingers intertwined.

Unlike the frontispiece of Don's volume of *Sonnets from the Portuguese*, the poems themselves emphasize the mutuality of the Brownings, as does Harriet Goodhue Hosmer's 1853 sculpture of their clasped hands. A replica sits on my desk, a gift from Sandra. Only the cuffs of the sleeves on the cast give away the identity of each hand: Robert Browning's below with a straight edge cra- dling Elizabeth Barrett Browning's on top with a scalloped edge, palm to palm, invoking pulses that "beat double." Handling the hands, I realize that there is no "below" or "on top." The sculpture can be positioned with either hand below or on top.

The verse grounded in Elizabeth's soul was inspired by Robert and would be cultivated by him. My Donald has also tended every phrase I have composed. Decades ago, he edited each of the chapters for which I was responsible in my collaborative work with Sandra; now he edits each of my cancer essays in my column for the electronic *New York Times*. Elizabeth's gratitude reflects mine at discerning my life and my life's work anchored in another's mortal existence. It was Robert Browning who wrote, "Grow old along with me! / The best is yet to be."

One of Don's scores of graduate students had been tormented about her doctoral dissertation on Robert Browning. How could she presume and who was she to make these interpretive claims? "Oh, Professor," she fretted. "Browning specialists all over the world will be reading this." Of course he did not disabuse her. Like me, she was lucky that he would be responding to every single word.

The Trace

THIS IS NO country for young people. Members of a dying generation lie comatose in single beds within darkened rooms or slumped in wheelchairs parked along hallways lit by overhead fluorescent panels. I stride down the long beige hall several times a day: first at 8 a.m., when I arrive, and then later at around noon, when I go on various errands, and then around 8 p.m., when I leave for home. No matter how breezy or bright the day, there is no weather in here. Just the beige walls and the stink of mortality. Would it be a courtesy to smile and nod at the dying animal wheeling herself forward by toeing the linoleum, gnarled talons on the hallway's handgrip? Or should I protect her privacy with an impassive downward gaze? It is a she, I can tell by a wig perched less convincingly on her head than on mine.

The errands vary. Dirty laundry must be taken home; warm sweatshirts brought in, since Don is always cold, and chocolate malts or the swill on the trays will result in weight loss. Shorts need to be bought extra-large to fit over the cobalt-blue thick cast that now encases his left leg from his upper thigh to his foot. A bottle of wine, smuggled within a discreet brown bag, gets me through sundown syndrome, when Don's depleted spirits plummet into sorrow at his complete incapacity, for he cannot use a walker, cannot take one step, cannot get into a chair. I sit between his hospital bed and a window overlooking the parking lot. We are determined to stay in this miserable place as long as necessary—four days, a week, ten days—but how we landed here still shocks me.

We had gone to the post-operative appointment with high hopes. After Don hauled himself into an examination room and onto its table with his legs outstretched, Dr. Licini took off the brace, probed the knee, and said, "It's not attached." The tendon is not attached? What could possibly have happened? Might it have been that second fall the first night home? Why had we been sent home with a flimsy brace and assured that the leg was weight-bearing with it?

Tears welled at the surgeon's office, in the car as I drove us to the hospital to sign admittance forms, during the reoperation, and intermittently throughout the three-night hospital stay, which (I was convinced) the doctor connived out of a guilty conscience or fear of litigation. For, as I kept on saying to Don and to his daughters and to mine and to anyone I could buttonhole, an eighty-seven-year-old man should never have been sent home after the first surgery. Two operations in two weeks: an outrage. If the first failed, would the second also?

After the first operation, Don should have been counseled on the need for therapy in a rehabilitation facility. The problem is that he looks much younger than his years—like Julie, who in her fifties looks twenty-something (and sometimes, in her skinny jeans and Humane Society T-shirts, twelve). It was my fault, too. In New York, I had no inkling how difficult recuperation with a torn tendon repair would be, much harder than a hip replacement.

Now, in a rehabilitation center called Bell Trace, the monthly calendar lists coffee ice cream socials, manicures, singalongs, church services, bingo, aromatherapy, balloon volleyball, puzzle tree crafts, and (much to Julie's delight) therapy dog visits. From his bed, Don can see mountainous or skeletal Hoosiers shambling or rolling slowly down the hall. He wonders, why aren't they screaming?

It takes me a while to realize he is reciting lines about inmates in a nursing home, Philip Larkin's poem "The Old Fools." What, Larkin asks, do the old fools think has happened to them? Do they suppose that their mouths always hung open drooling, or that they should be peeing in their pants, or that they were born crippled? Bewildered and shocked at relics of time's ravages, Don and I wonder, perhaps with more hope than Larkin had, if all these people inhabit clean well-lighted places inside their heads, rather than the beige smelly hallways.

Do pockets of memories of other voices, other rooms protect them from registering their inverted infancy of diapers and restraining belts and spoon feedings? With all their choices as well as the power of choosing gone, what must they make of their twisted hands, lined faces, flaccid trunks, and wasted or engorged limbs in this second childhood "Sans teeth, sans eyes, sans taste, sans everything"? Are drugs keeping them quiet? Why aren't they screaming? Larkin extends a tradition founded by Juvenal, who also decried the regression of the aged: "Doddering voices and limbs, bald heads, running noses, like children's, / Munching their bread, poor old things, with gums that are utterly toothless."

We are not screaming but waiting—for the paperwork, for the next pain pill, for the physical and occupational therapists, for the nutritionist and the podiatrist, for an attendant who might move Don onto a commode or help me give him a bath in bed. No matter how solicitous I am, though, his waiting diverges from mine. I can get up and go to the nurses' station to complain that the paperwork, pill, therapist, nutritionist, podiatrist, or attendant has not yet arrived. That our troubles differ troubles me.

We would never have landed in this place had I not gone to New York. Right before the first fall, Don was downstairs in the basement study working after dinner, which he would never have done if I were home. So I blame it on *Pride and Prejudice*. He was holding the edited manuscript in his hands when he stood on the first step and looked back to check that the door to the garage was closed. All the pages scattered as he tumbled down on his knee. Not one of them included any mention of later-life love. Austen could no more imagine late-life romance than could Philip Larkin, who convinced himself that he was born "too late" to experience sexual freedom. For me, it's easy to blame the second fall on Dr. Licini, whose second operation has resulted in Don's complete immobilization. It is impossible to walk on one leg. If the heavy blue cast must stay on for weeks or months, what are we to do?

Enter Tyrone: this is no country for young people, unless they are physical or occupational therapists. A fit Filipino who looks like Yul Brynner in *The King and I*, Tyrone brings all sorts of odd implements. With pride, he shows us a long pole attached to a grasper that can be used to obtain objects out of arm's reach. Then he holds out a plastic tube with strings; what do we think it might help with? Don and I don't have a clue. Tyrone proceeds to manipulate a bright yellow hospital sock on the tube, place it around Don's toes, and pull up with the string until the sock encases his swollen foot. How ingenious, we agree, although Don's hands cannot reach down to his toes and the soles of his feet have begun peeling. Yes, Tyrone nods, he was himself intrigued and did some research, and it is not patented because it was invented so many centuries ago.

"You must put safety first," Tyrone instructs Don, whom he positions sitting on the edge of the bed. "All your weight must be put on your right leg. We will practice the pivot."

He has looped a heavy safety belt around Don's waist and placed a wheelchair at a 45-degree angle right up against the bed. We are grateful that there is no one else in the room; the second bed is unoccupied.

"Susan, you will watch me carefully since this will be your role. You see I have my own feet planted firm, just so. I have my hands on the belt and can push this fellow back onto the bed, if I worry about his safety. You are not strong enough to hold him up. Safety first. No more falls. Another fall will land you, sir, in a wheelchair and it is very hard to ever get out of one once you get into one. We don't want that."

With his cast leg just touching the floor, Don is supposed to use upper body strength to push himself vertical. Jamming his fists against the mattress, he manages to rise and balance on his good leg. Then he must reach his right hand over to the right armrest of the wheelchair, swivel his right foot around, reach with his left hand for the left armrest of the wheelchair, and lower himself, again using upper body strength, slowly down into it. Tired, he gets befuddled. The right hand reaches for the left armrest by mistake. Or he swivels in the wrong direction. Or he collapses into the chair. Maybe we should try the pivot from the bed to the walker, from the walker to the wheelchair. We must do it over and over again, day after day—first Tyrone and Don, then me and Don—until he can master both sorts of pivots, and then it is time to rest.

If the move from the bed to the wheelchair remains dicey, walking seems impossible. Helped upright to a walker, Don hops on his good leg and must be instructed on how to position himself inside the frame of the walker, how to slide his right foot forward only an inch or two at a time, how to relax his shoulders, how to use long colorful rubber bands to increase the strength of his arms and wrists.

Tyrone and his peers become the highlight of our days, since Don does not want colleagues visiting in such a depressing place and Fran has neither phoned nor emailed. Besides, the difficulty of simply getting him washed or into the bathroom exhausts us both. Julie cheerfully runs numerous errands, but we don't want to subject her to the indignities with which we must cope. In some ways, I find it a guilty relief to tap the code that opens the door out of the Trace—05 (for the month), 15 (for the year), star (for get me out of here!)—and walk into a glowing sunset, to have the physical power to escape into the warm fresh air, knowing that Don will soon be given a medication to help him sleep.

Those surreal nights take on their own desolations, however. In the empty house, I remember the three rules Don followed when he lived alone after Mary-Alice's death: use a placemat, don't eat in front of the TV, and make your bed every morning. Without a smidgen of his flinty discipline, I instantly break the first and last. I don't eat in front of the TV because I have not mastered the remotes and eating has become a problem, unless I stand in front of the refrigerator and simply reach for a piece of cheese to accompany the wine needed in abundance.

I am furious at Fran. Probably all of my fears are projected into that rage. I had accepted her growing need for time alone at home, but this feels like being ghosted. I really never did comprehend what she expected from her deepened seclusion, but now I have learned exactly how much (and it is a great deal) I love her and how angry I am at her. That blood is thicker than water upsets me. Don's girls have been great, as have mine from a distance. I always wanted to believe Fran was part of our family, but I have been proven wrong. I fume over the many forms of support I provided her in the past—the errands run, meetings attended, advice given and received. A sense of abandonment shrouds me, despite the offers of support from others.

Should Don remain incapacitated, would we have to move into the assisted living quarters of a place like the Trace? He wanted nothing to do with relocating to New York or Boston, the cities where three of our girls live. Now I can no longer help the daughter in need of help, though neither she nor her husband has had a full night of sleep in months. When will I again see the Buddha-baby, sweet-tempered even when sick?

And what if the two back-to-back operations plunge Don into a state worse than incapacity? Were that to happen, how could I stay in this empty, remote house? With Fran gone, Mary and her family set to leave for Baltimore, Julie unsure how long she will stay in town, to whom could I turn? Even my oncologist was contemplating a move to another state. Joining the girls in Manhattan or Brookline would be beyond my means. Would I end up in the Trace alone? Since the cancer diagnosis, Don and I both assumed that I would die first. The alternative threatens to capsize me. Would my existence conclude like my ninety-six-year-old mother's?

"Do you still watch TV?" I asked during one of our twice-weekly visits to my mother's room in a place like the Trace. Don was putting away the laundry he did to keep her monthly bills down, as I struggled against reverting back into her churlish adolescent daughter and she began inching her wheelchair toward the stuffed animal she called Munchkin. I couldn't bear watching her stroke the chipmunk's tail.

"Oh, yes," she said brightly and veered toward the television to pick up a hairbrush precariously perched beside it. She grasped it, firmly placed its plastic bristles on the side of the blank set, and began moving them up and down, making a grating sound. Then she swiveled around to look triumphantly at me and Don.

"You see," she said, "I play with it all the time."

Better my mother's affection for Munchkin than her earlier distress that "they came and bruised me (look at my wrist!), and took me to that other place, where there was a replica of this very room." The brushing of the television occurred two years after we found her stash of certificates—"You Are a Million Dollar Winner!"—and months before her death. Earlier, she never got a second chance at late-life love; and if she had, she would have been too traumatized to accept it.

One of the saddest stories by Isaac Bashevis Singer, "Old Love," describes an awakening of desire that comes after grief has taken too much of a toll. In his eighties, the widower Harry Bendiner lives a lonely life, his social interactions confined to visiting an office of Merrill Lynch. Only in his daydreams does he fantasize about restored powers and masculine adventures: "The brain wouldn't accept old age. It teemed with the same passions it had in his youth." Unexpectedly, a new neighbor—Ethel Brokeles, in her fifties—knocks on his door to introduce herself, and their conversation switches into Yiddish, as he exults, "It could be nothing else but that heaven had acceded to his secret desires."

In his apartment and then in hers, where she serves him lunch, they share the tragedies that had befallen them. He, the death of three wives; she, the death of her beloved husband, and her breakdown and seven months in a clinic for nervous disorders. They speak of using their money to travel before they hug and kiss. Youthful urges throb through him, but she cautions him, "Wait till we've stood under the wedding canopy." Then, suddenly, he sees that her face has "grown pale, shrunken, and aged." Back in his own place, he spends the night dozing and waking, worrying about strange footsteps, doors slamming, until another neighbor rings his doorbell in the morning to deliver a letter from Ethel, who had thrown herself out the window.

"Dear Harry, forgive me. I must go where my husband is. If it's not too much trouble, say Kaddish for me." The prospect of a future husband's appearance brought home to Ethel the tragedy of her late husband's disappearance. Harry in his loss reminds me of my mother or she reminds me of him. No space in the Inverness seems comfortable, not the upstairs bedroom, not my study.

I sit with my legs outstretched on the blue couch in the family room, where I wrote my last two books, not writing now but listening to *Fidelio*, as I had decades ago in the house in town, after my first husband left me. Our petty power struggles and hurt feelings had not deflected my incessant pleas that we work it out, for I clung to the belief that I could change him and save the marriage. Although we were profoundly incompatible—not just "potatoes po-tah-toes, tomatoes to-mah-toes"—the breakup plunged me back into the desolation I had felt at fifteen when my father committed suicide on June 10, 1960. Carbon monoxide poisoning in the car in his shop. The inevitable questions inevitably went unanswered. Why did he do it? How had we failed him? My mother's lonely life as a widow began when she was in her forties. More than half her existence, the second half, she lived alone under the shadow of that horror.

During the divorce, while I listened over and over again to *Fidelio*, the character of Leonore enthralled me. Could I tap into her strength and fidelity? An unfair conjecture continued to nag me: Would my father be alive if my mother had possessed

Leonore's determination? Beethoven's only opera celebrates the conjugal love of the indomitable wife Leonore, who disguises herself as the manly Fidelio to rescue her unjustly imprisoned husband Floristan. "The devotion of true married love gives me strength," Leonore-Fidelio sings. The entire opera takes place inside a prison; its chorus consists of the prisoners; and at its climax Leonore-Fidelio must screw up her courage to descend into the bowels of solitary confinement to find her enchained and starved husband.

With the jailer, as she begins to dig Floristan's grave in the lower depths, Leonore-Fidelio encounters the evil man who conspired against him and who is now about to murder him. After revealing her identity, Leonore exclaims, "First kill his wife!" and then produces a pistol, when an urgent trumpet call interrupts. The Governor has arrived to liberate not only Floristan but all the inmates.

At the breakup of my marriage, I was in my forties, about the age I imagined Leonore, and more than anything I wanted to rescue my husband, our marriage and family, from the prison-house of misery that encased us. *Fidelio* reworks the mythic hero's descent into the realm of the dead by imagining a wife journeying down into the dark underworld, where she offers her buried-alive spouse sacramental sustenance—bread and wine—before leading him up to a sunlit, redeemed social order and conjugal reunion. Unlike Orpheus, she never looks back, never wavers or falters in her resolution.

In the only interpretive book I could find about *Fidelio*, a musicologist writes that "virtually every critic of the opera feels the need to interpret it, to ask what *Fidelio* is 'really' about, because the music tells us that it cannot simply be about a wife rescuing her husband." But I think the celebratory music is precisely about a wife rescuing her husband. This same scholar declares that because "Beethoven was a profoundly unsexual artist, with a sensibility of unparalleled austerity," the opera "is utterly untouched by eroticism," for "Leonore and Floristan are well past the ardours of the first love." The guy knows bupkes, I think, or, as my father would say, "*Qvatch!*"

First, consider the opening scenes where the jailer's daughter, in the grip of a powerful infatuation, gains the permission of her father to plan her wedding with Leonore-Fidelio. In the single most beautiful canon I have ever heard, "Mir ist so wunderbar," four hushed voices longingly express their desires, most quite at odds: the jailer's daughter imagines Fidelio reciprocating her love, Leonore-Fidelio worries about the infatuation, the jailer envisions the couple's bliss, the daughter's spurned suitor considers his miserable abandonment. The thrilling harmonies suggest that although the singers are encased in the urgency of different hopes and fears, they share our common yearning to voice, if only to ourselves, intense emotions that remain incommunicable to others.

Then, at the beginning of act 2, we encounter the enchained husband Floristan in his dank captivity, singing an ardent tenor aria in which he broods over the all-consuming darkness that has engulfed him and concludes with an ecstatic vision of Leonore as an angel beckoning him to freedom. The word *Freiheit*, repeated numerous times, is sung at the highest notes Floristan reaches, resounding over and over again, quicker and quicker, after which he abruptly falls asleep. Sandra's husband Elliot, who often lectured me on the significance of operas, had a hilarious interpretation of Floristan's rhythmic climax. Elliot argued that the aria mimics the progress toward orgasm, after which a man does often go instantly to sleep. I could never listen to it again without smiling and thinking of Elliot.

But now I am decades older than Leonore, older than Elliot when he died so unexpectedly, so tragically, and Sandra, after enduring that trauma, again feels traumatized, her current relationship in jeopardy. We commiserate on the phone, though it is impossible for me to express my fear that my cherished second husband cannot be liberated from incapacity, that I do not have the strength to free him from his fetid confinement. He has been catapulted into old age: a hale and hearty senior yesterday, but today an exhausted, depleted, immobilized trace of himself. I try to instruct myself: we have been lucky to have had as much time as we did to revel in a love that was sometimes as dramatic as a spring storm and sometimes as comfortable as a worn slipper. C. S. Lewis felt the same way when, in his late fifties, he married Joy Davidson. In *A Grief Observed*, he marvels at their gaiety even after her cancer depleted their hopes.

Yet during her illness, Lewis realized that there is a limit to "one flesh," because of the difficulty of sharing someone else's fear or pain: "I had my miseries, not hers; she had hers, not mine." Especially when I was hospitalized for cancer-related surgeries, I knew that my physical miseries were not Don's, and I was glad they were not. Now the cold truth that lovers can be set on different roads chills me. For Lewis, "this terrible traffic regulation ('You, Madam, to the right—you, Sir, to the left')" inaugurates the "beginning of the separation which is death itself."

Is our current separation the beginning of the end of Don and me? Had we been wrong to plan that my ashes would be buried in the plot next to Mary-Alice's grave and that his body would join me there when he died? Would I, not he, be visiting Rose Hill Cemetery to plant flowers or place a stone? Why must one predecease (a horrible word) the other? Joy Davidson once told Lewis, "Even if we both died at exactly the same moment, as we lie here side by side, it would be just as much a separation as the one you're so afraid of."

In his grief at Joy's death, the widowed C. S. Lewis imagines himself a one-legged man. After the separation, he will "probably have recurrent pains in the stump all his life, and perhaps pretty bad ones." My one-legged man's life has changed inalterably. He, too, will face pretty bad pains probably for the rest of his life. "All sorts of pleasures and activities that he once took for granted will have to be simply written off. Duties too." Will Don ever be a biped again? I worry as I gather up books and scraps of cotton to have something to do during the leaden hours of waiting at the Trace.

Inside the dungeon, Leonore digs a hole for the man whom she has not yet ascertained to be her husband. Impelled by the principle of freedom, she determines that whoever he might turn out to be, she will unlock his chains. That sort of wide-angled, humanitarian heroism seems beyond me now. My vision has narrowed to springing Don from the Trace. At the close of the opera, the prison choir is joined by townspeople because Beethoven wanted sopranos and altos, along with tenors and basses, to hail the hour, long yearned for but unforeseen, when justice in league with mercy appears at the threshold of the grave. His exalted music leaves me exhausted.

Props

INSIDE THE NARROW ground-floor bathroom, I maneuver around the walker to position a small end table on which I place a mixing bowl filled with hot soapy water and a washcloth. The soapy water must be replaced by clear water, a clean washcloth, and a bath towel. Shaving cream, a razor, aftershave, a small mirror, and a hand towel come next. Then I move the bowl, washcloths, shaving cream, razor, aftershave, mirror, and towels to the counter by the sink and place deodorant, a glass of water, and a toothbrush with toothpaste on the end table. Then I find clean underpants, shorts, a long-sleeved T-shirt, and another pair of the yellow, nonskid socks from the Trace.

Don sits naked on the raised toilet, squeezed between a bathtub on his right and a wall on his left, a cabinet just above his head, the end table positioned next to his uncast knee. To help dress him, I crouch on the floor at his feet. In the old days, he did these routines standing in the upstairs bathroom with the door closed while I snoozed. We are home, but the burden of care weighs us down.

The walker, jammed sideways through the door, gets Don to the wheelchair I have placed just outside the bathroom; it cannot fit through the door frame. I wheel him to the wingback chair next to a window in the living room—the wall-to-wall carpet slows us down—and then go back to get the walker so he can use it to rise and pivot to the real chair. Then the bathroom must be cleaned. We are both fatigued and I am still in my pajamas, but the breakfast dishes have to be done because the dishwasher has broken down and the sink is full of last night's mess. As I leave him with his iPad—it's about 11 a.m., so he has already consumed his raft of pills—he says, "Shake me up, Judy," to which I say, "This *is* a happy day!"

He's glum about his camper outfit. He's glum about the heavy cast, his dependency on the walker, the wheelchair, the pills, the visiting physical therapists, and me. Even with the extra-wide shoes with Velcro fasteners that Julie found at Kmart, we cannot get his feet shod. That they are not merely swollen but flaking tells me we must return again to his GP for some sort of antifungal cream. Last time the GP prescribed an antibiotic for a urinary infection and "water pills." Taking the pills requires recurrent blood tests in the hospital to be sure they are not damaging his kidneys and trips to the nurse practitioner at the kidney doctor's office. Weary and wary, Don hunkers down in his upholstered chair. He does not want to make the same mistake we made before. He keeps Tyrone's rule foremost in his mind; it makes him gloomier.

"Every mark of an old crock," he says. "Bibs, urinals, wheel-chair, safety belt, smelly clothes."

Coming and going on errands, Julie calls her father "Grump-arella," but it could be my nickname today too. I'm grumpy because earlier this morning, I was awakened by "an accident," the term I used to use when one of my kids had trouble with toilet training. Every once in a while accidents happen with the ostomy, no matter how careful I am about my diet and about changing the contraption that sticks on my stomach. Excrement oozes through the adhesive that attaches the pouch to my belly.

At the crack of dawn, I felt the messy seepage below, jumped out of bed, fled upstairs to the bathroom, cleaned myself up, showered, and put on a new apparatus. My mistake was looking in the mirror over the sink in which I cleaned the soiled under-pants. Every mark of an old crock: a tall scarecrow with a balding head, no eyebrows or eyelashes, a bump on my chest where a port was embedded, abdominal surgical scars, no pubic hair, a plas-tic bag hanging from my belly, what little flesh there is hanging downward too. I don't look like the person I used to be; I am not the person I used to be.

While I put on a clean pair of pajamas, I thought of the nar-cissistic wounds of aging and of horrific scenes of its accelera-tion when the destruction of time speeds up. Dickens's aged flirt Cleopatra whose hair drops off, her lips shrink, the skin becomes "cadaverous and loose; an old, worn, yellow, nodding woman, with red eyes, . . . huddled up, like a slovenly bundle, in a greasy flannel gown." Don had read the thickest novels by Dickens aloud to me throughout a succession of toasty winters: a blazing fire in the fireplace making the leeks and radishes flicker in the big painting on the wall as I glanced up from the quilting that enveloped me.

I'm so weary that I feel perpetually pulled down by gravity, encumbered—as if moving through muck—by the weight of the cast, the wheelchair, the walker, our bodies. For doctor visits, I have to prop open the broken screen door to haul them into the car. Except for these fraught trips, every day is the same—simply getting cleaned, dressed, fed, undressed, bedded takes up all our time and strength.

"If I hadn't married you," Don had said in the Trace, "I would be rotting in a ditch."

To prove that married people could also rot in a ditch, on our arrival home I ordered a DVD of Samuel Beckett's *Happy Days* from Netflix and then settled down with the play—since Don snoozes intermittently from all the drugs. The common notion of love conquering all and providing a safe haven from the miseries of the world—the powerful conviction that there's a place for us, somewhere a place for us—seems ridiculous to me, an old lover. If late-life love cannot make us invulnerable to everyday misfortunes, what conceivable purpose does it serve?

I had worried that watching the play might deepen our depression, but we both found Beckett's geriatric farce intriguing in its portrayal of a later-life love affair like no other. The play's unflinching honesty about the deterioration of the body is unexpectedly funny about inextinguishable language that just keeps on going on within the bizarre landscape of aging.

The arid wilderness of aging in Beckett's play invokes heat and gravity, the sweltering and swelling weightiness of flesh: a female character immobilized in a scorched mound of earth, a male character so incapacitated that he crawls on all fours. Winnie, in her fifties, remains buried up to her waist in act 1; in act 2 she is imbedded up to her neck, unable to turn or bow or raise her head. To her right, sixty-something Willie lies out of her sightline. She is stuck, immobilized, while he finds it difficult to speak or maybe he is losing his hearing.

Winnie cannot win and Willie cannot will himself to do much of anything during indistinguishable days that blur into a daze. At the opening of both acts, an insistent bell wakes them and Winnie begins her happy day or daze of incessant chattering, though in the first act she starts by praying while in the second she does not—perhaps because in the first act she has the use of the objects in her large black bag. Why are the contents of Winnie's bag so important to her? Rummaging in her purse and incessant grooming occupy most of her attention in the first act.

A toothbrush, toothpaste, a mirror, spectacles, a handkerchief, a bottle of medicine, lipstick, a brimless hat with crumpled feathers, a magnifying glass, a windup music box, a gun, and a nail file: Winnie takes one after the other out to use or inspect it. Some of these objects are running out (the toothpaste, medicine, and lipstick); others may not be available again (the parasol spontaneously combusts, the revolver is not replaced in the bag). She considers them treasures or comforts that help her get through the hours.

Winnie's props give her a sense of getting something done, of keeping calm while carrying on. "There is so little one can do.

[*Pause.*] One does it all. [*Pause.*] All one can." The objects in her bag keep her busy as she tells herself not to complain, for there is much to be thankful for, and there is hardly any pain. Trimming her nails or checking her teeth: "these things tide one over," she says. And so they do, when nothing else can be done.

Willie's props include his yellowing newspaper, a handkerchief, pornographic cards, Vaseline, and his boater. When Winnie instructs her partner how to crawl backward—"Not head first, stupid, how are you going to turn? [*Pause.*] Oh I know it is not easy, dear, crawling backwards, but it is rewarding in the end"—I am reminded of myself directing Don on how to move his unmovable body around.

Pauses make up a large proportion of their conversation, since Willie speaks for the most part in monosyllables. That too seems resonant: Don is losing his voice or he mumbles (or I am going deaf). Pestering Willie to communicate, Winnie cannot contain her joy when he does: "Oh you are going to talk to me today, this is going to be a happy day!" Yet the next stage direction reads "[*Pause. Joy off.*]" Is she acting, expecting pretense to make it so, or might she be bonkers?

Like Philip Larkin, Beckett could be accused of gerontophobia: fear and loathing of old people or of aging. Willie picks his nose and eats the pickings too; Winnie intones botched and irrelevant snippets of Shakespeare and Milton. It would certainly be possible to view the couple as fearful, garrulous, foolish, solipsistic, or senile. Useless and isolated, they are nevertheless also amusing and insightful. Nostalgic, Winnie exclaims over fond memories of a past lover in a toolshed, but then admits, "We had no toolshed and he most certainly had no toolshed." She repeatedly praises the blessings she receives, yet worries that there is "so little to say, so little to do, and the fear so great, certain days, of finding oneself . . . left, with hours still to run, before the bell for sleep, and nothing more to say, nothing more to do, that the days go by, certain days go by, quite by, the bell goes, and little or nothing said, little or nothing done."

A perfect encapsulation of existence at the Trace: how can I enliven Don's homecoming? I invite his colleagues to visit for a late afternoon cup of tea. Some of them were part of a lunch group—I called them the Wheezers and Geezers—he can no longer attend. Positioned in the living room with all his props out of sight, Don looks depleted, not the vital man he once was but a phantom of himself, encased in the cobalt-blue carapace and the weird camper outfit. I leave these men to discuss university affairs since their presence means I can quickly run to the grocery store, where I stock up on foods Don likes—Moose Tracks ice cream, cinnamon bread, jam—as well as my own staples: Nicorette gum and red wine. That's what I subsist on these days.

Winnie and Willie never eat or drink; neither do they pee or poop. This sort of inane observation seems inescapable on a day begun not with a bell but with an accident. Maybe Winnie should count herself lucky not to have to deal with my below-the-belt issues. Judith will bring over soup for dinner; next week Jayne will drive me to Indy for my monthly meeting with my oncologist; Jon and Jan have put up screens; Mary has stopped by with a fruit tart. Although grief-struck at the departure of her partner, Sandra sent treats mailed from Zabar's.

But I brood over four weeks of Fran's silence. While driving or cooking, I denounce her to the empty air, telling her how selfish she is. After the first operation, when she had asked if I was avoiding our phone chats, I had sent her an email explaining that I did not want to reproach her and we should just "let matters rest" for a while. Yet when Don had to have a second operation, I was worried about him and about the baby in New York and also about Fran herself—her eerie withdrawal. I emailed again, informing her of the second fall and the needed second surgery and hoping that she was not encountering difficulties of her own. In response, she trotted out a phrase of formulaic sympathy and then stated that she was fine, enjoying her gardening. Hello? She's enjoying her gardening? As for helping out, apparently she prefers not to.

Since then, whenever I dread running into her at a grocery store or drugstore, I rehearse my words—which should simply be "Nice to see you," since what I want to say sounds like the screech of an infant wailing for or raging against its mother. On the toilet with excrement dripping down my thigh this morning, I seethed thinking of Fran, though I had avoided discussing the ostomy with her because this was one problem that really could not be remedied.

On the day of an accident, the best strategy for me is fasting. Even if it means showering instead of bathing, even if I cannot conceive of going swimming ever again, the ostomy equipment, I realize, is the essential prop without which I could not function. With it—hidden under clothing so most people have no clue—I can look and act like a regular person, especially when I wear my wig and draw on eyebrows. This morning, didn't I clean myself up and help Don to dress? My situation seems far superior to Winnie's, I think, and then I hoot, for I am doing exactly what Winnie does: I'm encouraging myself to look on the bright side, to see the glass half full, to remark on another happy day. Surely this is not what Beckett means us to understand, that we are programmed to accept whatever nightmares come and to keep on going?

The question of what Beckett means us to understand is posed in *Happy Days* by the characters called Mr. and Mrs. Shower or Cooker. This couple never appears on stage, but toward the end of act 1 Winnie recounts their appearance. One day they had arrived hand in hand and Mr. Shower or Cooker gaped at Winnie: "What's the idea? He says—stuck up to her diddies in the bleeding ground—coarse fellow—What does it mean? He says—What's it meant to mean?" The last human beings to stray into Winnie and Willie's desert departed without effecting any change at all. Except they prod us to ask about Winnie stuck in a mound and Willie crawling around it: what are they meant to mean?

Winnie considers Mr. Shower or Cooker's question nonsense, drivel, tosh. And she is right, since there is no rhyme or reason for her condition, Willie's, Don's, or my own. Shit happens, my kids and stepkids would say. Don fell twice, I had an operation for ovarian cancer that nicked a bowel and led to infections that in turn led to an ileostomy: a bit of small intestine pulled out of the body and stitched onto the stomach. Whatever caused Winnie's immobility and Willie's incapacitation, it happened to happen and there's no good in it.

But Winnie and Willie's meaning on stage has something to do with their endurance as a couple. Because *Happy Days* concludes with the schmaltzy waltz duet "I love you so" from Strauss's *The Merry Widow*, I have an excuse to read it as a story of later-life love. Throughout Winnie's numerous requests for the sound or sight of Willie in the first act, she reiterates that his presence makes her ongoing existence tolerable. She entreats him to hold up a finger or repeat a phrase. She promises not to ask him for taxing responses, because "to know that in theory you can hear me even though in fact you don't is all I need, just to feel you there within earshot."

All the tried-and-true clichés about theater of the absurd tell us that the play emphasizes human isolation, the entropy that will doom each and every one of us to be engulfed in the tomb of mother earth's womb: ashes to ashes, dust to dust, we all fall down. And certainly Winnie, wondering where her arms and breasts have gone, looks even more immobilized in act 2. Though she repeatedly mentions great mercies, she has sunk deeper into the ditch. With only her head above ground, she has no hands to retrieve the contents of her bag.

Fretting about Willie's visible absence and audible silence, Winnie in the second act finds her head "always full of cries" that remind me of my worst fears of cancer and maybe also Don's fears of his disability: terrors of hosting an alien, of being violated or exposed, of losing body parts and control over so-called private parts. In a reprise of the Shower or Cooker story, Winnie remembers his asking, "Has she anything on underneath?" And in a tale Winnie fabricates, a little girl gets out of bed to undress her dolly when a mouse runs up her thigh and she "screamed and screamed and screamed and screamed."

As in act 1, where the words "Eggs" and "Formication" conflate reproduction not with fornication but with the sense of insects or animals crawling on or under or into the body, infestation worries a character rotting in a ditch. Winnie is rescued from these frights by the extraordinary vision of Willie on all fours and "*dressed to kill—top hat, morning coat, striped trousers, etc., white gloves in hand. Very long bushy white Battle of Britain moustache.*" As he starts to crawl up the mound toward her, she cheers him on and jokes about wanting to give him a hand: "You were always in dire need of a hand, Willie." After he slithers back but then rises again on his hands and knees to face her, Winnie gets what she has wanted all along: "Someone . . . looking at me still" with "Eyes upon my eyes." She has dreamed of Willie coming round to live on her side of the mound.

Will he use his props—top hat, morning coat, striped trousers, white gloves—to follow the advice of Shower or Cooker: to dig Winnie out with his hands? Or, as Winnie surmises, is he dressed to kill in order to reach for the revolver and kill himself or her? Or does he want to reach out to touch her face or get a kiss? Her fright at how he looks at her—she exclaims twice, "Don't look at me like that!"—indicates a new unknowingness of what might eventuate from this sustained reciprocal looking. She is startled at his unpredictable intentions.

His speaking her nickname launches her into the Strauss love song of the music box tune from act 1: "Every touch of fingers / Tells me what I know, / Says for you, / It's true, it's true / You love me so!" The curtain comes down on *Happy Days* with the couple alone in the wilderness, looking at each other with a wild surmise that we in the audience share, for they have changed. Even though Winnie has repeatedly said, "No better, nor worse, no change," Willie has changed his clothes and Winnie has changed her tune.

At the end of the show, he's about to put on a show that she cannot foretell. Somehow their remaining changed onstage—especially her tremulous, heightened uncertainty—trumps their stumped physical remains. However long we live together, however intimately, we are capable of being surprised by our partners and at how little we know them and what they might be capable of, or so I thought as I looked down at the ring on my finger. Isn't this the source of ongoing attraction, being reminded how strangely inscrutable our partner remains?

I'm waiting not for the curtain to go down or the bell for sleep but for five o'clock so I can begin drinking. Don teared up when we heard about the death of our friend Paul Zietlow, and then an email arrived from George: his wife has been diagnosed with lung cancer that has metastasized to her brain. On the Web, I read about the deaths of Shari Benstock and Jane Marcus, two feminist critics gone with so many of my generation. They bring back the terrible loss of Patsy Yaeger last year. Would Sandra weather the shock of her breakup? What month is this, what year? It is the season of sorrow, the year of grieving.

I gaze out at the steep driveway down to the garage, its edges covered by ivy and myrtle. Did Don and I really once take sleds and slide down it on moon-lit snowy nights, risking a smash in the ravine below? They were yellow and red plastic trays, flimsy things, sending us hurtling downward, fast and then faster, until we toppled over, laughing at having escaped colliding into encrusted tree trunks, their iced branches glittering in the lone, tall yard light. The thick, downy snowflakes clung to our hats, scarves, even our eyelashes as we embraced in a heap, warmed by our crunching up and careening down.

During one of this succession of difficult days, I ask Don, "Do you think we should have the bathroom renovated?"

"No," he says. "We won't be here that long."

"Where are we going?"

"That's a good question."

On another of these difficult days, I tell Don, "You need a new iPad. Yours is cracked and running out of juice."

"So am I," he says.

It's the vaudevillian pitter-patter of familiarity, as comforting as the chirping of birds. Once during the stroke fright, when I was informing Don about the taxing demands made by the families of the women in my cancer support group, he said, "You have the advantage of being married to an older man: joint decrepitude." After his first operation, Don recalled a time when he had been working a harvest in Oregon and heard a fellow laborer say about another, "He has as much of a chance as a one-legged ass-kicker." Every time I announce that I'm going to take a shower, Don says, "I believe there's one left."

Chitchat, babbling, nattering—that is what resilient Winnie excels at: phatic speech, sounds that may signify nothing, but neither are they full of sound and fury. The recycled routines of long married people: "Each couple is its own vaudeville act," the novelist Zadie Smith knows. The tick of "Say goodnight, Gracie" is followed by the tock of "Goodnight Gracie." (That's how I remember it, even though Gracie actually only said "Goodnight.")

Chirp, Winnie says, I'm here and are you there? Her prattling rattles on, it keeps her and Willie going on. Maybe this is why Winnie never fears the tug of gravity, of being sucked down into the earth, but rather surprisingly she worries about being "sucked up" into "the blue, like gossamer," should the earth yield and let her go. She asks, "Don't you have to cling on sometimes, Willie?" Indeed I do, Winnie, yes I do.

Old lovers know that love does not conquer all, that our intimacy cannot establish a safe haven somewhere, someplace for us. We are vulnerable to miseries that make us opaque to each other. Yet even if we are stuck or stumped, we are living and learning and loving. Despite everything, Winnie wants to be grounded in her newborn expectancy. She has turned into a role model. Beckett is probably rolling over in his grave.

At times Winnie considers the teasing incongruity between who she is now and who she had been then: "To have been always what I am—and so changed from what I was." At these moments, she knows, words may fail, and one must wait for them to return. And even though there are no remedies, transitional objects prop us up. The apparatuses of the aged—walkers, wigs, hearing aids—become part of us but also not-us. They may not be as treasured as toddlers' teddy bears or security blankets, yet they help us cope with loss. As a prominent scholar of aging, Kathleen Woodward, once speculated, the transitional objects of old age symbolize and mediate our separation from the lives we used to lead and maybe also our ultimate separation from life itself. Munchkin, my mother's chipmunk, takes on new meaning. The props at yoga for cancer patients—bricks, straps, bolsters, chairs—do too. "Shake me up, Judy": isn't that Dickensian tagline also an imaginative prompt and prop?

Tomorrow morning and the next and the next, I will maneuver around the walker in the narrow ground-floor bathroom to position a small end table on which I will place a bowl of soapy water and a washcloth.

PART II

grounded

Alterations

OVERNIGHT, THE RAVINE has crept closer. The trees moved in. The leaves on their branches extend out over the small strip of the grassy backyard, shadowing the back rooms of the Inverness. Light splashing through the windows illuminates the front living room, where Don sits with a book or the new iPad Susannah has sent. But I recline in the family room, where a lamp has to be turned on. It's not easy to do, because a knob has fallen off the light fixture, and I hurt my fingers twisting the little switch. Whenever the exhausting chores allow, I sit on the blue couch with my legs outstretched, a book or the laptop on them. Except in the joy of cooking, I am no domestic goddess, nor was meant to be.

I have always resented spending time or money or thought on upkeep. When in the past I went with Fran to look at new cabinets for her kitchen, I admired the interest she took. Now, when I awake from nightmares about her, my incompetence meshes with apathy about the broken handle on the front screen door. But I must pick out a dishwasher at Sears, run to the pharmacy or grocery, cook dinner, do the laundry and dishes, take out the garbage and recycling, and plan another dinner while it rains and clears and then rains again.

The boon of reading is like that of quilting: it can be picked up and put down and then picked up again. To be within reach of call, I am settling down for the duration with the books I have been collecting in my study, bringing them downstairs, one and then another. With Don less and less communicative, the books are my constant companions.

Reading certainly provides an escape, when I get lost in a book. But, Rebecca Mead reminds us, "a book can also be where one finds oneself; and when a reader is grasped and held by a book, reading does not feel like an escape from life so much as it feels like an urgent, crucial dimension of life itself." Besides grasping and holding us, books sometimes read us, clarifying the issues we confront. In the best moments, according to the playwright Alan Bennett, a perception or feeling "you had thought special and peculiar to you" is "set down by someone else, a person you have never met, someone even who is long dead. And it is as if a hand has come out and taken yours."

The hand reached out by Ovid steadies me. The boon of reading his tale about late-life love cannot be attributed entirely to its regenerative transformations. Every aspect of the brief section devoted to Baucis and Philemon in Ovid's *Metamorphoses* speaks of aging and deterioration, yet the fable glows with affection for its late-life lovers and then for its even later-life lovers. When we first encounter the couple, they are enfeebled by advancing age, and by the end of their tale they are thoroughly exhausted. Clearly Ovid's account has not been integrated into the tradition usually mapped as the history of love's discourse. Writing about love, meaning young love, Roland Barthes declared, "In no love story I have ever read is a character ever *tired*." But Ovid and those who follow him by producing stories of late-life love often describe fatigued lovers.

The teller of the tale, Lelex, is himself getting on: he exhibits judgment that "had been ripened by his years" (872). And he, in turn, first heard the story from "sensible seniors" (1014). He narrates the long-ago time when Jupiter and Mercury, disguised as mortals, were met with a thousand bolted doors in one town before being welcomed into a humble hut by "a couple equally advanced in years" who were wed in their house "and there grew old" (892). Baucis, the wife, and Philemon, the husband, grew old together in a relationship noteworthy for its reciprocity. Too impoverished to have servants, they therefore have no masters in the house, "for there were only two there, and the one / commanding was the same one who obeyed" (898–99).

Lelex emphasizes their equality, their poverty, and also how the couple has been affected by the passage of time. Their door looks ramshackle. Baucis huffs and puffs to resuscitate a flame from yesterday's coals. The "hunk of what had once been bacon," an "old chine," was "not at all improved by long-term storage" (914–95). Baucis trembles as she sets a table, which is rickety, requiring her to slip a potsherd underneath its shortest leg. Her cracked cups are repaired with yellow wax. Despite the couple's patched existence, they represent the sort of domestic harmony that would be associated in the eighteenth century with the elderly Darby and Joan: "He's dropsical, she is sore-eyed, / Yet they're ever uneasy asunder." The names Darby and Joan later became synonymous with social clubs for British pensioners.

Baucis and Philemon's ample hospitality contrasts with their scant means and results in a simple meal as well as a series of miracles. The opening course they serve is rustic—cabbage, ham, olives, pickles, endives, radishes, fresh cheese, and eggs; the next consists of nuts, figs, dates, plums, apples, and an oozing honeycomb. First, they notice that the earthenware bowl for the mixing of wine and water fills up every time it is emptied. Second, since the replenished wine tells them that they are hosting immortals, they resolve to sacrifice their only goose and exhaust themselves chasing it, but the gods keep the bird alive. Then Jupiter and Mercury decide to punish the inhospitable town by flooding it, but they exempt Baucis and Philemon, who, leaning on walking sticks, climb with their guests up a steep mountain. Finally, the gods save the cottage and transform it into a temple with columns, a roof of gold, doors of inlaid bronze, and a marble courtyard.

After the gods ask their wish, Philemon consults with Baucis to obtain their mutual decision. They want to be allowed to guard the temple as its priests and, more importantly, request that eventually "the same hour take us both together, / And that I should not live to see her tomb / Nor she survive to bury me in mine" (994–99). Neither Baucis nor Philemon wants to be widowed; they fear the survivor's grief and loneliness.

The moral maxim with which Lelex concludes his story—"Let

those who reverence / the gods be reverenced as gods as well"
(1020–21)—strikes me as close to the mark, until I think about
what exactly the gods have done in this fable. Jupiter and Mercury,
offended at not encountering an open-door policy, have obliterated an entire town and the multitude of people who resided in
it. Isn't this a case of overkill? The flooding reminds me of the
story of Noah and his wife, Lot and his, and of the destruction
of the Egyptians in the Red Sea, a part of the seder that always
disturbs me.

Although I resist the moral, the metamorphosis of the couple
strikes me as compelling and disquieting. After years spent tending the temple, Baucis and Philemon, depleted by older old age,
stand by its columns; they are speaking of their past

> *when Baucis saw Philemon come into leaf,*
> *and Philemon saw Baucis put forth leaves.*
> *Then, as their faces both were covered over*
> *by the growing treetop, while it was allowed them,*
> *they spoke and answered one another's speech:*
> *"Farewell, dear spouse!" they both cried out together,*
> *just as their lips were sealed in leafiness. (1005–11)*

The leafing wife and husband escape the grief and loneliness
of one predeceasing the other. But as C. S. Lewis's partner knew,
death—even if lover and beloved die at the same instant—still
constitutes the ultimate divorce . . . a farewell to life itself and to
each other. Ovid captures the shocking finality of that separation by depicting the couple's faces "covered over" and their lips

"sealed" at the moment of their final goodbye. The alarm of flesh turning into bark, of limbs turning into boughs, of faces turning into leaves troubles their fate—in part because the metamorphosis of Baucis and Philemon recalls the transformation of another mythic character in Ovid's book, Daphne.

After the virgin Daphne prays to be delivered from Apollo, the desirous god pursuing her, she feels torpor seeping through her limbs. Her trunk is girdled with a layer of bark, her hair turns into foliage, her head into the summit of a tree, her arms become branches, and sluggish roots staple her feet to the earth (1.756–72). When Apollo feels a breast trembling under the new bark, the novelist Jhumpa Lahiri points out, "It's not clear where the nymph ends and the tree begins; the beauty of this scene is that it portrays the fusion of two elements, of both beings." Daphne escapes the rape of Apollo; however, she had wanted to continue chasing through the forest, a chaste huntress. She can retain her chastity only by relinquishing the chase. Daphne, Baucis, and Philemon lose voice, volition, and mobility.

Or do they? I have heard the trees around the Inverness whisper and whistle, rustle and moan; once in a straight-line wind storm, I heard them shriek. They twine and bend like Elizabeth Barrett Browning's thoughts about the sturdy wood of her husband. After Don and I moved to the country, before a road was paved beyond the red shed and through the field and forest beyond it, we regularly tramped a rough path that meandered around a clearing of rocks placed in a circle—we called it the Shrine of the Virgin Sacrifices—and into tangled thickets with crowns that hummed and thrummed. We have watched trees closer to the house bow, turn, and twist their arms and also their trunks when they grew curved, lost a branch, or went up in flames, hit by lightning as was one of our giant fir trees. We smell the scents of their foliage, see them blossom, fork, wrinkle, shed, drink, wave, shelter birds, and heal their own wounds.

The pioneering thinker Eve Kosofsky Sedgwick believed that after her demise she would be "differently extant." Baucis and Philemon as intertwined trees—they are described as "an oak and linden, side by side" at the beginning of the tale (877) and "side by side, / sprung from a single trunk" at its close (1013–14)—are exactly that, differently extant. They are separated neither from each other nor from life itself. Although they can no longer speak in a language we understand, they remain braided on earth.

Nestled together permanently, they abide differently, which is what Don and I must learn to do, which is what the aging Baucis and Philemon must have learned to do even before their transformation, when they trekked with their sticks out of the drowned town to tend the temple. Now Don and I cannot leave the Inverness without difficulty. The heavy cobalt-blue cast keeps us mostly house-bound. The town hardly exists for us.

However, we have heard about a resource called Agewise Design. Its "Certified Aging-in-Place Specialists" suggest renovations to ensure the safety of older people in their own homes. We will invite them for a consultation. Maybe the ground-floor bathroom can be made more accessible. In other respects, I have made the ground floor habitable, though I miss our bed upstairs. Its old-fashioned wooden frame charmed me when we found it, probably because I had never before had a real headboard. Both

Don and I grew up in makeshift sleep areas—on sofa beds in our parents' apartments: his on an enclosed porch, mine in a living room. At our visit to a bed store, we were both amused when I tested out firmness by lying down on a succession of mattresses, and the salesman said to Don, "I'm sure your daughter will find one to her liking."

The bed in the ground-floor bedroom has no headboard. Getting into and out of it constitutes the single most difficult activity of Don's day. When Susannah arrived here for the second surgery, she bought a new mattress. The previous one really did need to be replaced. Don and I had purchased it two decades ago for my former husband. Because he could not live alone while recuperating from heart bypass surgery, he recovered in the ground-floor bedroom.

During the next twenty years, how many guests slept on that bed? Dyan or Rick visiting for a weekend, Jonathan when he was commuting from Chicago, my British cousins when they came to surprise my mother, Don's sister, our children and their partners, Mary and Andrew's kids, and Sandra. I have stuffed two pint-sized rocking chairs, a scooter, and a plastic frog full of Legos into the closets to make room for clean stacks of Don's camper outfits, a commode, a laundry basket, and all the lotions and potions that do not fit into the adjacent bathroom.

Ovid's tale charms in its depiction of the sort of hospitality Don and I used to relish—not formal, but easygoing and unpretentious: brunches for graduate students on the back porch, the sun streaming through the skylight; suppers in the dining room for newly tenured, retained, or departing colleagues. Even though Baucis and Philemon could not catch their goose, the appetizing meal they serve suits their beaming expressions of goodwill. Did the capricious gods save the goose because they were satiated, or did they relish the prospect of watching decrepit Baucis and Philemon chase after it? I no longer have the time or the energy to cook for others, and Don has neither the physical nor the emotional resiliency to be sociable. Will all that fine hospitality be relegated to our past?

The only socializing I do these days involves not immortals but memorials. Jayne stayed with Don when I went to speak the words he had written for Paul Zietlow's memorial. They were beautiful words spoken in a beautiful setting—a tent set up in a lush garden—but at the lectern I faced Paul's widow, who was sitting in the first row weeping. There was a hole in the tent's roof and when the rain started, it poured down right on the heads of my three most elderly and incapacitated colleagues.

As soon as I got back home, I searched for A. R. Ammons's poem "In View of the Fact," a consoling work about late-life lovers mourning the deaths and disabilities of their friends. Ammons begins by expressing his sadness at attending too many funerals. Then he catalogs friends in intensive care, or losing a limb to diabetes, or left alone in an empty house. His poem captures the sorrow of an address book with names and numbers scratched out, of holiday cards being replaced by sympathy cards, and yet he conveys the need to hang on to the ones still living.

What seems remarkable is not his vow that he and his wife will love every one of their losses, but the next step. Ammons imagines that after he and his wife die, they will "leave it to / others to love, love that can only grow brighter / and deeper till the very end, gaining strength / and getting more precious all the way. . . ." Love is not a limited substance (like a quart of fluid) that you can spill or that, given away, is gone. It is more like a blazing torch handed over in a relay or words whispered and transmuted in a children's game of telephone. This bountiful view of love—a prized activity that can outlive us, intensifying after us—heartens me.

Although our circumstances have nose-dived since I began this project, Ammons seems to be affirming my decision to prize the preciousness of my late-life love by learning how others have envisioned loving in later life. On the anniversary of my father's death, I decided to be more methodical about the books I have collected. I have amassed quite a few ambitious novels, plays, poems, and movies. I trust they will alter and deepen my understanding, and I can group them into a more orderly progression. For in these works the issues of late-life lovers fall into easily recognizable categories, some of which I have touched upon but all of which present new complications.

First of all, sexuality—in same-age but also in winter-spring relationships: sex involving older lovers arrives with its unique inhibitions, motivations, practices, and pleasures. And then problems related to inheritance and retirement, obstructionist adult children, the transformation of temporality in older age, the caretaking needed by ailing partners, and the subtractions or multiplications of memories in aging lovers. Each portrait in these quite different creative works will undoubtedly record a mutated facet of later-life love. Each will serve as a guidepost providing information on the highways and byways of my own later-life partnership.

I want the books especially—vibrant and nuanced—to take precedence over boring domestic routines during a period in which Don and I can at least intermittently hope for his partial recovery. I'm beginning again, but then when am I not beginning again? There have been comebacks before: after my father's suicide, after the divorce, after the terrible surgeries. After 2013, the predicted date of my demise, I became a sort of revenant. "Who would have thought my shriveled heart / Could have recovered greenness?" And I have a map now, marking tracks through the terrain, providing the pleasurable prospect of an evolving project.

Like Baucis and Philemon feeding the gods or relying on walking sticks, Don cannot move the way he used to, and to a lesser extent this is true for me as well. Is it age that covers us like a bark and puts down encumbering roots? Will we splinter like ancient trunks? Inflexible, he creaks and hesitates or groans before planting a foot down to rise or take a small step. While the bark thickens and the roots stiffen, arresting us, we must come to terms with the metamorphosis of aging. Here resides the difference between the fate of Baucis and Philemon, on the one hand, and the destiny of fleet-footed Daphne, on the other.

Like Don and me, Ovid's couple—setting the table in their cottage and then tending the temple—felt their own and each other's hearts pounding beneath the rind, the sap flowing behind the hide. Aging prepared them for their ultimate transformation into inseparably mingled limbs. Through their spoken wish to be taken together and their metamorphosis, Ovid hints at the release of exchanging the burdens of human form and consciousness for gnarled and mossy branches, enmeshed roots. Decades-long partnerships, according to one British academic, involve two people in "a process of growing into one another, of growing together like plants, of intertwining without entirely interlocking, and certainly without submerging." When the film critic Molly Haskell considered her long marriage—"Over the years we had grown together like two trees"—she worried about losing "our distinctness of outline" and determined to prune in order "to sprout new growth."

It is a comfort that I can continue to comprehend the thickening, stiffening, intertwining, and sprouting through a succession of characters undergoing similar alterations. In defiance of an overwhelming representational history that decries the deficits of aging and of a powerful culture addicted to eternal youthfulness, the trick will be to find gains in the quite evident losses of these inexorable permutations.

"People recover from tendon tears," my treasured oncologist remarked upon hearing about Don's second operation. Dr. Matei was undoubtedly acknowledging how depressing it was for her to deal with cancers from which many people never recover. I will miss her if she takes another job, but she deserves the excellent offers she is receiving. Tormented by the decision making, she is nevertheless pleased that if she goes, she will leave me at a juncture when the scans and the blood marker indicate a stay or pause we had never dared to hope for. At our last consultation, her use of the word "remission" startled me. Since I continue to take powerful medications daily, I had thought only in terms of a more modest word: "maintenance."

To be able to remain with the books, I will follow the advice that Fran would have given me—namely, to get more help. It was Fran who looked at all the weeds the previous summer and sent a gardener, whose coreopsis and cosmos now bloom between the short mounds of green grasses on each side of the brick walkway leading to the front door of the Inverness. I will ask one of the cleaners if she could serve once a week as a housekeeper to do whatever has to be done: not just vacuuming but also laundry and forwarding Project Divest by lugging unused but usable stuff from the basement to Goodwill, for surely needier people could benefit from some of the things that have amassed. I have to recognize my own limitations.

Just the other day, I received an email from a student who had read one of my essays in the *Times*. Now a physician, he remembered seeing me at the podium and wondering what he could possibly learn from "an old white lady." He must have attended one of the large freshmen lectures I used to teach regularly, introducing first-year students to a college experience most of their parents never had. They received "extra credit" if they recited a poem by heart. The last week of the semester, they lined the auditorium's aisles: once a boy grieving his ailing father brought the house down with a fervent recitation of "Do Not Go Gentle"; once a girl dressed as a shepherdess recited "Little Lamb who made thee?"— or was that in one of the courses for majors that Don and I team taught? I knew the freshmen had never been to either Boston or New York when they commented on my "great Boston accent." If I was old when I was still teaching, I must be ancient now.

The night I decided to get housekeeping help, I took a clue from Baucis and Philemon and made a rustic dinner of Ps—

prosciutto, peas, parmesan, and pasta—with lemon zest that made it as bright as the coreopsis and cosmos at the ramshackle front door. I am not mixing my wine with water, but I have a new way of thinking about the pattern of the quilt I am making for the baby: flying geese. I had supplemented fabrics my friend Dyan mailed to me with patterned cottons in every conceivable shade of green. The baby does not look well in the daily photographs his parents send, but he has returned home where he can benefit from their vigilant care. My geese are flying, I whisper over bits of cotton. They are not going to be caught or cooked. They augur health and recovery.

Later that night, I fell asleep thinking of fore-edge paintings. Don had explained the term to me—I had seen images on the Internet while seeking cover ideas for the cancer book I had completed—and they intrigued me. A fore-edge painting is a scene painted on the edges of the pages of a book. In some cases, it can be seen when the volume is closed, but in others only if it is open. In the last sustained image before sleep, an ancient tome fanned open to reveal a colorful picture of an old man and an old woman chasing a goose on a meadow bordered by entwined trees.

Lovesickness

AFTER A NIGHT of galloping thunderstorms, we were awakened at the ungodly hour of 9 a.m. by the phone ringing. I listened to the start of a recording selling funeral insurance, and then lurched back to fulminate.

"Very timely," Don said.

Our days are now chopped up by twice-weekly visits to the Trace for physical therapy at 1 p.m. The surgeon had used an electric saw to remove the cast, which he replaced with the same sort of black Velcro brace supplied after the first operation—except this one has a dial at the side of the knee, so it can bend. We will keep it locked except during therapy, when Tyrone's peers teach Don a series of exercises. Some he must repeat daily at home: marching in place in the walker, up on his toes, then down on his heels, sidestepping, ankle pumps, straight leg lifts on the bed, wheelchair pushups. They measure his progress with a sort of protractor. He can bend his knee only 30 degrees.

Before or after those sessions, we drive to the pharmacy for drugs or salves to deal with congestion, swollen feet, fungal infection, urine output, allergies. It seems urgent to escape into fiction, to choose a substantial, engrossing book. While Don works out in the Trace gym, I find an empty room down the corridor and start a novel that absorbs me for weeks. Gabriel García Márquez's sprawling *Love in the Time of Cholera* reads like the pièce de résistance, the grand slam of the late-life love tradition. I am transported because this book is like no other I have ever encountered—riveting, rollicking, and yet, in some way I could not quite figure, deadly serious about the unique sexuality of seniors.

Love in the Time of Cholera depicts the longevity of passion through a triangle of two septuagenarians and an octogenarian— a woman and two men living in a Caribbean seaport town at the end of the nineteenth century and beginning of the twentieth. At least it seems to be celebrating the heart of aging in a ribald, outrageous, and then startlingly ironic narrative. García Márquez has taken up exactly the themes that fascinate me: why, then, do I have the uneasy sense that he questions whether we should love later-life love stories?

At the opening, a corpse dramatizes the lethal power of the fear of old age that has many in its grip, a lonely dread that is contrasted with the contentment of an aging couple. The dead man had made an irrevocable decision not to grow old and therefore killed himself at the age of sixty. Eighty-one-year-old Dr. Juvenal Urbino pronounces the cause of death "gerontophobia," after he returns to the domestic and civic routines he shares with his handsome seventy-two-year-old wife, Fermina Daza: "they were not capable of living for even an instant without the other, or without thinking about the other, and that capacity diminished as their age increased."

In the brief introductory section of this long novel, García Márquez wryly celebrates the intimacies of a mature marriage. The doctor remains committed to his medical obligations and his cultural enterprises; however, along with his wife he plays the perverse games of collaborative domesticity. So, for instance, Dr. Urbino leaves their opulent house and starts sleeping at the hospital, outraged that he has been forced to bathe without soap for a week; Fermina Daza, furious that she had forgotten to replace the soap, protests that the soap has always been there. For three months, they "inflamed their feelings": "He was not ready to come back as long as she refused to admit there had been no soap in the bathroom, and she was not prepared to have him back until he recognized that he had consciously lied to torment her."

There is a whiff of ritual in this quarrel, as in my skirmishes with Don about his insistence that he alone knows the proper way to load the dishwasher. Dr. Urbino returns to their bed when he realizes that his wife wants him there, and he does so by saying, "There was soap." When they recall this episode, "neither could believe the astonishing truth that this had been the most serious argument in fifty years of living together."

The intimate details of García Márquez's descriptions touch me. A memory of Dr. Urbino's "stallion's stream" on their wedding night returns to Fermina Daza when "years weakened the stream, for she could never resign herself to his wetting the rim of the toilet bowl each time he used it." Dr. Urbino copes with his oblique stream by wiping the rim of the bowl with toilet paper and later by urinating sitting down. Refusing to retire, he realizes that "even the oldest people were younger than he was and that he had become the only survivor of his generation's legendary group portraits." This must have been Don's thought, too, when he attended luncheons at the Tudor Room in the Union, though some of the men with whom he helped to found Victorian Studies, the journal and the program, are still alive. Dr. Urbino explains his fidelity to Fermina Daza in exactly the terms in which Don explained his fidelity to his first wife and then to me: "he would say, it was more work than the pleasure of daytime love was worth to take off one's clothes and put them back on again."

Only much later in *Love in the Time of Cholera* do we learn that neither Dr. Urbino nor Fermina Daza married for love. He, an eligible bachelor, had been struck by her haughty ferocity; she, alone and impoverished at twenty-one, had reached a stage at which he seemed the suitable mate. Yet her love deepens with compassion for her husband as he suffers "the disadvantage of being ten years ahead of her as he stumbled alone through the mists of old age":

In the end they knew each other so well that by the time they had been married for thirty years they were like a single divided being, and they felt uncomfortable at the frequency with which they guessed each other's thoughts without intending to, or the ridiculous accident of one of them anticipating in public what the other was going to say. Together they had overcome the daily incomprehension, the instantaneous hatred, the reciprocal nastiness and fabulous flashes of glory in the conjugal conspiracy. It was the time when they loved each other best, without hurry or excess, when both were most conscious of and grateful for their incredible victories over adversity.

Don and I married only a handful of years ago—at the county law building that also serves as a jail. We had to pass through a metal detector, and the officiator, with the grand name of Noble Bush, wore a red Indiana University basketball sweater. But we often feel "like a single divided being," guessing each other's thoughts and anticipating each other's reactions. I had experienced enough "reciprocal nastiness" in earlier relationships to be grateful that it rarely mars the "fabulous flashes of glory" in our "conjugal conspiracy." Still, I have found myself overcome by "instantaneous hatred," when in a noisy restaurant Don mumbles words that I cannot decipher by lip-reading since he puts his clasped hands in front of his mouth. Only as I note their elegance do I say, "I must be going deaf."

At the end of the first section of *Love in the Time of Cholera*, Dr. Urbino falls from a ladder and his wife comes running. With "unrepeatable sorrow at dying without her," he speaks his last words of love. Because he had pioneered new methods of warding off cholera epidemics, his funeral becomes a public event that infuriates Fermina Daza, who explodes in a blind rage filling her "with the control and the courage to face her solitude alone." Without him, she feels like an amputee suffering pains and cramps in the limb no longer there.

How odd, then, that this hymn to "the conjugal conspiracy" concludes with the appearance of a former lover from her youth, seventy-six-year-old Florentino Ariza, who informs Fermina Daza that he has waited "for more than half a century, to repeat to you once again my vow of eternal fidelity and everlasting love." Odder still, after a night sobbing in her sleep, Fermina Daza awakens to the realization that she "had thought more about Florentino Ariza than about her dead husband."

The next sections of *Love in the Time of Cholera*, the bulk of the novel, consist of lengthy flashbacks, a structure that strikes me as a formally significant aspect of late-life love stories. Lovers in their seventies—even those who had a relationship with each other in their youth—need to process their complicated backstories. Those convoluted backstories make the flashback an especially important technique, enabling us to comprehend the burdens of history: here the breakup of the young lovers' engagement and then the courtship, honeymoon, and marriage of Fermina Daza and Dr. Urbino as well as the evolution of the lovelorn Florentino Ariza.

In the case of Florentino Ariza, García Márquez asks an intriguing question: is it possible to recover an early romance much later in life or, more difficult still, sustain a romance for half a century? Most of the pages of *Love in the Time of Cholera* tell the story of Florentino Ariza, who adores Fermina Daza for "fifty-one years, nine months, and four days" until he makes his second proposal of marriage. García Márquez enlists my affections for this quintessential romantic. But if the aged Florentino Ariza personifies the invincible powers of love, why—as I read—do my reservations about him mount?

Everything about illegitimate, impoverished Florentino Ariza reeks of sentiment. As a youth, he falls in love with Fermina Daza at first sight and begins writing her perfumed letters. After two years of "frenetic correspondence," he makes a formal proposal to which she agrees "*if you promise not to make me eat eggplant.*" Her thieving father, opposing the match on materialistic grounds, divides the couple by taking her on a "demented trip." Upon her return, the eighteen-year-old Fermina Daza experiences "an abyss of disenchantments" and breaks off the engagement. When her cousin subsequently sees Florentino Ariza, he looks like an "invisible clerk with his air of a whipped dog, whose clothing, worthy of a rabbi in disgrace, and whose solemn manner could not perturb anyone's heart"—and yet she says of him, "he is all love."

Throughout his life, Florentino Ariza remains enamored of Fermina Daza, though he hides his passion from her. After her marriage, he escapes first into serialized love novels, then into a series of affairs and flings, recording them in a coded book titled "Women." After fifty years, "he had some twenty-five notebooks, with six hundred twenty-two entries of long-term liaisons, apart from the countless fleeting adventures that did not even deserve a charitable note." In these sexual escapades, he revels in the game of love, specifically the game of hunting. A hunter of willing widows and adventurous wives and young girls, Florentino Ariza nevertheless "behaved as if he were the eternal husband of Fermina Daza, an unfaithful husband but a tenacious one." At the same time, motivated by a fierce determination to deserve her, he begins working for the River Company of the Caribbean.

The elderly Florentino Ariza, who finally gets his chance to court the widowed Fermina Daza, hardly resembles his younger self. While he aged, he battled baldness with "one hundred and seventy-two infallible cures," until "a barber's razor left everything as smooth as a baby's bottom." The need for false teeth, however, he welcomed "with an orthopedic smile." He endures the complaints of old age, like repeated crises of constipation, better than most "because he had known them since his youth." When he enrages the widowed Fermina Daza by returning as a moth-eaten wreck, she cannot imagine him as the boy she had known and writes him an insulting letter. Within a year, he wins her over with an extensive literary meditation on "love as a state of grace: not the means to anything but the alpha and omega, an end in itself."

García Márquez concludes his novel by exploring the treachery of the body and of family ties that people in their seventies must overcome to attain a sexual relationship. When they first meet again, Florentino Ariza flees his beloved's house because his "intestines suddenly filled in an explosion of painful foam" and he is terrified that she might hear his bowels "bubbling." Adult children also serve as a challenge. Paradoxically, anger that her children judge late-life love revolting leads Fermina Daza to determine, "If we widows have any advantage, it is that there is no one left to give us orders." She decides to take her first river expedition, which Florentino Ariza arranges on one of his company's ships, the *New Fidelity*. Despite her children's conviction that "there was an age at which love began to be indecent," the two begin their voyage out.

On shipboard, the lovers cope with inhibitions that often accompany lovemaking in older age. Florentino Ariza reaches with "two icy fingers," and the clasped hands of Fermina Daza make them both realize that "the hands made of old bones were not the hands they had imagined before touching." As they kiss, Florentino Ariza shudders because she "had the sour smell of old age," but then considers that "he must give off the same odor." The days pass, the river narrows, she loses her hearing, and they spend hours embracing, with him exploring "her withered neck with his fingertips, her bosom armored in metal stays, her hips with their decaying bones, her thighs with their aging veins." "If we're going to do it, let's do it," she says, taking the initiative, "but let's do it like grownups." He sees her wrinkled shoulders, sagging breasts, ribs covered by flappy skin "as pale and cold as a frog's," and undresses to her laughter.

Sexuality in old age requires a sense of humor as well as patience. When Fermina Daza takes the "final step," she finds her lover "unarmed." Yet the next day, refreshed, "his guard was up, and she realized that he did not expose his weapon by accident, but displayed it as if it were a war trophy in order to give himself courage." Though the rushed act of intercourse—the first time she has made love in over twenty years—leaves her disappointed, they are satisfied with the joy of being together.

But isn't there something sinister about the means by which the couple extend their shipboard romance? The only way to bypass taking on cargo and other passengers involves hoisting the flag of cholera. With the yellow flag raised, the *New Fidelity* changes course while Fermina Daza helps Florentino Ariza take his enemas and brushes his false teeth. After a dance, "they made the tranquil, wholesome love of experienced grandparents."

Florentino Ariza vows to sail with her up and down the river eternally, for their love "was more solid the closer it came to death." What they want is what many lovers want: "a little cosmos (with its own time, its own logic) inhabited only by 'the two of us,'" as Roland Barthes put it.

Though I rejoice in the antique lovers' union, I find all the signs of degeneration unnerving: the yellow cholera flag as well as the cold hands, sour smells, deafness, enemas, and false teeth. Are these aged lovers traveling on a ship of fools or a ship of death? Both seem oblivious to the erosive undertow that their author depicts. I quickly go online, because that current reminds me of John Betjeman's poem "Late-Flowering Lust":

> *My head is bald, my breath is bad,*
> *Unshaven is my chin.*
> *I have not now the joys I had*
> *When I was young in sin.*

Like García Márquez, Betjeman knew that the young have no monopoly on lust, which nevertheless undergoes a transformation in old age, for the deterioration of the body infiltrates the urgency of desire with thoughts of its demise.

At a reunion, when the speaker of Betjeman's poem embraces a responsive woman, the act of intimacy leads him to picture two clasping skeletons:

> *Dark sockets look on emptiness*
> *Which once was loving-eyed,*

The mouth that opens for a kiss
Has got no tongue inside.

Betjeman's haunted luster realizes how little time he has left and then what painful probabilities await him in the near future. The jaunty light verse rhythms and rhymes underscore the grotesque surrealism of late-flowering lust.

The late-flowering consummation that concludes García Márquez's novel conflates love and death, Eros and Thanatos, not only in images of bodily decay and cholera but also in a devastated natural setting for which Florentino Ariza is partly responsible. The uncontrolled deforestation undertaken by his riverboat company has razed the colossal trees, along with the parrots and monkeys who depended on the forest's foliage. By day, the lovers see "calcinated flatlands stripped of entire forests that had been devoured by the boilers of the riverboats and the debris of godforsaken villages"; by night they smell "the nauseating stench of corpses floating down to the sea" in a "ravaged land."

Florentino Ariza had ignored early reports about the alarming state of the river because his mind had been "clouded by his passion." Traveling up and down a spoiled wasteland, the lovers on the *New Fidelity* resemble the ghosts on the legendary ship of the Flying Dutchman, fated never to find port and sighted by sailors as a portent of doom. Was Florentino Ariza's love an obsession, a compulsion that effectively blinded him to the devastation he and his company were in fact effecting and that his own body was undergoing? Had his mother assumed that "the symptoms of love were the same as those of cholera" because romantic love is a disease? And what about her lovesick son's catalogue of "six hundred twenty-two entries of long-term liaisons"? What sort of newfangled, rinky-dink fidelity is that?

"Love is like a fever," Stendhal insisted; "it comes and goes without the will having any part of the process." "Love is a universal migraine," Robert Graves once declared. Robert Lowell likened it to delirium, Roland Barthes to the madness of wanting *"nothing but the two of us."* The Greek poets "represent eros as an invasion, an illness, an insanity, a wild animal, a natural disaster," according to the classicist Anne Carson. We yearn and ache for who we want. How my knees weakened, my palms sweat, my pulse raced, my stomach flip-flopped, my face tingled when (after the mistimed first kiss at Lake Ogle) Don stopped by my office—tipping his chair back at a precarious angle, an index finger propped at each temple—to propose another walk or lunch.

And then again at our first Valentine's Day dinner date, when I knew, but he did not yet know, that I wore a garter belt and stockings under my dress. A note that I had asked the waiter to conceal in his dessert—it said "Darling, you send me"—was illegible from melted chocolate. Which one of us had started that odd custom: his leaving a tender index card under the pillow or in a briefcase at my house, my sticking a Post-it note with endearments on the desk at his? Not even the embarrassment of my children blundering into our secret assignations stopped us from continuing them. Nor did living together put an end to the amorous messages. After our wedding in the jail, on our one-night honeymoon in Louisville's Seelbach Hotel, his postcard in my laptop case read, "Our love is here to stay." According to García Márquez, irrational love—"the alpha and omega, an end in itself"—encapsulates us, making us do what we should not do, obscuring vision and obliterating reason.

All sorts of sinister sexual escapades undertaken by Florentino Ariza and also by Dr. Urbino keep worrying me, while I pack Don into the back seat of the car and the walker into the trunk and then unpack them at the Trace or the Inverness, carrying García Márquez back and forth. Just as Florentino Ariza ignored reports about the ruined river, in reading the novel had I skipped to the consummation of his desire, ignoring upsetting information along the way? What did García Márquez mean when he remarked about this novel that he had set a "trap" for the reader? As I helped Don in the bathroom and the bedroom, I puzzled over the maze of García Márquez's multiple stories: I had been rooting for Dr. Urbino and Fermina Daza and then for Florentino Ariza and Fermina Daza. How can I process disturbing passages that seem to satirize their—and also my—romance with later-life romance?

It was a historic day—both joyous and heartbreaking—when we managed to tape a garbage bag around Don's braced leg, seat him on a plastic bench positioned half in and half out of the bathtub, and use the handheld shower that Julie had installed. On June 26, the Supreme Court ruled that gay people could marry and President Obama sang "Amazing Grace" in a South Carolina church where African American worshippers had been massacred. An epidemic of gun violence was devastating the country. That its victims were so often people of color might explain why the tradition I have so far found is overwhelmingly white. In García Márquez's novel, most of the darker-skinned characters do not live long enough to experience late-life love. Or is there a different attitude toward aging—toward its physical manifestations—in cultures less saturated by Catholicism or Puritanism . . . with all their suspicions about the body?

After watching the late-night news, after wheeling Don into the bedroom to help him get undressed, I started a load of laundry, recalling Don's story about a colleague who taught with him at Stillman College back in the sixties. Jim had arrived in Alabama from Connecticut with a sick wife and three little kids in tow. Relieved at finding a laundromat, he interpreted the signs "Colored" and "White" to mean that one set of machines was for colored clothes, the other for white. When his students learned of his mistake, Don said, Jim could do no wrong.

It was time to shut off all the lights and gaze out the windows facing the meadow. There they were, tiny gems of light, rising and glowing, flickering, floating here and there. Were there fewer of them this year than that memorable time when Don and I had brought out towels and lain down in the darkness to marvel at the mesmerizing light show of what seemed like an infinitude of delicate fireflies?

During the magical summer weeks that we spent at Bellagio—astonished by the majesty of the view of Lake Como from our window—a residency in a retreat for artists and scholars gave us a taste of the aristocratic life: maids cleaning our suite, chefs preparing our meals, a villa with gracious public rooms. In 2001, we hiked up and down the steep steps to the village, overwhelmed by the olive groves, the Alps in the distance, the gelato. Or was it 2004 at Bogliasco, where we had hilarious conversations with Italians who spoke as little English as we did Italian? We wondered whether we had missed the firefly season or if it was a Midwestern phenomenon.

Ah, I suddenly realized, García Márquez was thinking about Italy. It hit me that *Love in the Time of Cholera* nods at Thomas Mann's famous depiction of love in a time of cholera, *Death in Venice*. I had no desire to reread Mann's account of a fifty-year-old male writer's obsession with a fourteen-year-old boy. In the vise of gerontophobia, Thomas Mann linked aging with predatory sexuality and degeneration. But García Márquez was raising ominous questions about later-life love that I had not previously considered, or maybe I had marginalized them. Does love isolate us from the world outside its bubble? Should late-life love be judged and found wanting because it sequesters us from disasters in which we are complicit?

I had finished García Márquez's novel, but it hadn't finished with me. Further sobering reflection on the human capacity for perversity, delineated in many interpolated scenes within his profoundly disquieting magnum opus, might help me understand the wide range of roles Eros plays in the lives of the aging and the aged.

What's Love Got to Do with It?

IF *LOVE IN THE TIME OF CHOLERA* mocks late-life romanticism as harmful escapism, is García Márquez implicitly challenging the basis of this book and my life? Does his novel issue a warning that my absorption in later-life love, and my curiosity about stories of later-life love, might be misguided? Shouldn't I be attending to more important matters—like global warming, rising poverty rates, gun violence at home, and terrorism overseas?

Best to take a walk when reaching such an impasse, I decided on a hot afternoon free from the need to traipse to the Trace. With the help of the walker, Don got down the brick walkway and onto the circle of beauty with me at his side. The circle of beauty, a potholed oval driveway in front of the Inverness, gained its name by virtue of the dogwoods, tulip poplars, pear trees, towering firs, lilac bushes, and massive beech gracing its prospects, some outside and some inside the driveway.

"I've drafted a letter to Fran," I told Don, as we inched forward, "a real letter, snail mail. Every time the phone rings, every time the iPhone pings, I think it must be her. Every time I go to the mailbox, I think, 'Surely she's written.' In the letter I make it clear that I understand we have been on 'different wavelengths' and respect her commitment to seclusion, but I also say that her absence during your surgeries really upset me."

Don was looking down, not at me or out at the trees or up to the sky, a Mediterranean blue with the curlicue of a cloud. He had heard most of this before, interminably, but not about the letter.

"Basically I say that her withdrawal has hurt me; I needed more engagement from her than she seemed able or willing to offer."

To my chagrin, he was still looking down as we crept forward up a slight incline. I can walk short distances fairly easily, but for some incomprehensible reason—maybe the daily cancer medication—standing up while standing still makes my spine ache and I realized that I was stooping, waiting for him to progress.

"I end by grieving our 'abandoned intimacy' and admitting that I have no insight into what to do about it. Why are you looking down? Do you think I shouldn't mail it? Why are you wincing?"

"Every pebble, every twig and acorn hurts."

"You shouldn't have to walk in those socks. We need to buy extra-wide shoes."

"It might make you feel better, trying to resume the relationship," he said, not noticing the marigolds and zinnias that had just been planted near the cosmos by the front door.

As always, inside we parted ways, Don to the sunlit front room with its white carpet and wingback chair near the window bird-feeder, me to the colorful but dark family room where I used a tissue to protect my fingers while struggling to turn the tiny switch on the torch lamp. Like a magnet, García Márquez's novel drew me back to the septuagenarian libertine Florentino Ariza, whose fanatical obsession with love results not only in ecological but also in human catastrophes. Why had I sidelined these debacles, when they are so deeply offensive?

Florentino Ariza's adventures in eroticism over five decades involve his hunting some six hundred twenty-two widows, wives, and girls in bawdy encounters with lusty women delighted by his philandering, including one who reaches orgasm while sucking an infant pacifier. But two of his exploits, one in the middle and one at the end of *Love in the Time of Cholera*, prove that Florentino Ariza's career as a Don Juan caused the wrongful deaths of some of the women who reciprocated his advances.

After an exchange of love notes through pigeon carriers, Florentino Ariza pursued an affair with one Olimpia Zuleta, who "preferred to remain naked for several hours in a slow-moving repose that was, for her, as loving as love itself." After one session of voluptuous modeling or cradling, he dipped his finger in a can of red paint, drew "an arrow of blood pointing south," and wrote on her belly "*This pussy is mine*": "That same night, Olimpia Zuleta undressed in front of her husband, having forgotten what was scrawled there, and he did not say a word, his breathing did not even change, nothing, but he went to the bathroom for his razor while she was putting on her nightgown, and in a single slash he cut her throat." What distresses the monomaniacal Florentino Ariza about the event is not the shocking murder but "the misfortune of Fermina Daza's learning about his infidelity."

In the second, equally scandalous incident, fourteen-year-old América Vicuña, "entrusted by her family to Florentino Ariza as her guardian and recognized blood relative," is led with the "gentle astuteness" of "a kind grandfather, toward his secret slaughterhouse." A kind grandfather's secret slaughterhouse? A septuagenarian hitting on his teenage ward? For her, "the doors of heaven opened" and "she burst into flower"; for him, the affair has "the charm of a restorative perversion." Under the cover of their kinship and extreme difference in ages, "he loved her with more anguish than any other, because he was certain he would be dead by the time she finished secondary school."

When Florentino Ariza abruptly drops her because of his reunion with the widowed Fermina Daza, América Vicuña takes the initiative in bed—"she cut him into pieces with malicious tenderness, she added salt to taste, pepper, a clove of garlic . . . until he was seasoned and on the platter, and the oven was heated to the right temperature"—but he resists. Later, she discovers typed copies of his correspondence with Fermina Daza. And while the aging lovers sail on the *New Fidelity*, they receive a telegram: "América Vicuña . . . had drunk a flask of laudanum stolen from the school infirmary."

What's love got to do with a pederast who has served as an accomplice to suicide and murder, I worried as I waited for Fran's response to my letter and as the pastoral quiet of the Inverness was shattered night and day by what sounded like bombs and blasts before and during Independence Day. Especially the suicide of the resonantly named América, who leaves no note to impugn anyone, disrupts the happily-ever-after of *Love in the Time of Cholera*. Florentino Ariza's obsession with Fermina Daza insulated him within a fanatical quest that effectively drained other human beings of reality. At any age, it seems, love is blind. Oblivious to the vulnerability of the women he pursues and of the river his company exploits, Florentino Ariza stands condemned of the devastation of human lives and of the earth's natural resources.

Could serious ethical charges also be leveled against Juvenal Urbino and Fermina Daza? Their conjugal bliss culminates at a gala dinner when she relishes helpings of pureed eggplant, begins serving the eggplant she had previously forsworn, and embraces her role in the marriage as "a deluxe servant." In domestic servitude, Fermina Daza "was absolute monarch of a vast empire of happiness, which had been built by [her husband] and for him alone. She knew that he loved her above all else, more than anyone else in the world, but only for his own sake: she was in his holy service."

This love "only for his own sake" might be what D. H. Lawrence had in mind when he considered marriage a form of "*égoïsme à deux*." Iris Murdoch's husband, John Bayley, used the phrase "*solitude à deux*" to describe "the inward self-isolation of a couple from anything outside their marriage." García Márquez associates the cooing of couples inside their cages with love that quarantines us from "cholera" (all the various evils of the world). Within Dr. Urbino's "vast empire," he and his wife remain oblivious to and yet complicit in the economic inequities and color prejudice bequeathed by Spanish colonization. García Márquez criticizes the deeply imbedded racism of Colombian society in a sequence of scenes about a mixed race woman who turns out to be Dr. Urbino's single marital infidelity and the reason for a two-year separation from his wife.

Fermina Daza's habit of sniffing laundry leads her to confront Dr. Urbino, at which point the ghost of Miss Barbara Lynch enters the house. An "elegant, large-boned mulatta," whose "sex seemed more pronounced than that of other human beings," Barbara Lynch had inspired a "mad passion that could endanger the stability of [the doctor's] marriage." When Dr. Urbino visited Barbara Lynch in her home, she gave him "the opportunity to seduce her but not to penetrate her inner sanctum, even when she was alone. She would go no further than allowing him to repeat the ceremony of palpation and auscultation with all the ethical violations he could desire, but without taking off her clothes." To keep up the appearance of house calls, he stays only for the amount of time it takes to give an injection.

Their hurried meetings become unsatisfying when Dr. Urbino makes "panic-stricken love with his trousers down around his knees, with his jacket buttoned so that it would not get in his way, with his gold watch chain across his vest, with his shoes on, with everything on, and more concerned with leaving as soon as possible than with achieving pleasure." Although the doctor remains fixated on "the mound of her dark bush under her madwoman's skirt from Jamaica," growing terror of his wife leads him to ditch Miss Lynch. Fermina Daza fumes at her humiliation: "And worst of all, damn it: with a black woman." The doctor corrects her, "with a mulatta," to which she declares, "Only now I understand: it was the smell of a black woman."

What are we to make of Dr. Urbino and Fermina Daza's collaboration in racial fetishizing? The couple's dehumanization of Barbara Lynch—their stereotyping her as a smelly, hypersexualized madwoman—brought back a shocking conversation Sandra and I once had with a prominent African American colleague back in the eighties, when we met him on the lecture circuit. We were presenting material that would find its way into the three-volume sequel of *The Madwoman*. In a fancy hotel ballroom filled with rows of chairs and much to our surprise, he confided that a number of white people in his audiences had a tendency, during after-lecture drinks, to inquire quite seriously into the genital endowments of black people.

Using farcical and flagrantly racist details, García Márquez satirizes Fermina Daza as well as Dr. Juvenal Urbino, who elsewhere exhibits smug satisfaction in his civic reputation, his European education, his ornate carriage and livery, his modern ideas of progress, his complacent Catholicism, and even the smell of his own urine. Also guilty of racism, Florentino Ariza sees a woman on a trolley: "black, young, pretty, but a whore beyond the shadow of a doubt," he assumes. Yet he soon discovers that she wants not money for sex but a job, which he obtains for her and which, because of her remarkable competence, enables him to rise in the River Company of the Caribbean.

Why did so many reviewers of this novel dote over the longevity of passion in these characters and skip over their immorality? García Márquez makes me aware of the obvious: namely, that old lovers, like all people, internalize the misbegotten views of their society. Not only does love sequester us from disasters in which we are complicit, it serves all sorts of wretched needs and ends. In *Love in the Time of Cholera*, the main characters' addictive, predatory desires block out the consequences of their depredations. No matter how tightly quarantined, lovers inside an epidemic cannot inoculate themselves against it; instead they embody and spread the contagion. Love in a time of cholera sickens.

Throughout the novel's many pages, the narrator informs us of the civil struggles that perpetually bloody his country. Through asides in the novel, as in the daily *New York Times*, we read about the violence of the slums, about political corruption, and about shocking class disparities. The aftereffects of the sieges of the Spanish, the atrocities of buccaneers and slave traders, the ravages of recurrent plagues and wars: while their country corrodes, all three characters in García Márquez's triangle are found guilty of fiddling. Maybe love at any age is nothing but an infant pacifier, I thought, lulling us into the dreamland we crave as an escape from the waking nightmare of history.

As I helped my housekeeper get the Inverness ready for a big party, I put away the letter I received from Fran in a desk drawer in my upstairs study. It distressed me as much as her disappearance had. There was something ominous about it. Better to clear the decks for the party and consider how *Love in the Time of Cholera* recasts *Death in Venice*.

Prowling Florentino resembles Thomas Mann's Aschenbach, who stalks a beautiful boy and endangers him by refraining from warning his family of a threatening epidemic. Unlike Mann, however, García Márquez links pederasty not to his hero's homosexuality but to his heterosexuality. And age is not the culprit. Aschenbach, fixated on the youthful object of his desire, spruces up his attire, dyes his hair, and uses makeup to appear younger. In contrast, Florentino Ariza pursues his philandering throughout all the seasons of his life. He also accepts his own aging as well as Fermina Daza's. And at their advanced stage of life, what can they possibly do, after all, about the mess the world has come to—even if its state was partly their fault?

Oh, I realized, here is the "trap" García Márquez set for readers. I get it. It gets me. Not only is love blind: our love of love stories blinds us so we can enjoy the consummation in which we want to revel. Like Florentino Ariza and Dr. Urbino, I became so engrossed with their mission to unite with Fermina Daza that I shelved my misgivings about their flagrant wrongdoings. García Márquez tricked me into conspiring with his delusional and destructive characters, whose lives, like our own, are inexorably shaped by a world going to hell in a handbasket.

As a trapped reader, I become aware of my sins of omission. Omission, the erstwhile Catholic Don reminds me, is when you don't do something you should be doing. García Márquez is spot on about the sins of omission in my late-life loving. When the perilous public sphere feels overwhelmingly frightful, as it often does, I retreat into my nest with Don and also into my reading of late-life love stories, even though I know that I am turning away from injustice and that this nesting is a privilege unavailable to those more vulnerable to the world's violence. In fact, the older

I get, the more I cocoon myself, hoping that younger people will find the means to fight the injustice and inequity that imperil us.

But then García Márquez prods me to go on and ask: amid mounting fears of global warming, rising poverty rates, gun violence at home, terrorism overseas, how can we *not* love late-life love stories? Voilà: the thread running throughout his multiple narratives! There. It. Is. The genius of *Love in the Time of Cholera* consists in its entrancing us with the perseverance of desire in deeply flawed characters whose self-encapsulating obsessions captivate and encapsulate us. On the one hand, we recognize his lovers' abundant moral failures; on the other, we marvel at the scandalous extravagance of their exploits. Like them, we cling to love and love stories as a shield against error and degeneration. In times of contagion, love is both a sickness and an anodyne.

Along the ravaged way, García Márquez manages to represent what very few other authors do: namely, the many modes of nongenital eroticism in which older people engage. Through sex scenes that detach pleasure from potency, García Márquez suggests that eroticism without penetration may be the norm for aging heterosexuals . . . not only because procreation plays little or no role in late-life sexuality, not only because elderly men may be dealing with erectile dysfunction or elderly women with hormonal deficiencies.

The novel's portrayal of, for instance, voluptuous embracing or modeling and illicit palpations or auscultations stresses the delights of looking, touching, listening, kneading, massaging, squeezing, holding, stroking, fondling, patting, tasting. This list leads me to another new word: *frottage* means arousing physical contact in a way that does not involve penetration. It comes from the French (of course!) for rubbing or friction. It makes me think of the cuddling, cradling, and spooning that comfort Don and me during many long nights in bed together. Sometimes, just the weight of limb on limb solaces. Forms of pleasure like frottage must not be equated with so-called bed death or sexless relations. Sexual excitement comes in many forms. Late-life eroticism differs from youthful eroticism, though it may become just as complicated, compulsive, exciting, and destructive.

On the afternoon that caterers started bringing trayful after trayful of hors d'oeuvres, depositing them on the dining room and kitchen tables, the hoopla seemed a celebration of my springing García Márquez's trap. It was exhilarating: the euphoria of appreciating the genius of his novel—the networks of his labyrinthine plots falling into place. Nothing compares to this elation: gaining a bird's-eye view of an author's maze, perceiving the paths through the forest composed of all that foliage.

And then there was the payoff for my project. García Márquez gives me permission to ponder the manifold and sometimes nasty but nevertheless compelling motives of ripe loving. After all, there are zillions of stories about misguided, even reprehensible young lovers. Wasn't Eros born out of Chaos? And doesn't volatile eroticism promote excesses, disorders, voracious impulses, and outrageous acts—as in the adage "all's fair in love and war"?

The gathering seemed like old times, but not really, for it wasn't of my doing. In the past, I had done the cooking and serving for parties myself. That would be impossible for the celebration we had determined to co-host in honor of Mary and her family, to say goodbye to them and good luck at Johns Hopkins. Alexandra and Jonathan ran the show. She ordered the food and he lugged in the cases of beer and wine and soda, despite an infected wasp bite that would send him to the ER as soon as the festivities got under way.

Alexandra had put balloons on the mailbox and a stone gnome at the center of the start of the driveway so people would recognize the Inverness and park on the road, instead of around the circle of beauty, where they would block each other's departure. Since these guests were invited by Mary and her family, many would be unknown to Don and me, just as they were decades ago when Mary and Andrew celebrated their wedding with a big tent set up in the meadow between the circle of beauty and the road. It had poured that afternoon.

But this afternoon was bright and hot, as incandescent as the day we had a tent up for my older daughter's wedding: its white sails flapped on a sea of green. She had wanted her father and me to walk her down the aisle, a grassy space between the folding chairs assembled on the meadow. So Don escorted my mother before my former husband and I accompanied the beautiful bride out the front door and through the guests, many gussied up in startling hats since it was a garden party.

"There's a German word for the comfort of well-fitting trousers," Don said.

I reached for my laptop, triumphant that we had managed to get Don into long pants and the Velcro sneakers Julie had purchased months ago. And we had fixed on a gift for our departing friends, actually the re-gifting of a gift: a sign inside a wooden frame spelling out "BLOOMINGTON." While Alexandra and

Jonathan set up glasses and napkins for the seventy or so people we expected, Don and I sat together in the sun-drenched living room. The chartreuse finches at the birdfeeder, the fat robins chirping on the grass, and the cooing mourning doves said "Not you, not you." Our friend George had emailed me his favorite July poem: "It's hard to imagine how unremembered we all become," Charles Wright's poem begins. "How quickly all that we've done / Is unremembered and unforgiven. . . ."

"Sick people are not moral failures, but moral failures may be sick and sickening," I said to Don, who took my birdbrained pronouncements in stride. I was pondering kindly grandfathers luring young girls into their secret slaughterhouses.

"Physical dissolution, moral dissipation . . . late-life lechery."

Delighted by an assignment, I rose to greet the first guests, determining not to stoop, to lengthen my torso, to keep my spine as straight as possible, especially when I stood to propose a toast to our dearly cherished but soon-to-be-departed friends. The threads connecting them to us would be stretched, maybe thinned, but they would not snap.

Late-Life Lechery

TWO MANTRAS RESOUNDED during the remainder of that muggy month. At home nightly, I sang to a Handel tune, "Lift up your leg, and be lifted up," while massaging Palmer's coconut butter into the scar tissue on Don's left knee. Out of the house daily, I chanted, "Up with the good, down with the bad" so he would remember which leg to use with the walker at a curb or a step. The first was of my devising, the second came from Tyrone's female successors as they walked with Don up and down the halls of the Trace.

While I sat in an empty room, waiting to take Don home, it began to dawn on me that most of the late-life love stories I have recounted occur in all sorts of settings except here in the United States, where, as Leslie Fiedler proved a long time ago, romance often entails two buddies lighting out for the territories. Does America's commitment to and sense of its own youthfulness explain why?

In stories about late-life lechery, however, our nation reigns supreme; and no one creates the lechers we love to hate better than Philip Roth, though John Updike comes in a close second. Both consider *alter kackers* who hit on girls young enough to be their daughters.

During more than half a century in the academy, I have seen my fair share of sleazy faculty—sometimes nearing retirement—who avoid sexual harassment charges by waiting till the close of the semester to seduce a student who has completed one of their seminars. Roth's and Updike's tomes had been a godsend when Don was interned in the Trace; I returned to them now either there or back in the Inverness, where I began cooking in preparation for a visit from my grandson Eli and his parents. Late-life cooking for guests requires early preparations: refrigerating or even freezing sauces and doughs before they will be defrosted, reheated or baked, and served. Otherwise I become too exhausted to enjoy meals with visitors.

A number of novels by Philip Roth would have suited my purposes. I fixed on *The Dying Animal* because its main character is an aging academic describing an electrifying affair with a student who subsequently confronted a cancer diagnosis. I can relate to both of these characters. I am an aging academic, but I am young enough to have been my husband's student (though I was not), and I also deal with cancer (though not breast cancer). Needless to say, I wanted to avoid a prudish or priggish response to seventy-year-old David Kepesh's spoken account of his affair eight years earlier with twenty-four-year-old Consuela Castillo.

Moral outrage, after all, is exhaustively aired inside the book by David Kepesh's alienated son, who gives prudish priggishness a bad name. In *The Dying Animal*, as in so many of Roth's novels, the genius resides in the voice of the main character, whose hyperbolic monologue, mainly in the past tense, aggressively tries to justify his outrageous sexual license even while inadvertently mourning its futility. An aging roué, a Casanova, a Don Giovanni, a libertine, a rake, a sensualist, David Kepesh savors above all else "the delightful imbecility of lust."

Passionately dedicated to his erotic independence, determined after a miserable marriage never to return to the sexless matrimonial "cage," Kepesh preaches the boons of the sixties' sexual revolution, when American girls became "fully implicated in their own desire." A protestor against Puritanism, he believes in the power of sex: "Only when you fuck is everything that you dislike in life and everything by which you are defeated in life purely, if momentarily, revenged." Kepesh—who terms sex a formidable "revenge on death"—ignites my prejudice against Jewish men: the boys I grew up with in Brooklyn pampered as God's gift to the world; the Orthodox men rising at dawn to pray on our plane trip to Israel, waking every screaming baby on board—though I am beginning to realize how tormented Roth's protagonist is by his supposedly libertarian creed.

In his account of his affair with Consuela, Kepesh analyzes the sexual politics of May-December mating. Of course, masculine December begins by controlling feminine May, like a father directing his daughter, as he has in fiction from *Pamela* to *Jane Eyre*. A public intellectual, Kepesh attained some media exposure through an expertise in art, music, and literature that enchanted the naive Consuela. Because of her gorgeous, D-cup breasts and her "sleek pubic hair," he "pronounced her a great work of art," while weirdly designating his own consciousness her "awareness of herself." Like Pygmalion and Professor Henry Higgins, Kepesh became the artist, she the object of his gaze. At their start, his experience and knowledge lent him pedagogic power and gave Consuela the "license to surrender."

But according to Kepesh's retrospective recounting (which constitutes all but the last sentences in this novel), the vast difference in their ages soon fueled her dominance over him. Consuela must have realized that "the force of her youth and her beauty" overpowered a lover aware of body parts "doomed to dwindle" and therefore of "the wound of age." After she performed fellatio with "a relentless rat-a-tat-tat rapidity" and he pulled her hair, Consuela "snapped her teeth" and that "was the true beginning of her mastery—the mastery into which my mastery had initiated her. I am the author of her mastery of me."

Despite his smug claim of authority, Consuela's mastery means that throughout the affair Kepesh suffered mightily from jealousy, as aging libertines have been informed they should since Chaucer composed his Merchant's Tale about a youthful May who uses the back of her old and blind husband to climb a tree, where she cuckolds him.

Kepesh explains how obsessed he became about losing Consuela to a younger man, with the result that "the pornography of jealousy" ran constantly through his head. Naturally, he cast his younger self as his rival, although he also tortured himself with thoughts of her earlier boyfriends. Anguished at being turned into a supplicant, drained of confidence, he was surprised when Consuela ended their relationship. "She didn't desire me, never desired me," he decides: "she experimented with me, really, to see how overwhelming her breasts could be."

During the years he perseverated on Consuela's rejection, Kepesh had to remind himself that "attachment *is* my enemy." His pledge of allegiance to his rights as a sovereign, sexual agent led him to drown his sorrow in masturbation and in piano lessons to perfect his playing of Mozart and Beethoven sonatas. It also issued in the furious tirades of his son, who lambasts the seventy-year-old "as the very picture of a pathetic old fool": "'The long white pageboy of important hair, the turkey wattle half hidden behind the fancy foulard—when will you begin to rouge your cheeks, Herr von Aschenbach? . . . Manning the aesthetic barricades on Channel Thirteen. The singlehanded battle to maintain cultural standards in a mass society. But what about observing ordinary standards of decency?'"

Kepesh's vanity brought home to me Don's diffidence, especially while I sat with him in a room at the Trace equipped with a barber's chair. No "pageboy of important hair" or "fancy foulard" for him. Except during a quick hair brushing at the start of the day, Don has always avoided mirrors. While the salt-and-pepper curls at the back of his head were being clipped, he kept his lids lowered and shed a few years right before my eyes. I was touched that he submitted to the woman's hands moving his head back and forth, since he was used to the antiquated barbers who used to cut his hair in a hole-in-the-wall off Third Street.

Don's acquiescence, which surprised me, reminded me of the

piano lessons he had taken a few years ago at Smith Holden, a musical instruments store in town. He had always wanted to learn how to play the piano. He told the youthful instructor he hoped to perform "Your Cheatin' Heart" at the end-of-course recital, but she said it was too difficult. After a few sessions, he managed to plunk out the first half of "Ode to Joy" with his right hand. He was in the middle of doing that when, he later told me, the instructor took her hands and put them on both of his hands and moved them on the keyboard.

Somehow the act stunned him into the conviction that it was too late for him to learn. None of my entreaties could prevail over his view that he would have to satisfy his abiding love of music through the headphones, the CDs, the tapes, the vinyl, his collection of three hundred 78 rpm records. Why not try to make the next haircutting appointment at his funky barbershop, I thought, as Don went to the gym and I found a lawn chair by the Trace's entrance. And why should I be paying a pricey salon fifty dollars a pop for the little bit of scalping I need, when it could be done at Don's barbershop for a measly fifteen dollars?

In Roth's novel, not the insults of Kepesh's son but looming threats of mortality may finally undermine his hero's allegiance to libertine principles. When on a New Year's Eve Consuela returned to Kepesh, her cancer diagnosis put in crisis his commitment to detachment. Having suffered hair loss from chemotherapy, she returned because she needed him to love her body again before it was "ruined" by surgery. Taking charge of his touch, she had him feel the growths in her armpit—"two small stones, one bigger than the other, meaning that there is a metastasis originating in her breast": "hers was no longer a sexual life. What was at stake was something else." The thought brings to his mind Stanley Spencer's 1937 painting *Double Portrait*, depicting the artist and his recumbent wife, both naked, and in the foreground an uncooked leg of lamb and a small chop. Consuela's body will be butchered. Cancer has erased the age difference between them. "Consuela now knows the wound of age," for she faces a future more foreshortened than his.

Kepesh's genuine sorrow over her fate renders indeterminate the final sentence of the novel and his destiny. Throughout his monologue, he has been talking to a mysterious someone, maybe his next student-mistress, until finally it becomes clear that he is expecting a phone call from Consuela. When it comes at 2 a.m., he returns to explain that he must go to her because she is terrified of the mastectomy and needs him, but the nameless companion says, "Don't" and then says in the novel's final words, "Because if you go, you're finished."

The line can be read in a number of ways. If Kepesh goes to support Consuela in the hospital, his autonomy, independence, detachment are over, done for, kaput. Or if he goes to help her, the nameless companion with be finished with him. Or if he sees Consuela's post-operative condition, he will be done with her. Or if he goes to help her, his love for another human being may finally be completed, accomplished, and fulfilled for the first time in his existence. He will have moved from lust into a deepening, responsible relationship.

Once, when Don came to see me during a terrible stay in the Indianapolis hospital, he brought a portable CD player and a CD of the late Beethoven quartets. Inside the case, I found a note in his minute script: "I've got you under my skin." With hope for Kepesh, I sing, "Lift up your leg, and be lifted up," urging him to step "up with the good." But it remains impossible for Don to stand in the shower—he still must sit on the plastic bench in the tub—so the Agewise Design consultants come and go, talking about plans they will draw up for the ground-floor bathroom: a walk-in shower, handrails and a seat within it.

However, such renovations can neither widen the bathroom nor change its relation to the bed, where Don lies on my left, me on his right. I consider the commotion it would entail while making the foods that nine-year-old Eli will enjoy, but I have reread Fran's letter many times and the distress it gave me upon its arrival somehow seems underscored by the decision facing licentious Kepesh at the end of Roth's novel. Which, on the face of it, is absurd. Fran has nothing at all in common with Kepesh. In values and habits, she is more like his antitype. Why had her letter confounded me and how could Kepesh have anything to do with it?

Fran's letter elaborated on our "different wavelengths" by describing her challenges over the past twenty years: a series of familial and professional struggles, all of which enriched her interior life. What I found bizarre about this lengthy account was that I had lived through each and every one of these events with her and discussed each and every one in detailed, recurrent conversations. Had she forgotten those talks, or was she simply reiterating, over and over again, what she knew I knew? And if so, why? She designated her effort in the letter-writing "compassionate listening"; however, the substance of the writing had nothing to do with me. It was all about her until the final line in which she concluded that whereas I was seeking "more engagement," she, for her part, needed less.

There is the link to Kepesh: attachment as the enemy. We are used to thinking of promiscuity as a defense against emotional engagement, as Roth does. But Fran's letter made me consider spirituality another defense against personal commitment. While I reflected on my own and Don's impairments, Fran's spiritual goals seemed to sanction her decision not to reach out to me when I really needed her—not so much with an offer of help, I realized, but with the gift of her steadying presence. Like Kepesh, Fran resisted attending to the other according to the needs of the other. No, I will not respond. Anything I wrote would read like a foreign alphabet to her.

It is a source of sadness to recall that Fran had always fostered my attachment to Don when he was becoming more than a friend. Decades ago, the three of us embarked on an eating club, much to the amusement of my daughters. Once a week, one of us would cook a meal for the three of us to enjoy together, and afterward I composed parodic "Club Notes" to record our wacky conversations. Fran had seen me through the divorce, a more effective ballast than any lover could have been . . . a ludicrous comparison since friendship so intensely involves love between caring cronies.

In one of those club reports, I began kidding Don about his decision not to hire me. We had met at a Modern Language Association convention in 1971, when he was the chair of the

English department and I was a job seeker. But he offered the one available position to another candidate . . . worse: a man. After we started living together, I teased Don by introducing him as "my partner who once, long ago, refused to hire me." He would privately protest that he had alerted his successor in the chairmanship to seek me out the next year and in any case he preferred to be called "the mister." (Sometimes I think we finally married to simplify nomenclature for the grandkids.) That we were a May-December match indubitably contributed to my passionate regard. His quiet dependability reminded me of my father, while his steadfast commitment to life assured me that he would never do what my father had done.

The year after Don didn't hire me, he finagled an interview for me on campus. In midflight to Indiana, I stared in horror at an advice handbook's prohibition against traveling while pregnant in an unpressurized cabin. The faculty, mostly male, would be no help. They ignored my belly (or, I later learned, argued that I shouldn't be hired because of it). But the wives, including Mary-Alice, commiserated, and Don drove me to the Greyhound bus station so I could return home without putting in jeopardy the well-being of the unborn. We chatted throughout the car trip about the French theorists just coming out in translation. Friendship and then partnership effaced the age difference between us, and then cancer erased it as I faced a future more foreshortened than his.

The last line of Roth's novel holds out the possibility that Kepesh may attach himself to Consuela in her time of great need. Engagement with the living, especially the needy living, is, after all, a surpassing Jewish virtue, just as important as prayer. By giving over all but the last line to Kepesh's voice, Roth seems munificent in his willingness to suggest that he identifies with his reprobate—unlike John Updike, who remains aloof from his lecher, a paradigmatic loser. Updike's protagonist loses his car business, his house, his wife, his cocaine-addicted son, his healthy heart, and eventually his life, while Updike, like Roth, skillfully re-creates the social milieu of a slice of American life at the end of the twentieth century.

In John Updike's final Rabbit novel, the portrait of Harry Angstrom suggests that late-life lechery remains a futile protest against the wounds of aging—less a revenge on death than an inadequate defense against thinking about it. David Foster Wallace once castigated both Updike and Roth for using sex as a cure-all for their heroes' ontological despair, but surely Roth and Updike fully recognize the absurdity of this venture. In *Rabbit at Rest*, sex resembles the junk food Harry gobbles to stuff the empty void that recurrently threatens to hollow out his being and then be filled up with premonitions of death.

Toward the end of the novel, Harry consumes fried eggs and bacon, french fries and a hamburger and apple pie, deep-fried shrimp and onion rings with white bread fried on one side, a hot pastrami sandwich, fried catfish and candied yams and pecan pie, french toast and link sausages—and that's just on one road trip. Fifty-five-year-old Harry is fleeing his wife's judgment that he has done "the worst thing you've ever done, ever, ever," and that includes his running away with her best friend, "and that poor hippie girl, and Thelma—don't think for one moment I didn't know about Thelma—but now you've done something truly unforgive-able." "The worst thing" Harry did was sleeping with his son's wife, an event that occurred after an angioplasty: "I can't run, I can't fuck, I can't eat anything I like, I know damn well they're going to talk me into a bypass."

Before sex, when his daughter-in-law Pru produced a condom, Harry had "been afraid he couldn't keep up his own pressure against it," especially when his shaved pubic hair got caught at the base in the unrolling. As she "jiggled in pursuit of the second orgasm, he near to fainting with worry over joggling his defective heart," Harry felt put off by Pru's "matter-of-fact shamelessness" about pursuing her own pleasure: "To keep his prick up he kept telling himself, *This is the first time I've ever fucked a left-handed woman.*" Fornication and junk food help Harry forget what he always fears, that he "is falling, helplessly falling, toward death," that it "is truly there under him, vast as a planet at night, gigantic and totally his. His death. His purely own."

One of the epigraphs of *Rabbit at Rest* comes from the *Life and Times of Frederick Douglass*: "Food to the indolent is poison, not sustenance." The same may be true of sex. Late-life promiscuity—pursued to recover an unrecoverable youth, one's own unrecover-able youth—remains a doomed affair. Although Roth at the end of his novel offers Kepesh a way out of the snare of lechery and of the hectic first person as futile defenses against decline and death, Updike, steady in the third person, watches Harry flail in the increasingly grim pleasures of the flesh.

Of course America cannot claim a monopoly on stories of late-life lechery. The Japanese writer Junichiro Tanizaki's novel

Diary of a Mad Old Man is narrated by a seventy-seven-year-old whose only relief from aches and pains derives from washing the feet and sucking the toes of his flashy daughter-in-law. Tanizaki's protagonist understands that "even if you're impotent you have a kind of sex life." The pleasures of his nongenital sex life—his frottage with his daughter-in-law—provide him a reason to live, while her cheerful willfulness assures them both that she can set the limits she deems appropriate. She simply disappears from the ailing invalid whenever his needs become tiresome.

How come neither Roth nor Updike imagines old men as a turnoff rather than a turn-on? When I did my PhD training in Iowa, I was so enervated by the ancients pontificating at the front of classrooms that I had my then husband drive me to a cornfield, where I could mock them to ears that would keep the secret not of my erotic thralldom but of my profound boredom. But graduate school, with all the insecurity it instills, probably remains an alienating experience, I thought, as I considered the grueling seminars I have led: trying to convince apprehensive graduate students—they felt like imposters—that they did not need to pretend to know what they did not know.

Happily, Eli is an avid questioner, a curious pupil, and a good eater not just of pizza and meatballs and spaghetti but of every conceivable form of fruit, though it is cars (he recognizes every make and model) that he dreams about. Or maybe, like me, he dreams of characters, since he loves books.

After Eli arrives tomorrow, I will take him to a local hobby shop, where he can pick out a present and I can find a party tiara for my oncologist, who will soon accept the Diana, Princess of

Wales, professorship at Northwestern University, and then I will compose a blog posting in praise of her. I will scheme with Eli's mother to find an online site that will send weekly ingredients for a month of suppers to her sister in New York. Since my poor vision makes piecing the flying geese quilt difficult even with "Easy Threading" needles, I will settle for a crib-size quilt. I will devise a way to resume meeting with my cancer support group. I will accept Mary's offer to stay with Don and Jan's offer to drive me to the Indianapolis hospital. I will keep myself and Don from helplessly tumbling at the next curb or step.

Thinking of the torn tendon now healing, I know that detachment is my enemy.

Sunsets

THE SUN RISES out of the ravine in the back of the Inverness, but it sets behind the red barn. It became so spectacular with its diffused pinks and oranges and bands of yellow or blue that after dinner we stood outside the front door to watch its magnificence deepen. I can see the sun dropping into Lake Michigan while Don and I nuzzle, bundled under a beach blanket, shoulder to shoulder, hip to hip on the warm sand. I can see lowering rays glinting on the Mediterranean, turning Don's eyes bluer, as we bobble on the lapping waves and laugh over a customs officer who had asked each of us why we had traveled to Israel: "Don't you know business and pleasure don't mix?" he joked.

Actually, Don stood with his walker and I sat on the baked bricks by his feet, near the cosmos, which had put out delicate magenta and fuchsia blooms on fragile, straying stalks. Maybe the deer hadn't eaten them because they had been planted close to the front door. Or maybe they were one of the few flowers deer do not eat. I would have to look them up in my gardening book, *Not Tonight, Deer.*

"Would you rather sleep with Jonathan or Alexandra?" I asked Don.

"I have always disliked that Procrustean bed."

"Why are you impersonating an old man?"

"I am an old man."

"Yesterday Jonathan was bemoaning having two jobs and no wife," I tell him. "The commuting must be demoralizing them."

"Better than two wives and no job," Don said as I held the screen door open so he could go back inside and settle down to a Ken Burns documentary on PBS.

But the evening air was unusually dry and inviting. I lit several candles on the back porch and sat down in a rocking chair to listen to the crickets and the frogs while mulling: why are older men with girls socially acceptable, whereas older women with boys are not? When I was a student in Erasmus Hall High School, I had no idea that Erasmus, the so-called Prince of the Humanists, inveighed against "old women, so ancient that they might as well be dead":

> They are as hot as bitches in heat, or (as the Greeks say) they *rut like goats.* They pay a good price for the services of some handsome young Adonis. They never cease smearing their faces with makeup. They can't tear themselves away from the mirror. They pluck and thin their pubic bush. They show off their withered and flabby breasts. They whip up their languid lust with quavering whines and whimpers. They drink a lot.

Older women, made to feel the punishing shame of age, have had a bad rap.

Is the man supposed to be senior because girls—traditionally "given" by their fathers to their husbands—renounce their fathers' name to take their husbands' . . . or they used to? My younger daughter evaded conflicting loyalties to her father and stepfather by walking herself down the aisle in all her radiant splendor. Don and I sashayed arm in arm before her, for the very first time. One of my daughters married a younger man, one an older; one kept her maiden name, the other did not. On both occasions I was fussing about my costume. In flyover country, Mary said, they dump all the clothes that people on the coasts would never buy. Mothers of the bride could find only pastels of chiffon and satin flounces that would have made me feel like a transvestite. There was no dignified garb for the aging woman.

Probably the ridiculed or scorned older woman is related to the phenomenon Susan Sontag called "the double standard of aging": the unfortunate fact that maturation consolidates the authority of men while devaluing the worth of women. On TV and in movies, men get better with age (like full-bodied wine), but women become lumpy, rank, and sour (like spoilt milk). When Jane Juska, the author of *A Round-Heeled Woman*, took a male lover thirty-three years her junior, even those relatives who approved of her sex ad in the *New York Review of Books* judged her or her youthful lover sick. She was facing a prejudice with a long history.

After middle-aged Sappho was rejected by the beautiful ferryman Phaon, according to one prevalent myth, she threw herself into the sea. What did sixty-year-old George Eliot make of forty-year-old John Cross's flinging himself out of the hotel window and into the Grand Canal during their Venice honeymoon? For centuries, people have assumed that older women "pay a good price" for a handsome Adonis. When the forty-year-old heroine of Zora Neale Hurston's *Their Eyes Were Watching God* returns home, townspeople suppose that her youthful lover must have abandoned her and ask, "What he done wid all her money?"

Billy Wilder's grand movie *Sunset Boulevard*, about a has-been from the silent screen era, renders Gothic the bad rap on older women with younger men. It famously begins with a male corpse floating in a swimming pool. Then it progresses through a flashback to the meeting of the fifty-year-old fading star Norma Desmond and the youthful screenwriter Joe Gillis. Her failed suicide attempt prefaces a series of guilt trips that ensnare impoverished Joe in her clutches until she shoots him in the back as he tries to escape.

A classic narcissist, Norma Desmond never stops smearing her face with makeup and downing drinks, as she pays a good price—for a gold cigarette case, a vicuna coat, and sixteen suits—to enlist the services of her youthful Adonis in coauthoring a Salomé script. She wants to use it to recover her lost stardom. Norma's delusions of grandeur reach a climax when, at the end of the movie, she plays the temptress Salomé before a throng of news photographers and journalists who have arrived to report her arrest for the murder. Relishing the spotlight, convinced that her movie comeback has begun, she slowly descends the staircase toward the police, vamping all the way. Her neurotic attempts to retain her youthful allure have tipped her into insanity.

Like predatory Mrs. Robinson in *The Graduate*, Norma takes as her rival a girl young enough to be her daughter. But Billy Wilder provides a scene that explains a character grotesquely absorbed in her skin patches, chin guards, and face creams. On a movie set, Norma meets with Cecil B. DeMille, who has continued to work effectively in Hollywood. Not only his gender but also his job as a director explains his late-life productivity. After she leaves, he says, "A dozen press agents working overtime can do terrible things to the human spirit." The celebrity industry—with its overvaluation of nubile beauty—has created the monster Norma has become. A similar point is made in the equally famous movie *All about Eve*.

"Age still equals abandonment for women," the sixty-year-old heroine of Erica Jong's *Fear of Dying* believes as she considers a bevy of antiaging specialists: "from dermatologists who harvest and reuse your own fat to those who freeze your facial muscles with toxins. There are blasters and scrapers, injectors and fat-suckers. . . . There are plastic surgeons and acupuncturists and even hypnotists who regress you into false youth you dream is real." At what age does a woman judge herself in need of such treatments? Two of my friends, although only a few years older than their partners, have been mistaken for their husbands' mothers. According to Susan Sontag, women grow old "as soon as they are no longer very young."

When the crescendo of crickets and frogs, the chirps and croaks of courting, began drowning out my thoughts, I blew out the candles. Not once this summer had we eaten dinner at the round table under the skylight of the back porch—because of the four steps down to it. As I locked the porch door, it seemed to me that *Sunset Boulevard* could only imagine a younger man with an older woman if she paid him for his services. Maybe *Harold and Maude* changed all that, I thought, until I caught myself up. Decades before *Sunset Boulevard*, two revolutionary books—I had read them in City College—and what about Ben Franklin's supercilious advice . . . But there was Julie at the door with her dogs, Hazel and Schnitzel, come to stay while her house underwent renovation.

Schnitzel barks and snaps and threatens to attack, not realizing that he is a miniature dachshund who could fit in my purse; Hazel cowers and trembles and hides, not realizing she is a hefty bruiser for a miniature Schnauzer. Under Julie's loving auspices, these rescue animals have escaped from hellish abuse to heavenly succor, though we sometimes have to cage the Schnitz, who would otherwise attack Don's ankles in the walker. "Dogs don't know what they look like," Ursula Le Guin once explained in an essay on beauty. "Dogs don't even know what size they are." No matter how old they are, dogs do not appear to evaluate their own attractiveness. The power of physical attraction, tied to youth, presents the greatest challenge in representations of winter-spring relationships. If the older lover is a woman, reciprocity threatens to evaporate as youthful beauty fades.

With Julie going on numerous errands for us, I could settle down on the blue raft with Colette's two linked novels in a new edition. In the first, *Chéri*, the title character is a pampered twenty-four-year-old man who has been adopted as a lover by his mother's best friend, the forty-nine-year-old Léa. The novel opens as their erotic relationship is challenged by the news that Chéri's mother has arranged a marriage of convenience for him with a young woman as wealthy as he is. Colette's portrait contests the bad rap on older female–younger male relationships. Money has nothing to do with Léa and Chéri's bond, though they both relish luxury. Intimate looking and being looked at furnish the greatest delights of this transgenerational couple.

A courtesan, Léa enjoys gazing at her own body, "pink and white, endowed with the long legs and straight back of a naiad on an Italian fountain." She also takes pleasure in remembering Chéri as a little boy, "a marvel of beauty with long curls," and as a handsome young man, "naked in the morning on her ermine rug." A "sort of doting godmother," she lets him play with her jewelry, teaches him manners, feeds him, and corrects his speech, mentoring him as Norma Desmond does Joe. When Chéri walks down the street, they both know that "the eyes of women followed his progress with silent homage." Both would agree with Mae West that "It is better to be looked over than overlooked."

Would Colette have taken umbrage at Benjamin Franklin's "Advice to a Young Man on the Choice of a Mistress"? Back in 1745, one of America's founding fathers encouraged a correspondent to prefer old women to younger ones: they are more knowledgeable, more discreet, will not produce children, and "lastly they are *so grateful!!*"

After Chéri's marital plans have been announced, looking at aging women becomes a source of torment for Léa. At one social event, she finds herself dismayed by a seventy-year-old acquaintance who "walked with difficulty on round swollen feet, tightly swaddled in high-heeled laced boots with paste buckles on the ankle straps"; "a silver fox fail[s] to conceal" a neck "the shape of a flower-pot and the size of a belly." By embarking on a trip, Léa defends herself against being supplanted by Chéri's future wife. However, Colette revises a Continental tradition in which the older courtesan inducts the younger man into the mysterious rites of eroticism so he can then marry a woman closer to his own age. Although Chéri takes a young woman as his wife, he never extricates himself from the allure of his older mistress.

Léa's powers derive from the maternal role she plays. Far from being merely instrumental, the maternal-filial bond in *Chéri* and its sequel inaugurates a blissful paradise. Once lost, it can never be regained. Colette seems to be thinking about the incest taboo: the alluring prohibition against a man taking a mother surrogate as his lover, the frisson of the illicit.

When Chéri and Léa reunite, they collapse onto her bed. Their bodies "joined together like the two living halves of an animal that has been cut through," while she anticipates "with a sort of terror the moment of her own undoing"—which arrives in the clear light of the next morning, when it falls on the "soft flabby skin" on her hands and wrists "like criss-crossings on a clay soil when heavy rain is followed by a dry spell." Aware that her lover has returned to "find an old woman," Léa determines that Chéri must free himself "from perverted mother love." As she has done throughout the affair, Léa takes charge at its conclusion, relinquishing a young man twenty-four years her junior.

The great pleasure of reimmersing myself in Colette's sensual descriptions of a hedonistic heroine was made possible not only by Julie but also by Don, who has started to resume many chores. On the walker, he has begun getting his own breakfast and then unloading the dishwasher and making our bed, as he had always done before. As in the old days, Don wakes up with a song in his head: "Is you is or is you ain't my baby?" "Must be jelly 'cause jam don't shake like that." "I've been consulted by Franklin D. / Greta Garbo has asked me to tea." He cannot hum the tunes, but he knows all the words. And he looks like his handsome self again.

Exactly when did my rigorous efforts to look attractive decline into halfhearted attempts to pass as relatively normal? In midlife, I fussed over my frizzy hair, the shadows under my eyes, skinny appendages, crooked teeth, and that's leaving aside tortured considerations of my nose and chin. Did the self-lacerating scrutiny come to a close at the weirdly elated moment of diagnosis, when I thought I finally knew what would cause my demise? Or was it after the debulking surgery, when I was plucked, trussed, carved, and gutted, and then chemotherapy took away my hair? Or was it after the seventeen days in the hospital that resulted in the ileostomy?

Now when a workman is scheduled to check the inoperative garage door, Don reminds me to put on my wig. I do it to save the workman and me the tsuris of having to deal with his reactions. Surviving beyond my prognosis—some two years beyond my expiration date—has brought me the welcome relief of not caring so much how I look. Gladdened that Don found the garage repairman himself—apparently the door should be replaced, not just fixed—I wondered how long it would take Don to get used to the cane we had just picked out. He still has to recline in the back seat of the car, but the knee has reached a 60-degree angle. It amuses him that Julie attributes his increased mobility to one feisty and one fearful dog, who are the least therapeutic creatures anyone could possibly imagine.

Whereas *Chéri* is primarily told from the point of view of Léa, *The Last of Chéri* is narrated from Chéri's perspective. He has been poisoned by too much mother's milk and cannot become his own man in the sequel, which occurs six years later, after World War I. Repulsed by the public roles his mother and wife play after the Great War, Chéri resembles many disillusioned veterans. His mother therefore arranges a visit to Léa, who has morphed into a sight revolting to Chéri: "She was not monstrous, but huge, and loaded with exuberant buttresses of fat in every part of her body." Shocked, he longs to tell her, "Throw off your disguise! You must be somewhere behind it, since it's your voice I hear." But while he hopes for a flash of her real self, he suspects that she has made peace with her aging: "when she stopped smiling or laughing, she ceased to belong to any assignable sex. Despite her enormous breasts and crushing backside, she seemed by virtue of age altogether virile and happy in that state."

The person who suffers the horrors of aging is he, not she. He is the one who subsequently commits suicide. "Unsexed" in old age, Léa would nevertheless dispute Montaigne's caution that "The shorter the possession we give to Love, the better off we are." Granting Cupid an injudiciously long possession, Léa does not degenerate into a grotesque character. In the first novel, she achieves insight into Chéri's miserable fate and takes responsibility for it: "I should have made a man of you, and not thought only of the pleasures of your body, and my own happiness," she admits. "I am to blame for everything you lack."

How to measure the pleasure accrued against the damage done? In their final scene together in the sequel, Léa insists that she is neither ashamed nor regretful, for she had been in love. Léa has relinquished erotic desire and femininity, but she has gained virility and moral clarity.

Doris Lessing, in a novella called "The Grandmothers," depicts older women inducting young men into sex and then *not* thinking only of their own happiness but instead taking the initiative in renouncing the youths. Each of Lessing's maternal lovers realizes that she must surrender her Adonis for his own good, even though she wishes, like the Marschallin in *Der Rosenkavalier*, to tarry in the present of desire. Should such idyllic retreats in the rapturous Eden of maternal sufficiency be labeled pathological? Colette and Lessing ask.

On the surface at least, the difference between women writers (thinking about older women and boys) and male writers (thinking about older men and girls) is striking: the women estimate the damages done, while the men do not. (García Márquez is the exception.) Based on a tiny sample, this judgment cannot possibly be considered judicious, especially because it accords with my prejudices. But once, while I was writing my doctoral dissertation at the Newberry Library, when my first marriage had crashed and we had separated for a semester, before the first pregnancy and the move to Indiana, I had a brief fling with an undergraduate. OK, he was not "my" undergraduate, but still he was an undergraduate. He gave me my first and last acid trip; I worried then and later about the deleterious effect of the relationship on him.

Colette, who posed in her youth for publicity stills in costumes redolent of Salomé, went on to take her sixteen-year-old stepson as her lover after she published *Chéri*, thereby proving Oscar Wilde's point—that life imitates art. As her biographer Judith Thurman explains, "By impersonating Léa . . . Colette accepts maternity for the first time, however perversely, and graduates from being the slave of love to the master, and from the child to the parent." Through Léa, she studied what Thurman calls "a cruel trick of fate": namely, "that the state of erotic exigence—the last few years before a woman begins menopause—also coincides with the diminishment of her sexual allure." What a miserable combination for maturing women: heightened erotic desire and decreased sexual appeal.

Precisely this irony casts its shadow on fiction about the later-life loves of older women. The urgency of desire surprises the heroine of a grisly work by Doris Lessing, *Love, Again*, who at sixty-five believed that she had thrown Cupid out. When she falls passionately in love with two younger men, she feels as unlovable "as the innumerable people of the world who are ugly, deformed, or crippled." Insane with desire, sodden with grief at unconsummated longing, by the end of the novel Lessing's central character has acquired "grey bands" of hair and "that slow cautious look of the elderly, as if afraid of what they will see around the next corner." Her double in the novel is a man who has fallen in love with a dead woman: that is how inconceivable it is for Lessing to imagine a younger man reciprocating the desire of an older woman. (I would not recommend this punitive novel to the faint-hearted.)

Is the randy aging woman, like the single woman, feared as a kind of witch who must be punished? Was it 1980 or 1981 when a scorch mark appeared on my office door? Someone had used a lighter or a match to torch a poster announcing a program on lesbian studies. I was touched when Don quickly organized a workshop on free speech.

The only recent rebuttal I can find to the tragically desirous older woman is Olivier Assayas's movie *Clouds of Sils Maria*, which provides a gorgeous reinvention of *Sunset Boulevard* and also of *All about Eve* in a winter-spring story about two women. All of our sympathy goes to the forty-year-old internationally celebrated actress Maria Enders, who twenty years earlier played the role of a young temptress, but must now take on the part of the siren's dumped older lover. (Forty is old in the movies.) In the play within the movie, Maria Enders has to submit to the inevitability of being usurped by youth. Yet as she walks through the set to arrive at her stage spot on opening night, she has the look of a person who will give a powerful performance. It does not hurt that Juliette Binoche appears ravishing in the butch role.

Like Erica Jong's heroine, Assayas's may find herself at risk for spending her "sunset years without sex." For the older woman–younger lover story continues to resist happy endings. Is this because it invokes the mother-lover taboo, as Colette suggests: the recovery of a pre-Oedipal delight that is supposed to be thoroughly repressed? When Marge Piercy imagines an adult male without any prejudices against older women, he is a cyborg. An intelligent machine "is not breaking any Oedipal taboos, for he was not born of woman."

The heroine of Lessing's *Love, Again* hypothesizes that heterosexual desire pertains to mother hunger. "Am I really to believe that the awful, crushing anguish, the longing so terrible it seems one's heart is being squeezed by cruel fingers—all that is only what a baby feels when it is hungry and wants its mother?" Lessing also proposes a practical reason for the sad conclusions of some later-life love stories: "When Cupid aims arrows (not flowers or kisses) at the elderly and old, and brings them to grief, is this one way of hustling people who are in danger of living too long off the stage, to make way for the new?"

The thump, thump, thump of the cane as Don cleaned the kitchen brought to mind the Sphinx's riddle. What creature walks on four legs in the morning, two at noon, and three in the evening? Making a shopping list for the vegan meals I would concoct for Julie, I resisted the idea of reducing all amorous relationships to the family romance. After all, Kepesh is nothing like Consuela's Cuban father, and Léa hardly resembles Chéri's sarcastic mother. But if Roth and Colette are right, eroticism is imbued by special urgency and poignancy for those aware that Eros has one foot out the door.

In the poem "Last Love," the Russian author Fyodor Tyutchev describes love at the closing of the day glowing "brighter, brighter, farewell rays / of one last love in its evening splendor," for "The blood runs thinner, yet the heart / remains as ever deep and tender." Does the multicolored intensity of fading light infuse sundown symptoms of agitation, apprehension, and confusion in sunset lovers, I wondered in somewhat of a muddle. If the thumping of the cane, not to mention the barking of the Schnitz, was derailing my concentration, there was no way I would be able to live with the incessant banging of contractors, plumbers, tilers, and electricians. And since we were not using half the space of the Inverness and clearly the upkeep was beyond us, I nixed Agewise Design, determining to turn my thoughts toward real estate. We shouldn't renovate . . . the rundown house, too big for us, was pushing us out. We needed to move.

Cupidity

EVERY TWINGE SHOULD not conjure cancer. That's how I
was counseling myself when Don appeared on the ground floor,
waving a black object in his hand like a trophy. I had driven him
down the steep driveway so he could get to his basement study
and return to work on *Pride and Prejudice*. Apparently going up
steps was easier than going down. He caned his way to the blue
couch, stretched over me, reached up to the torch lamp, and
twisted a little knob onto the switch that had been bruising my
fingers every day and every night.

The knob, which he had taken off a broken lamp, reminded
me of all the junk in the garage: straw baskets, clay flower pots,
rusty hoes, snow shovels, a wheelbarrow, coolers, sleds, folding
tables and chairs, watering cans. In the basement: not just yards
of books on the planks Don had bracketed on two large walls,
but my mother's files and file cabinets, her two sofas and easy
chair, and a cabinet holding some twenty of her heavy photo-

graph albums. Then my younger daughter's exercise equipment, sheet music, CDs, knitting projects, clothing, and shoes, left from when she inhabited the basement during her high school years.

My older daughter's books, stuffed animals, journals, and sewing projects were lodged in an upstairs bedroom, along with the paraphernalia her son Eli had needed for visits: a humidifier, bed rails, a stroller. Mary-Alice's college luggage was stacked in a closet in the upstairs hallway. I had no idea what was inside the cartons belonging to Don's daughters, moved some twenty years earlier from the storage area of his old house. Most of it would not be missed, but the thought of trashing all this detritus—how does one get rid of so much stuff?—made me ill. "A dumpster," Julie enthused as she packed to return to her own house and I brooded over our wasteful materialism.

Even as I started to purge in anticipation of a move—boxing extra sheets and towels for Julie to donate to the animal shelter—I worried that it was a drop in the bucket. And how could we move, if it meant relocating to a small place with no room for the kids and grandkids to stay over? Still, it was time to remind our real estate agent to show us more apartments and town houses. Zak—a young journalist-turned-realtor who prides himself on his karaoke performances—would give us sound advice on what needed to be done before we put the Inverness up for sale. There were patches of carpet torn up in the musty basement, next to the door leading to the garage: the late demented cat Perkins must have been desperate to get out.

Real estate turns out to be a major issue in stories of later-life love. When Don and I obtained a mortgage for the Inverness, we had to remake our wills so that my half of the equity would go to my girls, his half to his. We needed to decide how long the survivor could remain in place before selling the property, though both of us felt we would be too lonely to stay on alone for very long. We owned no other property, but we have witnessed older couples tied up in knots over an apartment in Paris or a summer house in Maine: should it go to the surviving partner or to the children who expected to inherit it? Problems of inheritance become a rich theme especially in stories about aging characters dealing with avaricious adult children.

I knew I should open the Louis Begley trilogy that I had read in February, when I was sleeping in my grandbaby's hospital room, but I did not have the energy. In *About Schmidt*, which has nothing to do with the movie of the same title starring Jack Nicholson, a sixty-year-old retired lawyer inhabits a multimillion-dollar house in the Hamptons that had been bequeathed to his wife. Just thinking about the haggling that ensues after her death, over gift taxes and life estates, contributed to my wooziness.

A lonely widower, Schmidt feels isolated by his retirement from a prestigious Manhattan law firm and by the apparent distaste with which his beloved daughter treats him whenever she appears to extract his money. Charlotte has nursed childhood grudges against his sleeping with her babysitter and his garden-variety anti-Semitism, which may have motivated her to marry a Jew. We are given many reasons to judge Schmidt and find him wanting, although he engages in this activity best himself.

Most of Begley's characters are guilty of cupidity—a word, like "Cupid," that derives from the Latin *cupere* (to desire). Notwithstanding the anti-Semitism Schmidt himself worries about, he turns out to be less captivated by cupidity or greed, more entranced by Cupid than are his rapacious daughter and her equally merce-nary husband. Some Jews can be avaricious and some anti-Semites capable of moral evolution, or so Louis Begley suggests. By buying out Charlotte's share in the house, Schmidt manages to extricate himself from his daughter's clutches.

Schmidt has grown in self-knowledge, presumably because a gorgeous, twenty-year-old, half–Puerto Rican waitress has shown up to fulfill his desires: "She grabbed his erection and squeezed hard." But all the bickering over finances between Schmidt and Charlotte as well as the unlikelihood of a beautiful young woman falling for a man forty years her senior has intensified my queasi-ness. I am shivering in the heavy humidity and put on a second pair of socks.

Neuropathy from long-ago chemotherapies ossifies my feet, but now rigor mortis sets in. I understand that Louis Begley, him-self Jewish, intends to satirize his characters; however, the kitchen faucet has started dripping and Sandra grieves the loss of her part-ner of seven years. Our friend George writes anguished emails about his wife's brain metastases, Mary was in her car when it was rammed by a driver who ran a stop light, and at the last lunch with my cancer support group Carrol sounded fatalistic, Ilka looked frail. The phone, when it rings, delivers a cheerful recording about a diabetes panacea or a preemptory voice ordering me to protect myself from identity theft by immediately verifying the numbers on my credit card. I am beginning to feel wobbly.

Reclining on the blue couch beside Begley's novels, which

bristle with yellow stickers, I swaddle myself in a quilt. Despite the intense heat, I am frozen. Was I hyperventilating—like I did at a lectern once in DeKalb, or was it Urbana, when Sandra had to take over? Or way back when I was presenting a paper for her—she was too sick to travel—and my milk suddenly came down, coating the front of my dress? Regulating my breathing, I tried to consider how Begley's self-congratulatory analysis of winter-spring relationships contrasts with Colette's assessment of their damages.

According to Begley, transgenerational relationships enable not-good-enough fathers to redefine themselves as good-enough fathers to the lovers they adopt, nurture, and then relinquish. Wealthy older men can offer financial security to young women, as Schmidt does to his girlfriend. (Somehow this is not seen as paying for her services.) Eventually, when his girlfriend becomes pregnant either by him or her young fiancé, Schmidt knows that his love for her "had become paternal": paradoxically, she "would be a better daughter to him than Charlotte, just as he might be a better father to her."

But Begley seems self-conscious about this plot. He portrays an obnoxious novelist in *Schmidt Delivered*, all of whose books are about "this older guy who's screwing a young girl. Ha! Ha! Ha! What we all want to do." Phyllis Rose is right in her review: "One geriophilic young woman per novel might be credible. Not two." Plenty of Begley's codgers brandish amorous girls—eye candy— on their arms. Nor is this fantasy unusual in literature. Consider John Wilmot, Earl of Rochester, who created poems spoken by youthful girls adoring the "Ancient person of my heart," whose phallus can be released from "age's frozen grasp": "soothed by my reviving hand, / In former warmth and vigour stand."

Suddenly, bilious waves send me rushing to the bathroom, where I heave again and again into the raised toilet seat set up for Don, paroxysm after paroxysm, and then the splattering, a burning throat, tearing eyes, a drippy nose. I somehow cleaned it up and he somehow made me tea, but I could not keep it down. Did I have the flu or was the cancer returning with a vengeance? Had the trial drug stopped working?

Over the past few months, the blood marker had gone up and down, but only slightly. Maybe the marker has stopped being a reliable indicator. For two of the women in my support group, the CA125 blood test does not measure tumor growth. But why assume the wretched retching means cancer? When my cancer recurred in the past—before I went on the trial drug—there were no symptoms at all. Part of what earns some sympathy for privileged, prejudiced Schmidt is his caregiving, as well as his grief over his wife's painful demise from cancer.

Though frozen, I am clammy all over. (It does not help that the word *clammy* inspires Don to mention Galway Kinnell's poem "Oatmeal.") There's a bowl by my couch and a towel at hand. My body shudders through swell after swell of nausea with no comfortable position possible. This must be what Carrol and Ilka contend with as they deal with recurrences. Alone with poor Don as impotent witness, my oncologist hours away, I loathe the idea of the local emergency room. Except there is no I—only a battered container that quakes and curls up and then stands and then slides down the slurry slope, with nothing but breathing to get me through another surge of misery. Wet with sweat, my chest pounding, grasping the bowl, I feel my bladder or kidneys breaking down, and oh! I realize: I need to alert my guardian angel in Indianapolis, Alesha Arnold, Dr. Daniela Matei's research nurse.

My email prompted Alesha to prescribe Compazine, which Jayne rushed to pick up. It takes time to die with cancer. Maybe we should move into a Trace cottage like the one Jayne's mother has; Jayne was spending most of her evenings there. The idea of yet another operation and more chemotherapies seems palpably idiotic. What would be the point? They would only escalate and then prolong the agony.

Who will take care of Don, as he took care of me? Instantly, I picture us seven years ago, after interventional radiologists had stuck a thick tube, attached to an output bag, into my right buttock: I am prone on my stomach on our bed upstairs. Don unwraps the bandages, pats soothing ointment around the wound, drains the bag of fluid, measures and records it, and applies clean bandages on my bottom. I can neither see nor reach the area that aches no matter how many pain medications I swallow.

Waiting on the blue couch to see if the Compazine would work, I mourned the watershed summer coming to a close. Don, who used to run marathons, hobbled. The grandbaby in New York incapacitated by eating and sleeping disorders. In California, Sandra's devoted daughters were helping her adjust to a single life, but it was not easy. Mary and Andrew, their children, and my oncologist were leaving. Ilka, looking skeletal, attempts last-ditch medical interventions, but Carrol has begun considering hospice. And Fran has left a hole in my heart.

The trembling ceased while Jayne took her leave and I checked that the ostomy bag was securely attached, emailed assurances to Alesha, and wrapped the quilt under my numb feet. (How can I thank them for being so instantly available?) Maybe Fran had been trying to distance herself from me for longer than I realized. Was she envious of my publications or jealous of my family? No, I thought as the nausea receded and I could wiggle my toes. Fran has always made it abundantly clear that she prided herself on her successful career and cherished her single life.

Her books had established a scholarly field and in retirement she found inventive outlets for her energies. Though living alone could be difficult, she acknowledged, she relished meeting that challenge creatively. She could come and go as she pleased, she could dress as she liked and mess up the house and eat beans out of a can, she could listen to music as loud as she wanted whenever she wanted or putter over a jigsaw puzzle and not speak for a week. If I found her recounting of her exercise regime boring, she probably found my absorption in my writing boring. Our conversations had devolved into reports on her nephews and my kids or reiterations of our past. She had reasonably not wanted to go on performing a façade of friendship. I dozed through that afternoon and then through the night. By the next morning, what must have been an infection or food poisoning had passed.

"I guess it wasn't a recurrence," I told Don. "I'm becoming a cancerchondriac. But there is no bodily function I loathe more than throwing up. Even the words are revolting. Vomiting. Retching. Heaving. Hurling. Puking. Spewing. Barfing. Upchucking. Remember how I would start gagging whenever Perkins or Sam threw up?"

Don's response—"'Lord, Lord, where's his little cap?'"—made me laugh.

It was the punchline of Sandra and Elliot's joke about the old woman who took her grandson in his Saturday finery for a picnic at the beach, where a huge wave came up and swept him into the sea. "Lord, Lord," she says. "He's my treasure; please, please give him back." Instantly, a huge wave rose up, depositing the little boy safe and sound—in his playsuit—right next to her on the beach blanket. "But Lord, Lord," she says, "where's his little cap?"

Trying to cultivate gratitude that I was not at the moment dying of cancer, I remembered the casualties of our fused families when we moved into the Inverness. Perkins, Mary-Alice's orange cat, had never made peace with Sam, my younger daughter's Siamese, and vice versa. We had tried to give them each their own spaces, but while Perkins tore up the basement, caterwauling Sam peed in the dining room. Even feline Valium did not solve their territoriality. Eventually Perkins lit off into the ravine and Sam spent her declining years as a pampered geriatric guest at a nearby veterinary clinic.

At least Don's kids get along with me and mine with him, though at the start of our families' fusion all of them must have had their doubts. We were hardly the Brady bunch. My girls were mortified at an early Thanksgiving get-together when decorous Don and his daughters witnessed my antics. To a blaring trumpet fanfare, I had insisted on our usual ritual of parading the roasted

bird on a rolling cart, but it fell off—not once but twice. At his
house, my kids knew, the furniture, dishes, silverware, and towels matched. His family did not scoop turkeys off the floor. Why
did we have to be so bohemian? Yet over time his oldest and my
youngest, his youngest and my oldest have become friends. And
all of them support our union . . . in stark contrast to the merci-
less offspring in a story Sandra had just composed.

In "Shiksa," elderly Abe and slightly younger Marina attend
a Passover seder at which his adult children rise up in righteous
wrath, ostensibly over Marina's religious difference: like his kids,
Abe is an observant Jew, Marina a lapsed Catholic. Actually,
the children want to divide the couple in order to gain control of
the old man and his possessions. Sandra's story was grim about
"the most good-for-nothing bunch of kids that were ever raised."
This memorable phrase, spoken by one of the good-for-nothings,
comes from a classic Depression film that Orson Welles said
"would make a stone cry." In *Make Way for Tomorrow*, which certainly made me cry, an old, happily married couple must split up
to live with their crummy kids, and we are left wondering if they
will ever lay eyes on each other again.

The devolution of Schmidt's relationship with his daughter
Charlotte in the third volume of Louis Begley's trilogy hinges on
filial antipathy, even wrath. After an accident causes Charlotte's
miscarriage and hysterectomy, she blames Schmidt for the loss of
her baby and her reproductive future. Although "the temptation
to disinherit can be powerful," Schmidt pays all the bills for a long
hospitalization to deal with her depression and obtains legal services to extricate Charlotte from her unhappy marriage.

As I recuperated, I knew that I should consider the main plot in the conclusion of the Schmidt trilogy, where Begley's hero finally embarks on a serious partnership not with a chicklet but with a woman closer to his age. Unmoored by the purposelessness of retirement, he also finds a second vocation. However, I needed prose more restorative, like the warming baths I continue to crave. The title of Kent Haruf's *Our Souls at Night* promised just that. I read it in a few hours, tranquilized by its tenderness for two widowed characters who find late-life intimacy in the simplest of ways.

Seventy-year-old Addie Moore visits her contemporary and neighbor Louis Waters one evening to say, "I wonder if you would consider coming to my house sometimes to sleep with me." Lonely in her house, she imagines him lonely in his and therefore proposes that they get through the nights by talking and sleeping together. In a small town in Colorado, the widow and widower converse during a succession of luminous evenings in which they disclose the tragedies and disappointments of their previous marriages. Exultant that they are "not finished with changes and excitements. And not all dried up in body and spirit," they eventually "tried to do what the town thought all along they'd been doing but hadn't."

Even in this quiet paean to the boon of companionship, however, the precious connection between Addie and Louis is broken by an adult offspring. "I want you to stay away from my mother," Addie's son tells Louis. "And forget about my mother's money." With their small-town rootedness, Addie and Louis are worlds apart from Begley's elite, East Coast characters. Yet Begley also emphasizes the long backstory that late-life lovers must convey in order to connect with each other while keeping adult children at bay.

In the last book of Begley's trilogy, Schmidt embarks on a relationship with an equal and on a new vocation. He has profited from the advice of a multimillionaire who gives him a job managing an overseas foundation. With his private jets and hotel suites, the millionaire—outrageously imperious, ridiculously boastful, astonishingly tactless—melds in my mind with the bullying blowhard Donald Trump, who has begun appearing on television: extravagant egos plumped and pumped by colossal affluence. That this friend and Schmidt's love interest are Jewish, however, dispels his earlier anti-Semitism.

At seventy-eight, Schmidt fusses: is his "late-onset puppy love" for sixty-three-year-old Alice Verplanck a reasonable basis for cohabitation on "a satisfaction-guaranteed trial basis, with assurances he would creep away quietly if she found him wanting"? Between the first chapter, in which Schmidt awaits his reunion with Alice in the Hampton house, and the last, when they pledge their bond, we are given a flashback of their affair thirteen years earlier. In this case, the flashback underscores the commitments we have in later life—to people, to countries, to networks of professional obligations and settled habits that make it difficult for an older person like Alice to move in with a prospective partner. Plus, she has understandable reservations about Schmidt's character, specifically his capacity for aggression.

At their reunion, Schmidt and Alice must cope with how their earlier affair ended. When Schmidt learned that Alice was concealing a longtime sexual relationship with a colleague, he punished her with a furious "night in the sack": "he made love to her without uttering a loving word, without tenderness, transforming each caress into an assault." His violent attempt to claim or shame her triggered Alice's fury, his contrition, and the long rupture. During a few of those years, Schmidt whiled away his time in "friendly, unalloyed carnality" with the wife of a podiatrist whose ad in the *New York Review of Books* he had answered: "If I see you again, and if you're still nice, we'll do anal," she promises at their first meeting in the Carlyle. (My estimation of the *New York Review of Books*, which continues to arrive periodically in Don's office mailbox, has undergone a sea-change.)

The epigraph of *Schmidt Steps Back* comes from Yeats: "nothing can be sole or whole / That has not been rent." Presumably, Begley's main character becomes sole and whole because he has been rent by paternal grief. Eventually, as Schmidt withstands his daughter's irrational hostility, she makes a slow recovery and embarks on a new life. Schmidt has mellowed in kindness, even if his author has not, for Begley finds a particularly gruesome way of killing Charlotte off. Upon hearing news of the death of Alice's colleague, Schmidt makes his modest proposal. That he accedes to Alice's terms and timing manifests his maturation. But Begley's decision to decapitate Charlotte in a car crash testifies to his authorial anger at the ungrateful, mercenary daughter. Shakespeare would have called her a pelican daughter (for the pelican was believed to feed on its parents' blood).

Don and I were discussing selfish adult kids in the movie we had watched the night before, *Elsa and Fred*, when I brimmed with pleasure at his being able to get into the passenger seat of the car for our first expedition together to Kroger's in half a year. Late-life grocery shopping used to mean that we would divide up the aisles so neither one of us had to cover the entirety of the massive building. However, he was only strong enough to shamble into the supermarket, sit at the Starbuck's café, and sip a cup of coffee while I did the marketing. But again, after we managed to locate my car in the parking lot, he bent his knee sufficiently for him to be sitting beside me.

"Christopher Plummer got a second chance," I said. I was thinking about Fred's decision not to give his money to his shrewish daughter, to use it instead to take antique Elsa (Shirley MacLaine) to the fountain of *La Dolce Vita*, though the comparison with Marcello Mastroianni and Anita Ekberg was jarring.

"If we had to choose between our kids and each other," Don said, "we would choose our kids." He was examining the glue he had asked me to buy; it would keep the knob affixed to the torch lamp.

The remark, though true, smarted. But happily our daughters do not resemble Schmidt's or Christopher Plummer's. Although Schmidt managed to stand by Charlotte even while she exploited and reviled him, at the moment she castigates him for the loss of her baby he "wasn't sure he had heard of any father having been addressed by a child with such bile. Goneril? Regan?" He has nurtured her, but she repays him in venom. As a Renaissance adage puts it, "Love doth descend, but not ascend." The viperous offspring of King Lear, who strip him of all vestiges of power, stand as a warning to aging people, telling them not to relinquish their property too soon or else they will surrender their autonomy and possibly their lives.

Wrinkled in Time

MY STEPDAUGHTER SUSANNAH had been to the post office, the donut shop, the grocery store, and the farmer's market. She had cleaned the vegetables and put away the groceries and started planning the meals she would cook and either serve or stock in the freezer, when she looked up from her iPad to declare, "Hey, there's an apartment house that is going to go up downtown, just one block west of the square. High-end condos."

As she reached for her phone to call our real estate agent, I plunked down another playing card and considered the energy of people in midlife. What would have taken me a day or two, she had accomplished in an hour or two. My daughters evince the same strength. Was it adrenaline, drive, will, sheer physical stamina? Their speed and vigor underscored my more tentative pace as I slowed down in older age. How does that need to decelerate distinguish later from young loving?

On our way to the Trace, just the other day, I had noticed the vitality of the parents unloading huge SUVs at the dormitories. Don and I had rented a van to take first my older and then my younger daughter to college, a grueling experience for any parent who dreads crowds in Target (which my kids pronounced as if the word were French). Teaching is a profession that accentuates aging because the freshmen stay the same age, whereas their teacher does not. When I began as an associate instructor, I was a few years older than my undergraduates. As a professor, I was old enough to be their mother. Now I am old enough to be the grandmother of the kids sweating in the crowded driveways over their computer equipment, mini refrigerators, and bedding.

The brash dynamism of people who can take for granted the robust resilience of the body: there should be a word for it. Directly after cancer surgery in 2008, I lost that vitality, though I suppose other aging people feel it draining away less dramatically. The early twentieth-century author Vita Sackville-West describes how a healthy woman of eighty-eight, endowed with a mind alert to make the most of the time she has left, experiences the sensation of age: "the body was a little shaky, not very certain of its reliability, not quite certain even of its sense of direction, afraid of stumbling over a step, of spilling a cup of tea; nervous, tremulous; aware that it must not be jostled, or hurried, for fear of betraying its frail inadequacy." Is this a body capable of desire, sex, or frottage?

"When you and Jack finish that game," Susannah said as she got off the phone with Zak, "I'm taking him to buy a skateboard and some Hoosier wear and then out to lunch with Julie and maybe a meeting with Zak. Not to worry. We'll be back in plenty of time to make supper."

I was beating my fifteen-year-old grandson at gin rummy, but he had trounced me the night before at presidents and beggars, an insane card game in which the rich get richer and the poor poorer. So we finished our hand and they were out the door. I admired their ebullience—"restless modern youth," Mary-Alice used to say—just as Sackville-West's Lady Slane contrasts her children's striving ambition with her own wish to sit still and savor and simply be.

My copy of *All Passion Spent* came from Judith, who was surprised by its sophisticated insight into the newly widowed Lady Slane. We agreed: it's as if the novel lets us imagine what might have happened in *To the Lighthouse* if Mr. Ramsay had died in the night and Mrs. Ramsay had survived him. Like me, I suppose, Judith had been misled by Virginia Woolf into undervaluing Sackville-West's literary talents. Now her novel remains sadly out of print.

Judith, who sometimes stops by at the end of the workday, had come across a term she applied to *All Passion Spent*: *Altersroman*, a novel about age or the aged. Lady Slane finds that younger people display "a slight irritability, dawdling rather too markedly in order to keep pace with the hesitant footsteps" of the elderly, which is one reason why she thoroughly dislikes the company of her adult children. Another is their patronizing attitude toward her, for they simply assume, after their father's death, that "Mother had no will of her own": "she had not enough brain to be self-assertive."

"How sharper than a serpent's tooth it is / To have a thankless child." Adult children in stories of late-life love display their fangs by mocking or obstructing their parents or by exploiting them financially. King Lear's lamentation resounds throughout the opening pages of Vita Sackville-West's unexpectedly delightful novel, whose title would seem to rule it out of any study of later-life love and whose heroine evades Lear's miserable fate. Would King Lear—who seeks attestations of love from his daughters—have escaped his terrible destiny if he had lived with a wise partner? Would he have heeded such a companion? Sackville-West does not pose these questions, since her heroine is a widow.

Instead, she considers the need of older people to separate from their children. *All Passion Spent* explores the temporality of the aged, which alienates them from their families while transmuting hectic romantic love into the sedate pleasures of the sociable companionship that Don and I enjoy daily.

The novel begins with Lady Slane's covetous children expecting her to live out her widowhood by residing with each of them in turn for a two-week period and compensating them financially for the privilege of doing so. Much to their surprise, this previously dutiful mother and wife refuses a proposal similar to the one made by Lear's pelican daughters. She determines to move to a rental house that had entranced her thirty years earlier. "If one is not to please oneself in old age, when is one to please oneself? There is so little time left!" With all her passion spent, she wants to be visited only by those who "are nearer to their death than to their birth."

But is all her passion really spent? Judith had warned me that the only passion Lady Slane sustains revolves around the Hampstead rental, which represents her release from the domestic duties she had shouldered with Victorian rectitude for a politically prominent husband and a gaggle of demanding kids. Emancipated by her husband's death and her children's adulthood, she greets old age: "Those days were gone when feeling burst its bounds and poured hot from the foundry, when the heart seemed likely to split with complex and contradictory desires; now there was nothing left but a landscape in monochrome, the features identical but all the colours gone from them, and nothing but a gesture left in the place of speech."

More predictable than the novel's opening, the middle section of *All Passion Spent* emphasizes the need for retrospection that arises in old age. Inside the renovated Hampstead house, present time slows down during Lady Slane's remembrances of things past: her reflections on her long marriage to a man who became viceroy of India. Being a proper wife and a mother—becoming Lady Slane—had effectively slain her identity by forcing her to renounce her early dreams of becoming a painter. She considers the marital and domestic projects that consumed her attention as well as the ways they foreclosed other, less traveled roads that might have been taken.

The habit of recollection in later life, which certainly has me in its grip, was a subject Montaigne addressed: "Let childhood look forward, old age backward; was not that the signification of Janus's double face?" With a past far longer than the future she can expect, Lady Slane appears to agree with Montaigne's proposition about the Roman god of gates and doors. Looking backward enriches her existence: "to be able to enjoy one's past is to live twice," Montaigne believed.

In the final section of the novel, Lady Slane finds herself visited by a man who had fallen in love with her many years ago, and perhaps neither his nor her passion has been entirely spent. The narrative reminds me of our friend Ken who, after being widowed, reunited with his college sweetheart. The appearance in Hampstead of Mr. FitzGeorge, whom Lady Slane had met in Calcutta, surprises her with an unanticipated crackle or lick of desire: "She was eighty-eight, but the man-to-woman mainspring still coiled like a cobra between them. Innumerable years had elapsed since she had felt that stimulus; it came as an unexpected revival, a flicker, a farewell, stirring her strangely and awaking some echo whose melody she could not quite recapture."

For a number of people, late-life love involves reinventing earlier infatuations. Mr. FitzGeorge is an eccentric millionaire: a bachelor who collects art treasures, a miser who buys cheap and hoards his finds. Lady Slane nevertheless decides to continue receiving him, for they were "so old that they were all the time age-conscious, and being so old it was agreeable to sit like two cats on either side of the fire warming their bodies, stretching out hands so transparent as to let the pink light of the flames through them, while their conversation without effort rose or fell." He admires her face and her tranquility: "Youth could never sit as still as that, in absolute repose, as though all haste, all movement, were over and done with, and nothing left but waiting and acquiescence."

Together they remember an intense moment they shared

decades before while visiting a deserted city in India. One glance from him "had exploded a charge of dynamite in her most secret cellar. Someone by a look had discovered the way into a chamber she kept hidden even from herself. He had committed the supreme audacity of looking into her soul." The youthful Mr. FitzGeorge was saved from the indiscretion of confessing his love (to a married woman with children) by the intoxication he experienced while going about the business of collecting art treasures. Since the two agree that this long-ago passion cannot be revived, they become friends.

Companionability in later life was extolled to me by both my grandmother and my mentor. My grandma cherished a very dear "gentleman friend" whom she met in their retirement facility; they ate all their dinners together until he died. Carolyn Heilbrun advised the elderly to "leave romance to the young, and welcome friendship."

But youthful thinkers about love sometimes judge sexless relationships to be failures. The scholar Laura Kipnis, for example, assumes that "a 'good relationship' would probably include having—and wanting to have—sex with your spouse or spouse-equivalent on something more than a quarterly basis." Reflecting on the affection that kicks in when desire flags, she likens it to "denture adhesive. Yes, it's supposed to hold things in place; yes, it's awkward for everyone when it doesn't; but unfortunately there are some things that glue just won't glue, no matter how much you apply."

Yet reverie and conviviality are adhesives, powerful glues that can meld later-life partners. Like my grandma and her gentleman friend, Lady Slane and Mr. FitzGeorge neither marry nor move in together. Either action would be too complicated and, anyway, beside the point. For some older couples, neither sex nor frottage plays a part in successful unions. For others, cohabitation is not in the cards. LAT is the current term for people living apart together: partners with separate addresses who maintain a close relationship with each other. Vita Sackville-West envisions the companionability of seniors who are tame, humble, and wait upon judgment. She implicitly disagrees with the assumption that love must be wildly impetuous and intensely erotic. Perhaps she was able to do so because she relished a succession of passionate affairs with women while remaining deeply devoted to her husband of many decades.

Divorcing gratification from sexuality, *All Passion Spent* portrays two characters sharing recurrent, quotidian activities. They have relinquished goal-driven projects ("telic" is a word my philosopher son-in-law uses) for aimless but enjoyable routines (my son-in-law calls these "atelic"). Lady Slane and Mr. FitzGeorge have nothing left to achieve, accomplish, finish. Instead, they want to float on a sea of silence stippled with schmoozing. When not warming themselves like two cats before the fire, Lady Slane and Mr. FitzGeorge enjoy strolling on Hampstead Heath, wandering over to Keats's house, "that little white box of strain and tragedy marooned among the dark green laurels":

> Like ghosts themselves, they murmured of the ghost of Fanny Brawne and of the passion which had wrecked Keats; and all the while, just out of reach, round the corner, lurked the passion for Lady Slane which might have wrecked Mr.

FitzGeorge, had he not been so wary an egoist (unlike poor Keats), just too wise to let himself float away on a hopeless love for the young Vicereine, just unwise enough to remain remotely faithful for fifty years.

The slam of a car door and the rumble of skateboard wheels informed me that Susannah had returned and Jack was speeding down the driveway, so I grabbed my iPhone, determined to take a little movie. He dutifully started again at the walnut tree, which had already begun to lose its leaves. I was relieved that he did not attempt to skateboard down the steep driveway to the garage, but instead veered at the beech tree around the circle of beauty. Then it was time for us both to become sous-chefs for the complicated ratatouille Susannah was constructing, to set the table and welcome Julie, the Schnitz, and Hazel.

"Have you girls ever heard Don's story about W. H. Auden?" I asked as we settled around the kitchen table. After I explained to Jack what a famous poet Auden was, I asked Don, "Why was he in Indiana?"

"He had been asked by people in Columbus to stay for a week to bring cultural energy to the town. They had it all planned out, but he wanted a break so they phoned and asked if we could entertain him in Bloomington. I rounded up some people for lunch, including Bill Cagle, the director of the Lilly Library, and after a really stimulating conversation—Auden in his prime, talking about Continental philosophy—Bill and I asked him if he would like to visit the rare book library. He had a car and a driver so he was driven to the Lilly while Bill and I walked over."

"What did he look like then?"

"He was in his sixties, with his famously seamed face. He got out of the car and entered the library and Bill asked him if he wanted to see the most precious treasures of the Lilly, which were kept in a windowless, basement vault. We rode down in a small elevator and Bill showed him the Gutenberg, a copy of the Declaration of Independence autographed by all the signers, and John Keats's letter to Fanny Brawne, telling her he was dying. Auden began shaking and turned red. He said, 'This is obscene . . . that other people should read this letter and that you should have it in your library.'

"He turned and instead of taking the elevator, he stomped up an iron spiral staircase without a word of goodbye. Bill and I were really frightened that he would have a stroke or something."

"What do you think set him off?" someone asked, as the Schnitz started barking at Jack rolling around in the wheelchair.

"We thought then that he was thinking of his own impending death and the ghastly prospect of his privacy being invaded by some fool biographer or archivist . . . at some future time when he couldn't protect himself. His vulnerable posthumous existence. Later we found out that Auden objected to all personal papers being released so that strangers could read them."

The ghosts of Keats and of his wrecked passion for Fanny Brawne dimmed when Don mentioned Yeats's visit in 1903 and Dylan Thomas's in 1950 and Susannah began telling Julie about The Foundry. Apparently some architectural firm in Indianapolis was planning a four-story condominium just off the courthouse square. Zak was excited because it was intended for retirees who wanted to be within walking distance of shops, drugstores, and restaurants.

"Zak's going to drive you two up there to see the floor plans. Since it's still in the design phase, you could have a say in choosing flooring or making decisions on grab bars and a walk-in shower, that sort of thing."

I got up to get ice cream out of the freezer as Susannah turned to Jack. "Tomorrow, before we leave, you can bring that wheelchair down to the basement for Poppy. He doesn't need it anymore."

Then she turned back to us. "Daddy, if you can get into the passenger seat of the car, you can get into an airplane seat and you know Susan wants to see the baby . . . and you know how comfortable my guest room is. I'll arrange a wheelchair at both airports. Why not consider it?"

Putting bowls and spoons on the kitchen table, I rejoiced in Susannah's contesting the distinction between young and old people that Montaigne had emphasized and that the owner of the Hampstead house had discussed with Lady Slane: "Young people compel one to look forward on a life full of effort. Old people permit one to look backward on a life whose effort is over and done with. That is reposeful." In another month, Don would reach the age of Lady Slane, but I wanted us to look forward as well as backward. While Julie took out the dogs and Jack hauled the garbage bin out to the road, I considered the ghosts of Mr. FitzGeorge and Lady Slane, Keats and Fanny Brawne.

After the sudden death of Mr. FitzGeorge near the end of *All Passion Spent*, it becomes clear that he has left his considerable art collection to Lady Slane. She determines to give the artwork away to benefit hospitals and museums, in part because she wants nothing more than quiet, in part because she knows the act will shock her greedy sons and daughters: "Think how much I shall annoy my children!" Finally, a visiting great-granddaughter thanks Lady Slane. Not having an inheritance has made it easier for her to break an engagement that would have hindered her from developing her passion for music. Seeing "one last opportunity for annoying" her children, Lady Slane encourages her great-granddaughter's artistic ambitions and dies in repose at having found a surrogate who may lead "the unled life"—a resonant phrase from my friend Andrew—that she had relinquished.

The tranquility Lady Slane values above all else would often elude turbulent John Keats, as it does many young people, as it sometimes does me. "My mind has been the most discontented and restless one that ever was put into a body too small for it," he confessed to Fanny Brawne in March 1820. But in loving her, he achieved a respite from agitation. "I never felt my mind repose upon anything with complete and undistracted enjoyment—upon no person but you. When you are in the room my thoughts never fly out the window: you always concentrate my whole senses."

Impecunious, tormented by thwarted poetic ambition and sexual desire, the twenty-five-year-old Keats struggled with disease and despair. It was very late in his life, though he was very young and troubled by the figure of Fanny "eternally vanishing," as he prepared himself to step through death's door: "I always made an awkward bow." The hemorrhages from his damaged lungs, along with the miserable treatments of tuberculosis, led to his tragically early demise. Pondering Keats's great suffering, Fanny Brawne resigned herself to the death, or so she claimed in a letter mourning only the fact that Keats had died so far away from home, for "he might have died here with so many friends to soothe him and me *me* with him." While contemplating Keats's final days in Italy, was she lamenting his losses or her own? Would it have soothed not only "him" but also "me *me*" to have him dying at home?

Give and Take

IN THE GRIP of self-revulsion, in need of guidance, I stared at the six lines, read them silently and then aloud, reread them, and then reread them again, for days on end. On the page of the hardcover book I had found in Don's study, the six lines appear set off, framed by a space break symbol—the word for such a symbol is *dinkus* or *dingbat*, he tells me—within a long poem by Donald Hall about his relationship with his cherished wife, Jane Kenyon. I copied them by hand into a notebook, paying attention to the line breaks and centering.

> *Why were they not*
> *contented, four months ago, because*
> *Jane did not have*
> *leukemia? A year hence, would he question*
> *why he was not contented*
> *now? Therefore he was contented.*

I admired the slightly archaic "contented," instead of the usual "content," which could be mispronounced and misunderstood. Just a snippet in a longer poem, I gave it the title "Contented." The last phrase became a refrain to reprimand myself for impatience and irritability, to remind myself that I should be contented, contented, contented. For I had become visibly exasperated: grouchy about the interminable rounds of blood work, doctor appointments, physical therapy, and pharmacy trips. I had been getting progressively more peeved at how long it took to get the Velcro sneakers on Don's feet. Worse, at a rare social outing—we had been invited to a close-down-the-pool party—and within earshot of a number of young colleagues, I had asked Don if he needed to use the bathroom before our trip home.

The discourteous remark became my very own Box Hill. I was wedged in the gulch associated with the shameful incivility of Jane Austen's Emma . . . even after I apologized profusely. It was a worse moment than when, years ago, in a highly inappropriate setting, I had inexplicably called Don by the name of my first husband. Surely now was the time to try a secular version of *lectio divina*—the practice of "divine reading" that involves not fast but slow, very slow reading. In monasteries and convents, students of the Bible for centuries approached reading as a meditative, devotional practice. One passage would be reflected upon, prayed over, and contemplated.

Why would my impatience grow when Don was clearly getting stronger? And why when we were actually out of the house and among friends after such a long seclusion? Somehow being shaded by an umbrella on a sunny back deck, conversing with young people and being interrupted by their children's antics, he had looked so brittle, so tentative. But why would that have sparked feelings of anger . . . at him . . . that blemished, and then blighted the day?

"Contented," Donald Hall's six-line secular catechism, reflects on what remains. While Hall ministers to Jane Kenyon in the hospital, the disease that threatens her teaches him about their earlier relationship, when they took for granted their being healthy together. During our everyday interactions, of course, most of us do not congratulate ourselves on not having a mortal disease. But while dealing with Kenyon's leukemia, Hall realizes how grateful they ought to have been for the time before the diagnosis. And just as he understands the plenitude of the past through the privations of the present, the privations of the present swell with significance in contrast to the prospect of a diminished future without her.

The book in which these six lines appear is titled *Without*. Part of it meditates on Jane Kenyon's death. However, I ignore the elegies. As the short mounds of grass by the front door feathered and tasseled, as the Eupatorium Chocolate at the edge of the back yard put out tiny white flowers glowing against burnished brown leaves, I was caught up in the first half of the volume, where Hall suggests that there is a reason why we use the words *caregiver* and *caretaker* interchangeably. Nor is he alone in pondering the paradox that the caregiver receives caretaking by caregiving, a perspective I thought I knew, but must learn again. Opsimathy: it turns out to be an unexpectedly useful idea.

I was contented by our plans to fly to New York and grateful that Don would undertake what would feel to him like a hazardous journey. I was contented that he was well enough for me to leave him alone at home while I lunched with my cancer support group. Though Carrol was accepting hospice help at home and Ilka looked fragile, the rest of us were scheming to improve community cancer care. I was contented that I could continue composing my *Times* columns and correcting the first pass proofs of a book about cancer I had not thought I would live to see into print. Yet as the town teemed with students and Mary emailed pictures of her new house in Baltimore and thousands of refugees poured out of Syria but were barricaded out of Europe—the photographs were devastating—an intermittent rash of irritability kept on breaking out.

Donald Hall's poems, composed with the sort of clarity that comes from having experienced caregiving in both directions, do not gloss over the anger, claustrophobia, and estrangement that can burgeon when one must take care of an invalid. Nineteen years older than Jane Kenyon, who had been his student, Hall assumed she would outlive him, especially after colon cancer metastasized to his liver. Like my Donald and me, they continued to presume that he would die first, until her leukemia disabused them. The intensity of her fifteen months of treatment is recounted in the poems of *Without*.

Anger is contagious, I am somewhat relieved to be reminded. It may be impossible not to resent disease or disability that threatens to take over the lives of the well and the unwell alike. Sick or disabled people take out their distress on those most proximate. When Hall's wife no longer knew the month or year, she had to be moved from a clinic back into the hospital, where the return of normal consciousness was accompanied by depression that caused her to erupt in fury. In one poem, he quotes her saying, "I wish you could feel what I feel!" After a stanza break, Hall describes how her rebuke triggered his nightmare:

> *At Eagle Pond, Jane*
> *sprayed his body with acid*
> *from a booby trap. He was dying.*
> *He followed her in his rage*
> *to Connecticut and his mother's house.*
> *Just before he woke, he saw*
> *Jane crouched in terror at the bottom*
> *of the cellar stairs while he*
> *crept down, his hands clutched to choke her.*

"There's nothing more selfish than sickness," Don once remarked. Jane Kenyon, furious at her disease and its terrible treatments, lashes out in the physical attack of the dream-Jane who sets out to murder Hall. At the house of his mother, the dying caregiver wants to strangle his terrified wife, to put an end to their torment. Toward the close of the most beautiful movie about elderly caregiving, Michael Haneke's *Amour*, Georges (Jean-Louis Trintignant) smothers his beloved wife Anne (Emmanuelle Riva) with a pillow, knowing that the end of her life means the end of his own as well. Of course, the physical confinement of caregiving can make people stir-crazy.

Near the beginning of *Amour*, we see the aging couple at a

concert; in a dream sequence at the end, they put on coats to go outside. But all the other scenes take place inside their apartment, where Georges bathes, dresses, undresses, feeds, medicates, moves, and massages his increasingly immobilized wife. Georges and Anne weave from the kitchen to the bathroom to the living room, where the grand piano evokes the fulfilling teaching career Anne had to relinquish. By spitting out food, by pushing Georges away, Anne repeatedly mimes the rage she cannot put into words about her intensifying incapacitation. At one point, he becomes so frustrated that he slaps her.

Donald Hall captures a claustrophobic year in hospitals and clinics when the seasons were obliterated by sickness. The disturbing title poem "Without," which he read aloud to Jane Kenyon—" 'That's it, Perkins,' she said. 'You've got it. That's it.' "—describes a world without color, without seasons, trees, animals, or garlic, which have all been annihilated by the war against cancer: "provinces invaded bombed shot shelled / artillery sniper fire helicopter gunship." It is a poem without punctuation that repeats the words of loss—"without" and "no"—to protest the "pain vomit neuropathy morphine nightmare / confusion the rack terror the vise."

An incomprehensible, medicalized vocabulary erupts to swamp the "we" of the opening line: "vincristine ara-c cytoxan vp-6" would be impenetrable without the next line about "loss of memory loss of language losses." There is a moment of possibility, a stanza about the potential return to the normalcy of sun and moss and leaves and a market and a dog, but it is overwhelmed by "the sea unrelenting wave gray the sea" with its successive surges of unmitigated negativity. "The days were endlessly the same in the way that the ocean is the same," Hall noted in a prose memoir: "When you are so sick, there is nothing wherever you look that is not sickness."

"Without" reminds me of the seventeen days I spent in an Indianapolis hospital on TPN (total parenteral nutrition)—tube food, I called it—in February 2009 and how the indistinguishable hours slipped by without the punctuation of meals or even of night and day, since the window slats were broken. When Don arrived with a bouquet of yellow roses, I could not believe that there was a world elsewhere celebrating Valentine's Day. "They didn't call it off," Don said. The scene that shocked me in *Amour*: Georges standing at the kitchen sink with a bouquet of flowers. Instead of cutting off the bottom tips, he chops the heads of the blossoms off their stems. It seemed a desecration until I later saw them strewn over the face of his dead wife.

As I took Don to a shoe store where we could not find any extra-wide shoes, as I drove us to the post office to return the shoes he had ordered online, "Without" brought back another day without the punctuation of weather, in August 2012. A week earlier, I had signed a sheaf of papers informing me that the medicine in a Phase 1 clinical trial would not cure me of ovarian cancer but could kill me and that neither the clinicians nor the pharmaceutical manufacturer would be held legally responsible. I had decided to become a guinea pig.

Don and I arrived at 8 a.m. at the research wing of the hospital, where my blood and vitals would be checked every half hour, then every hour, then every few hours after I took four pink capsules of the experimental drug. By late afternoon, it became clear that my magnesium or potassium levels were insufficient. We waited through the ordering of the prescription and then through the long infusion and by 9 or 10 p.m. I was cranky, petulant, but some other test had to be done before Don would find our way to a motel for the night so we could return back to the hospital the next day at 8 a.m. for more testing. I was antsy to get out, snarky, and, yes, in need of a glass of wine.

Don somehow found an app on his iPad to get a succession of the most beautiful tenor arias—by Puccini, Bizet, Verdi, Donizetti, sung by Pavarotti, Björling, Domingo, Caruso—one after another soaring, throbbing with such passion that I was drenched in the pleasure of listening. And then he found "The Slow Drag"—a joyous chorus from Scott Joplin's opera *Tremonisha* that could not fail to lift anyone's spirits—and we replayed it over and over again and an aide crept in to listen with open-mouthed amazement.

That the experimental pills have continued to work for three years astonishes us. No more stressing about medical bills: clinical trials cover most of the costs of treatment. Last time I had a blood test, the nurse took an extra vial of blood, and I could not figure out why. "They want to sprinkle it on the sick," Don said. "Test its magic powers."

Jane Kenyon managed to buoy Donald Hall's spirits—"'That's it, Perkins,' she said. 'You've got it. That's it.'"—even when her immune system was so compromised that she had to be quarantined. During a perilous bone marrow transplant, Hall had to suit up in sterile gear to enter her hermetic cubicle—a floppy hat, yellow mask, a paper gown, long white booties, and sterile latex gloves: "Jane said he looked like a huge condom." The line, written (as throughout the sequence) in the third person, testifies to the poet's self-alienation and also to Jane Kenyon's retained sense of humor. Perhaps that is why the character Alice in the movie *Still Alice* says, "I'd rather have cancer."

Absorbed as I was in the concentration of all this slow reading, it came as somewhat of a shock that two dates on the calendar suddenly drew nearer and then in a flash were gone. On September 18, Zak drove Don and me to Indianapolis to meet with the firm constructing The Foundry, the apartment building that would be erected along the B-line trail downtown.

The pretty girl who met with us knew nothing about the design layouts she showed us: not which direction the windows faced, not the size of the rooms, not the materials planned for the floors, cabinets, or countertops. At each of our questions, she looked stunned and then left to confer with some mysteriously unavailable authority only to return with indeterminate information . . . except she promptly answered our final query about the price of the three-bedroom unit we liked.

Our jaws dropped.

"Eight hundred and seventy thousand dollars?" one or the other of us exclaimed. "Who would pay that in Bloomington? To live around the corner from the Irish Lion and across the street from Chase Bank?"

"Dentists," she said.

On September 21, I drove the two of us and Julie to Jonathan and Alexandra's for a celebratory dinner. Don did not want any gifts on his eighty-eighth birthday, so Jonathan made a lavish meal with plenty of vegan dishes. On our return to the Inverness late that night, we found a package propped against the front door. It turned out to be a replacement of the framed Bloomington sign we had given away to Mary. How generous, I thought as the phone rang—my son-in-law in New York, calling to congratulate Don on reaching the number of the keys on a piano. In two years, he would be a nonagenarian, a word that alarms me.

"There was a Dick Tracy villain named 88 Keyes," Don said. "I'm switching to the organ."

That is why the character Alice in the movie *Still Alice* would have rather heard a cancer diagnosis than the Alzheimer's diagnosis she receives. She wanted to retain her sense of herself. It is hard enough to imagine one's own degeneration and death, harder still to imagine dying witless.

When I settled back down to the literature I had collected on caregiving, I realized that the experience changes radically for couples dealing with senility, Pick's disease, Lewy body dementia, Alzheimer's, or brain damage. The best-known autobiographical and imaginative works on this subject—John Bayley's *Elegy for Iris* as well as the movie *Iris*, Alice Munro's story "The Bear Came over the Mountain" as well as its film version, *Away from Her*—depict the sorrow and frustration of loving a person whose body has been increasingly evacuated of subjectivity.

John Bayley always understood that he did not understand the beautiful mind of his wife, the philosopher and novelist Iris Murdoch, whose youthful confidence contrasts with the "omnipresent anxiety typical of Alzheimer's patients." To Bayley, the "lion face" of the Alzheimer's patient "indicates only an absence: It is a mask in the most literal sense." His memoir about Iris Murdoch jux-taposes a joyous Iris, enjoying daring swims, with the terror that engulfs him when he worries that she might forget and let water "pour into her mouth as she opened it in a soundless appeal." In the movie, then-versus-now is emphasized by cutting back and forth between the young Iris, played by Kate Winslet, and the older Iris, played by Judi Dench.

A sexually and intellectually adventurous Iris Murdoch underscores the deterioration of an agitated, frightened Iris, as the squalor of the pigsty she shares with John Bayley begins to seem downright unhealthy. According to Bayley, the "omnipres-ent anxiety" typical of Alzheimer's patients "spreads to the one who looks after the sufferer." Exhausted by her urgent questions and physical needs, Bayley asks, "Does the care-giver involun-tarily mimic the Alzheimer's condition? I'm sure I do." Only to this extent does he suggest the grueling grind that can wear down and indeed totally deplete caregivers.

While caring for her brain-impaired husband, Alix Kates Shulman believes they are "becoming mirror images of each other," as if "his illness has infected me." The doubling of the caregiver and the ailing partner occurs with other diseases as well. Again and again, Donald Hall misspoke the sentence "My wife has leukemia"; it came out "My life has leukemia."

Still, dementia poses its own specific problems. My Donald remembers sitting down to dinner with Mary-Alice, when she turned to him and asked in her most polite Oak Park voice, "Do you have any children?"

"What did you say to her, Bear?" At my diagnosis, I was horrified that my cancer would propel him back into the caregiving role he had undertaken for years with Mary-Alice.

"'Yes,' I said. 'We have two wonderful daughters.'"

Taking care of a partner who does not recognize you . . . that must be the hardest. Would you recognize yourself? How can longtime companions prove their love if they cannot remember their shared past?

Alice Munro contemplates the demise of memory and of love in "The Bear Came over the Mountain." When Grant is allowed to visit his wife in the nursing home (one much nicer than the Trace), Fiona barely remembers him and has found a new friend, Aubrey, on whom she dotes. Serves Grant right, one might think, for his philandering. But Alice Munro's ironies reach beyond such a judgment as it becomes clear that Aubrey's subsequent removal from the nursing home, his return to his wife, threatens Alice's well-being. Because she is pining, Grant tries to facilitate his wife's infidelity by means of his own: by starting a relationship with Aubrey's wife (so he can persuade her to return Aubrey to the nursing home). Yet when Grant manages to reunite Aubrey with Alice, she has forgotten him.

At the end of the narrative, does Alice's affection for her husband awaken, or it is just another ephemeral caprice of her unpredictable mind? The bear goes over the mountain to see what he could see; and what he could see was, in my childhood version, another mountain and, in Don's, the other side of the mountain. Don thinks the title means "you just keep going, mountain after mountain, one foot in front of the other." That's what he did for Mary-Alice. But the title makes me think of great lines by Gerard

Manley Hopkins: "O the mind, mind has mountains; cliffs of fall / Frightful, sheer, no-man-fathomed." (Clearly, between the two of us Don has the better disposition.)

John Bayley, more than Alice Munro, suggests that love can be proven with partners who cannot remember their shared past. Alzheimer's brings John Bayley and Iris Murdoch closer together. Decades earlier, Murdoch had defined love as "the extremely difficult realization that something other than oneself is real." During her illness, this realization, on both their parts, could not be more evident. Their previous "closeness of apartness has necessarily become the closeness of closeness," for the "terror of being alone . . . is a feature of Alzheimer's."

The "closeness of apartness"—the pleasure of solitude in tandem—strikes me as an often ignored but exquisite benefit reaped by healthy companions. For satisfying hours on end, each solo and yet connected: no need to cleave together, being so closely conjoined. No need for ordinary communication either. Don and I often sit in separate rooms at home or together at a table in restaurants, not talking but companionably silent. We overhear elderly partners who bicker and babble in the call and response of Winnie and Willie, in slang, chitchat, prattle, phatic chirping. Or as Bayley and Murdoch did, in nonsensical phrases, baby talk, encoded colloquies. Before the onset of illness, Bayley and Murdoch shared "a whole infantile language of our own," a "private" one. After Murdoch became ill, they communicated in "snatches of doggerel, song, teasing nonsense rituals" that functioned "like underwater sonar, each bouncing pulsations off the other, then listening for an echo."

By means of quirky dialects, many people revive unextinguished sensations and emotions. Without overt meaning or substance, sometimes addled and recycled allusions, punch lines, and jingles elicit a shared past with a multiplicity of eccentric associations that have accrued over time. Such linguistic shortcuts enliven a relationship that can be imperiled by disease, especially if it threatens the mind.

When Marion Coutts realized that a brain tumor had taken away most of her husband's words, she worried, "What of our private language? How can a language endure if it has only one to speak it and another to give it context?" Before cancer, "we were proximate even when apart"; after its ravages, their language "diversifies again and becomes a repertoire of homemade sighs and groans. We are in the versatile region of tone and touch and pitch mapped by light pressure to the skin or a hand circling the face."

As the reference to touch and pressure suggests, "the closeness of closeness" relates more specifically to the intimacy created by disease: "If Iris could climb inside my skin now, or enter me as if I had a pouch like a kangaroo," Bayley states, "she would do so." Alix Kates Shulman's husband and Donald Hall's wife confused their caregiving partners with their mothers. Caregiving can recreate the nursing couple: mother and child. For a woman, therefore, caregiving may require more of the same, but maybe not for a man.

A memoir by Brian Aldiss explains why many published testimonies come from male caregivers, when statistically most caretakers are female. Tending to his wife of thirty years, Aldiss finds himself baffled by the shopping, cooking, and cleaning that he must learn to do. He writes his account in order to understand his perplexity. Taking on his wife's tasks sensitizes him to her past existence. In the process, it instructs and changes him: "Our two lives had become one life."

According to Bayley, illness has made him and Murdoch "inseparable—in a way, like Ovid's Baucis and Philemon, whom the gods gave the gift of growing old together as trees." After Jane Kenyon's death, Donald Hall looked at the trees near her grave, wishing she were a birch, he the gray oak alongside it.

Earlier in *Without*, when Hall fully expected his wife to dress herself and drive herself in a matter of months, he found himself discomforted by the thought of her renewed independence: "He felt shame / to understand he would miss / the months of sickness and taking care." Hall had first learned how caregiving intensifies intimacy when Jane Kenyon had nursed him after he "lost two thirds of a liver and nine-tenths of my complacency": "I have come so close to Jane that I feel as if I had crawled into her body through her pores—and, although the occasion of this penetration has been melancholy, the comfort is luminous and redemptive." Daily, as she would massage him, he felt "an interdependent fusing together of our bodies and spirits."

My Donald also suffered the loss of arduous caregiving's redemption. He was in a rage at himself when Mary-Alice died. He phoned me with the news. "I've failed, I've failed," he kept on repeating, despite my assurances that he had nursed her devotedly throughout her long illnesses. Was our friend George—now grieving the death of his wife in New Jersey—tormenting himself with gratuitous self-recriminations? The husband of Carrol—she would no longer be attending our cancer support meetings—was contented, I was convinced, while he drove her around the neighborhood through which she was now too weak to walk. On their last drive, she confided, they had counted fifty-six rabbits, a personal best.

That conversation caused me to reach down to the stack of books accumulating on the floor next to the blue couch and find the last collection of Jane Kenyon's work that she managed to organize. It strikes me that the title poem is a precursor and a companion piece to the six-line catechism by Donald Hall, the one I titled "Contented." Also a memento mori, "Otherwise" was written when she was his caregiver and begins with two declarative sentences:

> I got out of bed
> on two strong legs.
> It might have been
> otherwise.

Through a morning of eating cereal and taking the dog for a walk, through the noontime ritual of lying down with her mate, and then later eating dinner together, and then getting into bed and planning another identical day, the refrain resounds: "It might / have been otherwise." The shift to the future in the poem's concluding, unbroken line—declaring that one day "it will be otherwise"—admonishes us to continue being contented with the work of love before the rhythm of successive days is stayed.

Tequila Mockingbird

VIVID GOLDS, BLAZING oranges, burnished reds first came into view through the airplane window and then danced before our eyes all the way home. We had not missed the peak of the glory. The flamboyant leaves flamed before they would cascade and drop down. "East, west," I said, as I always do, and then I tipped our driver for "heroic driving." What a whirl the past week, what fun. Images swirled in my head: Don toasted at a music stand, the fox crawling and the monkey strutting around Susannah's apartment, the pavement under my feet during brisk walks alone as the city sky blued into that blacker blue that always takes my breath away.

The maples at the Inverness were gold, the bushes orange, the dogwoods red, though the pear trees remained as green as ever, while the walnut was bare. "I miss you most of all, when autumn leaves begin to fall": Nat King Cole's voice issued from a fax Don once sent me when I was away in England, lecturing.

Of course our trip to see my daughter and her family was the high point for me. During the weeks leading up to it, I was sure we would not make it. We had come down with such terrible colds that the night we were supposed to take Judith out for her birthday, she brought us garlic soup and some Emergen-C packets. Too many signs were alerting me of my advancing imbecility. One day, I noticed that I was wearing mismatched socks. On another, I forgot to pay at the salon for a trim of the few hairs growing at the back of my head and had to return with apologies. The ingredients I took out of the refrigerator for our supper that night turned out to be rancid. When I informed Don that our colleague Ross had been named a finalist for the National Book Award, he said, "Susan, we learned that a while ago, last week in fact." (It's never a good sign when he uses my name.)

Yet we managed, with much trepidation, to get ourselves to Susannah's apartment. Don did not have the energy to negotiate the bustling Manhattan streets, but I could walk the seven blocks to my daughter Simone's place, where the chaos of life with a two-year-old and a one-year-old astonished and exhausted and delighted me. The baby was well enough for us to pack them both into strollers and take them to the park, where Sam could prance before the street musicians, while Jonah inspected and tasted the toys, teething rings, and binkies we put in his hands. The joy of seeing my younger girl so very competent and confident as a mother gladdened me, made me giddy with pleasure.

Like most mothers, I feel a unique tie to each of my kids. Shy and sensitive as a child, my younger, in the second grade, had convinced herself that people died in their birth order and would, if they had their wallets on them, find their way back to their families. Simone represented a challenge, since my extravagant highs and lows frightened her. She was the only child to live with me and Don during her school years. We listened weekly to a musical quiz show on the radio, "Ether Game," and guessed the titles of songs or the names of composers; she phoned in our answers to the local station. On mystic summer nights, we would sit at the table on the back porch and she would bring out her cello and play a gorgeous movement of the Bach suites to the accompaniment of the crickets and frogs.

While I walked the seven blocks back to Susannah's apartment with the sort of brisk stride that Indiana streets, lanes, and roads never inspire in me, I wondered if it was the pace of the young people passing me by that quickened my steps, or some trace remembrance of hustling from the Norton office to a restaurant, deep in book talk with Sandra; or maybe it was the chill in the air as nightfall brought out lights here and there in the towering buildings; or perhaps simply the exhilaration of returning to a place of origins. That I could be walking alone in the city, exulting in the toddler's chirpings of "Hickory Dickory Dock" and the baby's wet smooches, elated me, as did the sky darkening into the midnight blue I had chosen for many of my quilts. Amid throngs of people of every conceivable color and from an inconceivable number of foreign countries and with inconceivably various customs and costumes and cuisines, my relish at the pied beauty was qualified only by Don's inability to venture out.

The bracing vitality and variety of New Yorkers and some satisfaction at the trip's having been accomplished sent me to one of the happiest late-life love stories I had found, a contemporary novel that explores the special link between an aging parent and an artistic younger daughter in the multicultural capital of the world, London. Bernardine Evaristo's *Mr. Loverman* foregrounds the obstacles to late-life love for people lumped together in the category "diversity": its central character is an aging man of color, an immigrant, and a homosexual. Don and I were going out after months of imposed hibernation; Evaristo's protagonist struggles throughout *Mr. Loverman* to come out after a lifetime of enforced subterfuge. His progress, like my own, proves that children may facilitate rather than obstruct their parents' second chances.

Seventy-four-year-old Barrington Jedidiah Walker tries to extricate himself from his fifty-year-long marriage because he has always loved and been loved by Morris, ever since they were boys in Antigua. But Barrington fears the homophobia all too evident in Caribbean society and also in the cosmopolitan British world where his girls were born and raised. I love the photograph of an aging dandy on my paperback copy of *Mr. Loverman* and its elegant French gatefolds: flaps extending the front and back of the cover that can serve as page holders. Though Barrington wants to live with Morris, he has witnessed verbal and physical violence against anyone labeled a "Batty man! Bum bandit! Poofter! Anti-man!" The prospect of coming out makes him feel "like climbing Kilimanjaro with no clothes, crampons, rope, pick, or SOS flare." Besides, he explains to Morris, "I am an individual, specific, not generic. . . . I ain't no homosexual, I am a . . . Barrysexual."

In addition, like me he dreads leaving his home of many decades: "to leave here will be like dismantling and remantling myself in some strange, cold place. Houses don't turn into homes straightaway." In the family room, I gaze at the fireplace around which so many heartfelt conversations bound us to our four girls, at the two paintings by Jan of the red shed, at the wall covered by a huge acrylic of leeks and radishes. I cannot conceive of this house emptied of what has made it a home.

Shades of Don and me inhabit it inside and out: caressing in the bed with the wooden frame, conducting a blindfolded knish-tasting test with a grandchild in the dining room, racing the wind-up little-old-ladies-in-walkers on Don's study floor, chopping and baking in the kitchen, doing what we keep to ourselves in one of the living-room armchairs, watering "Splat," the chartreuse hosta that recovered only to be eaten by deer.

It would have been fun to teach *Mr. Loverman*, since it resists and spoofs the politically correct discourse that students bring into classroom conversations these days. An outright misogynist and too old to want to mend his ways, Barrington invokes Aristotle's declaration "that the female is a female by virtue of a certain lack of qualities," remonstrates that women "menstruate twelve times a year, or, as I like to say, *mentalate*, which incapacitates them physically and psychically," and argues that childbearing "likewise incapacitates them for nine months and thereafter for eighteen years of motherhood." No wonder he is banished from a course on feminism.

Vain of his "indestructible ivories," of his heroic drinking capacity, and of his retro finery, Barrington flaunts his faith in his own exuberance: "Nobody can be depressed around me for long. I am the Great Mood Levitator. I am the Human Valium." Since all his teachers in Antigua came "from the colonial mothership," he can speak the Queen's English, but "so what if me and my people choose to mash up the *h-english linguish* whenever we feel like it, drop our prepositions with our panties, piss in the pot of correct syntax and spelling, and mangle our grammar *at random*? Is this not our *postmodern, postcolonial* prerogative?" He has been taking evening classes for decades and likes nothing better than putting on display the linguistic gymnastics that make him such a boisterous and likable character.

Because family considerations torment Barrington with "second thoughts about his second chance," he is surprised when his younger daughter turns out to be pivotal in helping him come out of the closet. At a moment of great stress, Barrington tells Maxine "about me and Morris since way back in St. John's and how we been carrying on ever since like agents in post-war West Berlin." Her response—"Nothing gets past my gaydar, and you are *beyond* camp"—astonishes him.

Maxine teases her father and Morris, but she also introduces them to a gay bar, where they touch each other in their "first public display of physical affection in sixty years." I have some small inkling of their pain at not being touched in public, since Don has always been very private about displaying his affection. Bernadine Evaristo also reminds me how valiantly my girls—then seventeen and thirteen years old—supported my growing commitment to Don, even when the three of us felt dowdy at social events with his family. In photos of Susannah's wedding, we look like shtetl denizens beamed into the beau monde.

Like many late-life narratives, *Mr. Loverman* uses the flashback, in this case a series of interspersed chapters from the point of view of Barrington's long-suffering wife. But she, too, gets a second chance in Evaristo's generous tale, for in *Mr. Loverman*, older people have a better shot at love and happiness than do youngsters. Barrington's daughters find that "the good guys are all taken and the rest are either commitment-phobic dogs . . . or too ugly, too old, too poor, too badly dressed, too unfit, too uneducated, too boring, too low-class, too gay, or too into white or nearly white women." Although I have noticed commitment phobia in young white men as well, Barrington ascribes the problem to the ongoing legacy of slavery—"when we wasn't allowed to be husbands and fathers."

Even while his girls browbeat him with the smug sense of superiority that apparently comes with young adulthood, Barrington continues to support them. He spends some of his time figuring out why by "contemplating how those Ancient Greek eggheads came up with four categories of love: agape is unconditional love; eros—intimate; philia—brotherly; and storge—a deep, familial affection." The first three of these terms were familiar to me: *agape* associated with God's unreserved love, spiritual devotion, or charity; *eros* with sexual desire; *philia* with friendship. But *storge* was new, a term that apparently pertains to relationships within the family, affectionate ties to parents or children that sometimes become strained, but that we struggle to maintain because of abiding loyalty.

Storge had been the supreme pleasure in New York, when Susannah made a meal for my two British cousins, who were visiting from London. With the help of Jack, she served a tasty supper of coq au vin and (my favorite comfort food) mashed potatoes for our reunion. Watching my cousins getting to know Susannah, Jack, Simone, her husband, and boys—after the cataclysmic diaspora that our family had suffered—assured me that I would not be the taut, flimsy tightrope providing the sole connection to our common but shredded ancestry.

Despite his misogyny, Barrington excels at storge with his daughters, at eros and philia with Morris, and at agape with a female friend of Maxine's who came out of the closet but then wound up homeless. Since Barrington had made a good amount of money in real estate and Maxine's friend exhibited the sort of courage that eludes him, he moved her into one of his flats. Fear motivated him to invest his money in broken houses, which he bought, repaired, and rented: "Any time this country starts Nazifying itself and another Shitler comes to power, I can relocate somewhere safe, émigré myself and my loved ones." When Morris calls him paranoid, Barrington replies, "No man, I *prepared*. Look what happened in Germany in 1933."

What happened in Germany explains why I feel so strongly about storge. On the day after *Kristallnacht*, November 11, 1938, my maternal grandparents escaped from Germany to Palestine. They evaded an arrest by the Gestapo when my grandfather displayed his uniform, revolver, and medals: he had served as a medical officer in the German army during the Great War. My mother and my brother (then a baby) fled from Hamburg to New York, also in 1938. Impoverished, she had to work as a live-in maid; she immediately weaned my brother and put him into what she called "a baby factory." My father, who subsequently joined her, and his brother, who escaped to England, left behind their parents, who did not survive. In my paternal grandmother's last letter, she wrote to her children, "May fate save you from such raw brutality." Two decades later, my brother and I were distraught over our father's suicide. Had the miseries of forced immigration contributed to his death?

Unspoken grief bruised the air in the Brooklyn apartment. How to explain calamities that cannot be understood? A niece's rape, cousins gone up in smoke through the chimneys. My parents vowed never to forget, but could not remember. Like Barrington, my father—whose accent marked him as an alien—feared another Hitler coming to power. During the McCarthy hearings, he thought the family might have to relocate again.

Did he look gaunt in the photographs taken right before his death because he had cancer? (I probably inherited a genetic propensity for the disease—a BRCA mutation—from him.) Did worries about preserving the savings he had managed to squirrel away contribute to his refusal to consult physicians? At fifteen, I grieved. I did not question then if his suicide might have been the result of anxieties about health care expenses draining the family of the little bit of security he had managed to safeguard. Because my family suffered the toxicity of German culture in the thirties, I cannot judge Barrington paranoid.

Also, all the Republican candidates currently campaigning for the presidency are homophobic, with the possible exception of the porcine Trump, who seems less like a bully, more like a fascist when he incites the crowds at his campaign rallies to shout "Build the wall." There are plenty of preachers today delivering sermons like the one Barrington wife's recounts: "All about philanderers, homosicksicals, and moral reprobates." And the alarming number of unarmed black men shot in the past year more than justifies Barrington's fear of enmity.

When, a week or so before we left for New York, Don led a book conversation for the fans of *To Kill a Mockingbird*, the people attending were distressed by the racism of a folk hero: Atticus Finch in his first incarnation, in *Go Set a Watchman*, an early draft of Harper Lee's classic that had just been published. I was stressing over how we would get out of the restaurant. Upon our arrival at Topo's, a waitress pointed toward a steep staircase; there was no elevator in this restored Victorian house.

Throughout the short lecture Don gave and then during the longer discussion he led with people from the community, I worried about the stairs and also about his vulnerable position. The organizer of the event, the publisher of *Bloom* magazine, had put a bar stool and a music stand in the door frame between two crowded rooms. Don had to swivel with a hand mike as he addressed first the people in one room and then the people in the adjoining room. It was a speaker's nightmare. I could not hear the questioners from the other room and they probably could not hear the comments coming from mine.

At the close of the event, *Bloom*'s publisher approached to ask if I would be willing to lead such a discussion in the future. "No way," I blurted out, flustered at my discourtesy. I could not imagine having the adrenaline needed to lecture and lead a productive conversation. Nor could I envision negotiating the impossible spatial configuration of two audiences, one to my right, the other to my left. Or a bar stool. Or a handheld mike. Or a rickety music stand. Don deserved the toasts he received after the talk. Raising bright blue cocktails, Tequila Mockingbirds, participants pronounced the event a smashing success, and so it was. With Julie at my side, I was relieved and happy for Don to have recovered this part of his life. How many book clubs and adult education courses had he conducted in the public libraries of small towns scattered across Indiana during the past half century?

After the three of us negotiated the staircase and landed in a bar to celebrate, Don said that he'd do it again, if he were asked. As we rehashed the event, I told them that seeing Don at the music stand brought back many memories of our team teaching together. Once in London, when I relinquished the lectern to him, I sat down with our students and realized they were thoroughly wasted by their weekend jaunts to Paris or Dublin. I had a conniption during the break—something about my dissatisfaction with the number of undergraduates not actively participating and the need to change our pedagogic tactics.

Although the adrenaline seeped out of Don in New York, after our return he accompanied me and Julie to the Jo-Ann Fabric and Craft store; I needed their eyes to choose the border panels for the baby's flying geese quilt. Between rummages, Julie hauled bolts of cotton over to the table on which we had laid the quilt top and finally she chose a solid green—somewhere between kelly and parakeet green—that I would never have considered and that we all agreed set off the patterned geese perfectly. As I washed, dried, ironed, and cut the solid green panels, I reflected on Don's skills at Topo's and the hilarious fashion designs described in *Mr. Loverman*.

Maxine creates the costumes for a commercial venture in the hope her father will finance it: an evening gown made of leather strips that can be deconstructed into a stool, with edible buttons and lace, the material of the bodice composed of family photographs. In her sales pitch, she explains, "Basically, what I have is the idea that food, family, and friends equal sustenance, along with the idea that people *wear* their loved ones, dead or alive, when they go out, or can even sit on them?" Maxine's follow-up plan for the "House of (Maxine) Walker" asks for thousands of pounds for marketing, models, and seamstresses, to which Barrington responds, "I will be sole investor in the House of *Walker* (no *Maxine* about it), which makes me the sole proprietor. Your role will be that of (mad genius) creative director. Take it or leave it." She will fleece him, but only to a degree he can control.

Aided by the resolute strength of his wife, who dumps him, and of his partner, who sticks by him, the hero of *Mr. Loverman* eventually comes out as a septuagenarian "Barrysexual—correction, *homosexual* (la-di-dah)—grandfather." Aging heightens his relief at shedding the lies, secrets, and silences that encumbered him for decades as he marvels over a young man making a pass at Morris: "What is he, a gerontophile?" Morris matches his partner's verbal hijinks when he terms Barrington's love of his 1970 Buick Coupe convertible a case of "motorphilia" and then defines "dendrophilia": "People turned on by trees." Philia has a supple linguistic longevity superior to that of agape, eros, or storge.

But philia continues to bedevil me since I have not seen Fran since before the spring falls, more than half a year ago . . . it seems inconceivable. I kept on combing through memories to understand how things could have gone so wrong. One moment in particular puzzled me: a scene in early December, maybe two or three years ago, when she came into the house, saw several bouquets of flowers, and asked about the occasion. "I feel bad about forgetting your birthday," she said, "but not as bad as you would have felt, if you had forgotten mine." What could that bizarre remark possibly have meant, I wondered. Should it have alerted me, delivered a warning signal?

The doorknob fell off the front door when I opened it to Hazel and the Schnitz, who showed up dressed in the Halloween costumes that Julie had chosen in Jo-Ann's: motorcycle gang leather jackets (fake leather, Julie assured me). As the Schnitz raced around and Hazel cowered, I savored my memory of the high point of the high point of the New York trip. Don and I, Susannah and Jack were lounging around her apartment when the doorbell rang and there were the monkey and the fox in strollers propelled by Simone and her husband.

The tan and brown monkey, who was holding a monkey, immediately scrambled out and lurched around the hall; it took longer to release the red fox, who crawled after his brother. Since the mountain could not come to Muhammad, Simone and Jeff had decided to bring the boys to Don. Their Halloween costumes, purchased early, served as perfect protection in the chilly air.

Julie's visit and that memory inspired me to do what Jack had forgotten to do. I got up determined to heave the wheelchair down into the basement. It clattered at the base of the stairs, its wheels spinning. Then I threw down the plastic tube with strings, the grabber, the security belts, the colorful rubber bands, and the toilet seat raiser. We eyed the remaining walker and cane with a genuine sense of release and relief.

"I'm tempted to buy a book I found on Amazon," I told Don as I privately acknowledged that my resolve not to acquire books had broken down. I wanted to find out how to make the Lime of the Ancient Mariner, the Last of the Mojitos, Rye and Prejudice, and the Yellow Wallbanger.

"We'll have to stock up on liquor," he said.

"Onward to Mucky's!"

At fifteen, Don had a job at Thrifty Liquors. He had loaded a truck with Black Gold whiskey for two men who were found shot dead the next day. It was during the war, and liquor was hard to get. In one of their pockets was a piece of paper with the address of Mucky Glasser's store. The FBI turned up to investigate and questioned Don, though not about his working illegally. After they left, Don went down to the basement: the FBI guys had stolen twelve bottles of scotch. Being upstanding citizens, however, they had taken the serial number off the box, as was required by law.

PART III

vacating the
premises

Wintering

YOUNG LOVERS CANNOT imagine the people they will become, but old lovers remember who they have been, or so I thought as I glanced down at the copy of *The Winter's Tale* in my lap and our conversation about moving petered out. Especially if youthful or midlife passion inflicts shocking damages, late-life love can right grievous wrongs. Suffused in the light streaming into the family room, Don stood by the window, recalling a college class.

The hunt for a habitable apartment was intensifying. We had traipsed to condos as far out in the country as the Inverness. On a circular lane of identical brick cottages, a unit for sale included—in addition to a kitchen, bathroom, and bedrooms on the first floor—a bedroom, bathroom, and galley kitchen in the basement. The place seemed too big and too remote. Zak had also taken us downtown to a building where the available apartment looked out on nothing but the concrete and asphalt of a busy thoroughfare: no green space in sight.

Don began reciting the first poem that taught him how poetry worked and what verse would mean to him for the rest of his life. Decades ago, a professor at Loyola had explained to him how Shakespeare's Sonnet 73 moves from the end of a year to the close of an evening and then to a dying fire.

> That time of year thou mayest in me behold
> When yellow leaves, or none, or few, do hang
> Upon those boughs which shake against the cold,
> Bare ruined choirs, where late the sweet birds sang.
> In me thou see'st the twilight of such day
> As after sunset fadeth in the west;
> Which by and by black night doth take away,
> Death's second self, that seals up all in rest.
> In me thou see'st the glowing of such fire,
> That on the ashes of his youth doth lie,
> As the deathbed whereon it must expire,
> Consumed with that which it was nourished by.
>   This thou perceiv'st, which makes thy love more strong,
>   To love that well which thou must leave ere long.

A fine poem for late fall: just a few crisp leaves clinging to shaken boughs. Its late-life speaker asks to be viewed as a testament to time's passing. The first eight lines evoke autumn and the setting sun as well as the dark night of sleep that captures in miniature the eternal obliteration of consciousness. The final image of embers glowing on the ash bed that will put them out portends the speaker's death. Intimations of mortality strengthen or ought to strengthen the bonds of love for those who realize they will soon be left alone.

"That's a good one," Don said, and then he grasped his cane and poked off to struggle with his socks.

While warming stews or soups simmered on the stove and no-knead bread rose on the counter, I recalled Shakespeare's Cleopatra, who knows herself to be "wrinkled deep in time." Her passion intensified after she left behind her youthful "salad days," when she was "green in judgment: cold in blood" (1.5.30, 77–78).

Midlife can also become a stage inimical to love, if manic fixations pervert passion. In *The Winter's Tale*, after a midlife obsession murders love, Shakespeare considers how an older and wiser husband and wife, miserably separated for sixteen years, reunite to reconstitute their family. More, this late play portrays an older couple, divided by the death of the wife, reuniting. What? How can that be? One of Shakespeare's strangest works depicts the labors of midlife love lost and then the labors of later-life love found and resurrected in the flesh by means of the dexterity of friends.

The fault of the separation lies squarely on the shoulders of the paranoid Leontes, king of Sicilia, who embodies Shakespeare's most stringent criticism of masculine insecurity. Leontes' anxiety about his inability to control women and therefore his lineage issues in irrational cruelty. Implacable but groundless jealousy convinces him that his pregnant wife Hermione has been unfaithful with his best friend. Obsessed with his paternity, Leontes accepts his existing son as a rightful heir, but decides that the baby in Hermione's womb proves him a cuckold. He judges the queen a whore at the very start of the play, when his entreaties to persuade his friend to remain in Sicilia fail and hers—undertaken at his urging—succeed. Unlike Othello, truculent Leontes needs no Iago. He's quite simply a mental case.

The closest I have come to such madness was the most terrible moment in my teaching career. Don had driven me to give a talk at Knox College, where I was informed that my graduate student Susan Clements had been murdered in a Bloomington dorm by an ex-boyfriend. Don kept hold of my hand or rested his arm on my shoulder throughout our stay. Long ago, he had lost a brilliant graduate student, another Susan . . . hit by a truck. My Susan was twenty-three; it was the spring of 1992.

The speech at her memorial was the hardest I ever had to give as I grieved with her family over the promise lost and I realized once again that our graduate students are of course not our off-spring, but they too should inhabit our posthumous future and the bonds should remain strong long after they have gone off to launch careers of their own. At the retirement event that Mary organized in 2010, many of my former graduate students and even one for-mer undergraduate lined up at a microphone to recall in a phrase my most ludicrous moments of mentoring. Susan Clements had been dead eight years; she would have been thirty-one years old.

The green-eyed monster blights the world of *The Winter's Tale*. The king's diseased imagination builds an unsubstantiated case that leads to a series of disasters and seems mulishly impulsive when he ignores the judgment from the Delphic oracle, which declares Hermione chaste, Leontes a tyrant, the baby legitimate.

The oracle concludes: "the King shall live without an heir if that which is lost be not found" (3.2.133–34). The king banishes his infant daughter, his son dies, and his wife faints. Leontes orders her to be taken away to recover, and then immediately repents his unwarranted accusations. After her friend Paulina announces Hermione's death, Leontes determines to bury the queen with her son in a grave that he will visit daily.

In the early afternoon, when I drove over to Carrol's house, I decided to skip over the middle of *The Winter's Tale*, though I love the name of the king and queen's daughter—Perdita means "lost"—and the most famous of Shakespeare's stage directions (to punish the man who leaves her in a foreign land): *"Exit pursued by a bear"* (3.3.57).

Carrol, who had stopped eating but continued to sip water, was sitting in a hospital bed set up in what used to be her dining room, looking surprisingly hale. On a table next to her, she had laid out some of the products of her loom. She showed me "Woven Iridescence," a blue shawl shot through with waves of purple, as well as two cotton dishcloths, traditionally striped and in need of repair. These told her, she said, that she had led a patchy life, full of mistakes she somehow managed to mend. Decades ago, she had been an undergraduate in a senior seminar I had taught. She deserved the poor grade she received because, she confided, she had been stoned on drugs when she gave her final report. The last year had been the best, she felt: a trip to Italy with friends and family, when she realized her disease was terminal; the Last Chance to Dance party she had thrown. Her rare type of ovarian cancer did not respond to treatment.

In a sage-green room flooded with winter light, Carrol adjusted her covers and reached for a little bulb attached to a rod—a tahkli spindle, she explained, from India—and a plastic bag full of fluffs of white cotton. With her right hand she held the spindle; with her left, she somehow twisted and pinched and pulled a puff of fiber taut, creating a long, thin thread. In ancient times, she informed me, there was not only a stone age but also a thread age. She contemplated Egyptian shrouds woven so thin that "you could see through them." The tiniest filaments of cotton are considered "as fine as frog hair," she said. "Thin threads are so full of energy they want to jump together."

When I arrived back home, I called out to Don. "Didn't Peter Lindenbaum own a bear costume?"

He mumbled something that I couldn't hear, so I went to stand before him.

"What did you say? I'm sorry, I'm going deaf."

"It doubles the conversation," he said. "Peter kept a bear costume in his office and enlisted a series of graduate students to chase him out of the classroom, pursued by the bear. That's how he concluded every one of his final lectures on *The Winter's Tale*."

The conclusion of *The Winter's Tale*—after a fast-forward in which Time appears on stage to "slide / O'er sixteen years, and leave the growth untried / Of that wide gap" (4.1.4–5)—presents the second chance of later-life love as a miraculous resurrection: the dead live and the lost are found, all in the nick of time. Leontes arrives at the house of Hermione's friend Paulina with the daughter he now accepts as his own and only heir: his object is to view a statue of the queen. Like a stage director, Paulina draws a curtain to reveal a lifelike effigy. Leontes exclaims, "Hermione was not so much wrinkled" (5.3.28–29). After Paulina explains that the artist presented his wife as she would look sixteen years after her death, she offers to make the statue descend.

Calling for music, Paulina proclaims—in a voice remarkable for its powerful authority—"be stone no more," and Hermione steps down to embrace her husband. Hermione's first words after sixteen years in hiding and her last words in the play ask the gods to grace her daughter. She wonders how Perdita was saved, and promises that she herself will recount how she, "Knowing by Paulina that the oracle / Gave hope," had "preserved / Myself to see the issue" (127–28). Wanting to see the oracle's issue as well as the child who issued from her body, Hermione establishes both her own agency (she preserved herself) and the primacy of her desire (to see her grown offspring), but she also hints at her dependency on Paulina for survival.

The question of whether a destructive tyrant deserves this happily-ever-after shadows the play's ending, especially because Leontes actually makes a pass at his daughter, before he understands who she is. His adoration of the stone wife contrasts with his earlier vilification of the fleshly wife. Given his control issues, wouldn't he prefer his woman to be a mute, immobile thing on a pedestal—like Pygmalion's Galatea not after but before she comes to life? While the reunion of mother and daughter echoes the mythic reunion of Ceres and Proserpine, which brings about springtime renewal, Shakespeare's mother and daughter inhabit the wintery realm ruled by the king who had split them apart.

Still, what makes the ending powerful is surely a miracle, the rebirth of the dead. The audience is meant to accept the death of Hermione in act 3—reported by Paulina and accepted as a fact by the king. Paulina's successful efforts to establish the illusion of Hermione's death and her expert efforts, sixteen years later, to establish the illusion of Hermione's rebirth are created and validated by her author. The power of illusion is what Shakespeare shares with Paulina, whose authoritative utterance "be stone no more" performs a theatrical act of magic not dissimilar from those of her author. Although Paulina has been accused of being a witch, she is a wizard like Prospero and an artist like Shakespeare. The play's the thing whereby Paulina captures the conscience of the king.

After the wide gap of sixteen years, both the king and the queen are quite different creatures from who they had been before. He has lived with remorse and regret, she with proof of her uncanny survival skills. They remember but no longer incarnate the rash, furious despot and the tongue-tied, pregnant consort of the first act. The second chance of their reunion holds out the promise of a more equitable union between people who have outgrown disabling identities.

Yet surely Shakespeare knew that after the opening night of *The Winter's Tale*, most audiences would view the statue of Hermione as a sort of tableau vivant: not stone but a woman looking like stone (more precisely, a male actor looking like a woman who looks like stone). Besides dramatizing Paulina's and her creator's artistry, what does Paulina's injunction—"be stone no more"— signify? The phrase eludes and needles me, though it surely does more than underscore Shakespeare's most potent portrait of female friendship, or so I thought until I remembered the date: our appointment that afternoon and the fact that we would soon have to fall back, relinquishing daylight saving time. An additional hour of morning light was a boon for little kids at school bus stops, but it hastens nightfall at the end of the day.

As about so many eccentric preferences, Fran and I had adamantly disagreed on this point. She was glad to see the sun go down at supper time so she could go to sleep. But I loved daylight lasting as long as possible before I turned into a night owl. Would next month, my birthday, or the upcoming holidays bring some sign of reconciliation or even a reunion? Might these events inspire one of us to send a peace offering and perhaps then arrange a meeting, I wondered.

Memories of our time together flooded me: running at the gym and then sharing an apple with a wedge of cheddar, sitting in the camping chairs she set up by Lake Monroe, admiring her efforts at composting and her volunteer work at a homeless shelter, marveling at the Susie-sing-along she organized for my—was it my fortieth?—birthday, singing carols as she groused about the out-of-tune piano, laughing together over old Bob and Ray radio routines or Danny Kaye's movies ("The pellet with the poison's in the vessel with the pestle; the chalice from the palace has the brew that is true"). Like Paulina, Fran helped me survive the miseries of divorce and encouraged me to take a second chance.

What was lost, could it be found? Fran always set her clocks back the day before one had to. Anticipatory mourning: had she begun to withdraw from me to protect herself from the grief she feared feeling once she heard my terminal diagnosis?

A cry of pain propelled me into the living room.

"My leg just gave out," Don said, slumped in his wingback chair by the window.

"The good one or the bad?"

"The good one is also a bad one."

Then, just before renewing his efforts to stand, he said, "Ole rocking chair got me . . . with my cane by my side. Fetch me some gin, son, or I'll tan your hide."

"What watch, Liebchen?"

"In a few minutes," he said.

Returning to the blue couch, I knew that Don had determined not to undergo another knee surgery . . . and also that he believed he had four years left to live. His father had died at ninety-two. But I had met his father when he was in his late eighties, and he was not nearly as vigorous as Don, who has gone outside without the leg brace and started up his old Honda after more than half a year of disuse.

"Be stone no more," I realized, enjoins the resurrection of the spirit after traumatic loss. It could be the meme emblazoned over the stories of later-life lovers who have suffered shocking setbacks, privations, or heartaches before they found a way to recover emotions they had feared were dead and gone. Winter to spring, stone to flesh, suspicion to trust, spite to tenderness: Shakespeare holds out the promise of transformative renewal.

Certainly, most audiences know that Hermione is not really a statue. She had been stoned by suffering into a numb, dumb replica or simulacrum of herself. Becoming aware of her numbed and dumbed self, Hermione then brilliantly, over the course of years and out of a yearning to be reconnected, taught herself to stonewall. The suspension of disbelief Shakespeare invokes has to do with art—our willingness to imagine ourselves through characters conjured by words—but also with faith in human resilience after great pain: our unanticipated capacity to resist injustice and regain sentience after stunning disasters.

After the cataclysm of the Great War, after the poet H.D. lost her marriage, her father, her brother, and a stillborn baby, she fictionalized her plight through the character of Hermione and gave birth to a daughter she named Perdita. That daughter, Perdita Schaffner, once gave me permission to quote her mother's words. At Yale's Beinecke Rare Book and Manuscript Library, studying H.D.'s papers, I had been introduced to a personage who turned out to be a descendant of Ezra Pound's. She looked up from her desk and said, "H.D., who was she? She was nothing compared to Pound!" But we were going to be late, if I didn't rush us out the door.

Twice weekly in the late afternoon, I had to take Don back to the Trace, not to the gym but to a smaller facility, full of all sorts of machines for people who could afford a personal trainer. The therapists paid by Medicare had gotten his knee to bend to 79 degrees. Wanting to work on greater strength and flexibility, he signed up for regular sessions with an energetic woman who always kept him longer than the assigned hour. I grabbed my dog-eared copy of a contemporary novel that rewrites *The Winter's Tale* and hustled us into the car. On the way, we passed a succession of houses and mentioned their former owners. It was "a street of the deceased," Don said. Wasn't that bungalow on the corner the one in which Jim Jensen fainted dead away at a bris for one of Al Wertheim's sons? That must have been when? Maybe the sixties . . . before I arrived.

Since I did not need to pick up prescriptions or groceries, I plunked myself down on an uncomfortable love seat inside the lobby of the Trace, near a fireplace with a fake burning log. Nicholas Delbanco's *The Years* begins during a cruise tour of Pompeii on which two people, who had been college lovers, independently embarked. Within ruins preserved by ash, Lawrence and Hermia recognize each other after the lapse of forty-two years. Lawrence, at sixty-four and recovering from angioplasty, had dreamed the night before about "a woman [who] was a statue, and the statue was marmoreal but warmed to his hot touch." Sixty-three at their reunion, Hermia fears that she has been "alone too long to yield her hard-earned privacy."

The Years delineates the losses that have hardened Hermia: the breakup of her college romance with Lawrence, her wretched marriage to a physically abusive husband, her flight from him to protect herself and her child, and, after a life in hiding, the disappearance of the daughter she had attempted to save. By splitting Leontes into two characters—Lawrence (who is a feckless youth, but not crazed) and Hermia's first husband (whose violence springs from paranoid delusions about her infidelity)— Delanco skirts the scandal of *The Winter's Tale*: the idea that a woman might determine to be reunited with a man who had effectively killed her son and set out to murder her and their daughter.

Hermia thinks of "the school of second chances" when she

invites Lawrence to visit her Truro house, possibly to resume their relationship after the forty-two-year gap. At lighthearted moments, she believes they are finding in each other new as well as old friends. "We wait and wait," thought Hermia, "and sooner or later the thing we wait for does in fact appear: the statue moves . . ." When her missing daughter reappears, Hermia's stony face expresses her recriminations. Quickly, however, she embraces the runaway and commits herself to Lawrence with the words "'Tis time. Descend."

Hermia's "passion," she discovers, "was not spent": "everything was restored, made whole, old treacheries forgiven and old arguments resolved. What had been lost was found. They were gentle together now, slow." To him, marriage means "getting things right only forty years later, well, more than forty, but who's counting." What would have transpired if he had proposed back then? Regret permeates the lost years, for it is impossible not to wonder what might have happened if they had married back in the sixties. "'Better late than never,'" he concludes. Yes, that was Shakespeare's point too.

"Let's not go home," I said to Don when he finally emerged from his workout. "Let's go to T.J.Maxx and look for some extra-wide shoes with laces instead of Velcro."

He was wincing from a pulled muscle, but agreed. I wanted to put off poring over the second pass of my cancer book. I am a terrible proofreader, since instead of fixing typos or grammatical errors, I generally judge each sentence a mistake in need of recasting.

"They used to be called galleys or proofs or tegras," I said.

"I used to lug them on planes, but soon all the copyediting and proofreading will be done online, don't you think?"

"There used to be Continental, Eastern, Pan Am, Northwest, Allegheny, Southern. I took TWA to California, you had to change planes in St. Louis."

In the car, as Don told me a story about being at dinner with the poet Josephine Miles in a crowded Berkeley hotel restaurant, I thought about the stone woman I had been during my divorce. The grief was so stultifying that I could not eat, could not read, could not write. Stupid with pain I was down to about one hundred pounds, which happened again during the months of reoperations and infections, when everyone thought I was dying, as I did too.

But the divorce in the eighties had been a worse period than the initial cancer treatments . . . possibly because it involved more self-recrimination. It was my fault that I had embarked on a mismatched marriage. I had ricocheted off the trauma of my father's death. Regardless of my incompatibility with my first husband, the stresses of midlife marriage—we had no money, the children were demanding, the tenure clock was ticking—had overwhelmed me. We were each too self-involved, too vain, to sustain a conjugal conspiracy that the poet Marianne Moore considered an "amalgamation which can never be more / than an interesting impossibility."

There are fewer obstacles for empty nesters, I thought, as the realization dawned on me: Don and I would never have clicked in midlife. We were both too riveted by our political commitments and professional ambitions. In our thirties, we each of us needed a wife. And neither of us then would have been willing to undertake the renunciations required by that role. In late life, we excavate "the temporal *layers*" of all the different people we have been and share a yearning to remain connected amid threatening circumstances. He tells my jokes; I keep his silences. In sync now, "two by two in the ark of / the ache of it," we have acquired the patience to accommodate each other.

Apparently, Josephine Miles's wheelchair had been knocked over by a waiter and the poet along with it. After helping her back in, the waiter returned with a red rose. When she eventually left the restaurant, Josephine Miles wheeled herself out, to the applause of her companions and many of the other patrons, the long stem of the rose in her mouth.

Silver Threads among the Gold

"TURN ON THE TELEVISION," my friend Shehira shouted into the phone. "It's terrible, terrible. First Beirut, now Paris." It was the day before my mother's birthday. She would have been one hundred. With the flying geese neglected on my lap, I watched the replayed scenes of slaughter: explosions at a sports stadium, bloodbaths in restaurants, outside bars. Then the so-called analysis: talk of suicide bombers and gunmen with assault weapons, counterattacking police troops and triage teams. Then the mounds of flowers and the civic grieving. We had seen it before and we would see it again. Shehira, who had recently returned from Paris, worried that her son might be there, though his family was secure in the Dordogne.

"Just because you wander in the desert doesn't mean there is a promised land." Where had Paul Auster written something like that prescient sentence? Would American hucksters of hate seize on this tragedy to preach a xenophobic doctrine nearly as toxic as the ideology of ISIS, whose name desecrates the Egyptian goddess? When Shehira and I became friends back in 1973, a month or two after Sandra and I arrived in Bloomington, she showed us pictures of the Egyptian god Horus—he looked like a falcon— and recounted the myth of Isis gathering the torn body parts of Osiris to reunite and restore him and to bear their divine son. In the somber days that followed the attack, we did not dwell on Don's muscle spasms or the oddly returned envelope containing the check for our real estate taxes.

It was Zak who caught our attention when, during a visit, he relinquished his usual jokey manner to hammer home the need to begin repairing the Inverness for sale in the spring. There was mold in the basement, a telltale bowing of beams in the garage that meant structural stress on an external wall, cracks in the foyer, and bubbles under the paint over the door to the back porch: maybe water damage. Tuck-pointing should be done on the brick in the back, and did we realize that the storm windows were broken? Yes, Don conceded. Last summer, the screens had been put in, but the storms never raised. Who knew that youthful Zak—he cultivated a sort of punk hilarity—could be so meticulous and demanding and depressing?

"We should keep the house, make the kids in Boston and New York move their families out here; it could be a safe haven," I said.

"We'd be sitting ducks, if someone came out here," Don said. Then he added, "Who would want to come out here?"

I had no idea if he meant the kids or the terrorists or both, but I wanted to contain the violence while honoring the middle of the country; so I returned to the pellucid prose of Marilynne

Robinson. Undoubtedly, there was something robotic or neurotic about my binging on another text. Verbomania, graphomania, bibliomania—better, I suppose, than clinomania (the acute craving to stay in bed) or gamomania (the compulsive issuing of odd marriage proposals) or drapetomania (the obsessive desire to run away from home). But there was something missing in the secular works I had studied so far. They exclude the role of late-life love in deeply religious people like the faithful characters in Marilynne Robinson's books.

Would I find a way to raise my spirit in response to such a serious author, to pay homage to the gift given? Yes, I would, for there is a balm in *Gilead* that helps me transcend the sorrow, anger, and fear, if only for the silent minutes of following words on the page . . . and then putting the book down to ruminate before resuming. Robinson's prose instills the sort of slow reading that poetry often requires and that moves me as close to prayer as I am likely to get. Writing serves a purpose similar to that of praying for the novel's clergyman narrator: "You feel that you are with someone."

Marilynne Robinson emphasizes deepening spiritual and familial commitments in an aging character so high-minded that it is hard to picture how he engendered the child he adores. At seventy-six years of age, Reverend John Ames composes a diary-like letter to his young son whose birth he experienced as an unforeseen grace, but whose maturation he does not expect to see. The child of old age is "unspeakably precious," because an aged parent can no longer hope for more children, and also "because any father, particularly an old father, must finally give his child up to the wilderness."

Diagnosed with a heart condition, Ames does not expect to live long enough to tell his history to the boy. He needs to record the "begats" of his and the child's ancestry: tales of his volatile abolitionist grandfather, who fought with John Brown in Kansas, and of his pacifist father, also a minister; stories of his own dutiful evolution in the pastoral profession and his long friendship with Robert Boughton. Within Ames's poignant awareness of his limitations as a father—he has neither the life expectancy nor the money to protect the boy's future—his devotion intensifies while he seeks to convey his reverence for the values his genealogy has bequeathed, for the sacraments he offers, for the plains he inhabits, and for the child's mother, Lila, whose appearance in his church on a rainy day seemed miraculous because at sixty-seven he had resigned himself to an empty house.

As in other accounts of autumnal romance, *Gilead* depicts the loneliness preceding an unanticipated encounter that leads an older person to a second chance: "Not that I hadn't loved people before. But I hadn't realized what it *meant* to love them before." A fine distinction: of course we have loved before, but without the realization of what it means to love, which may deepen in the breeding ground of loss or isolation. Robinson's characters associate loneliness with looking into the lighted windows of other people's houses.

After the early death of his first wife and of their baby girl, Ames walked the roads of his small Iowa town, covetous of other families, especially the large family of his best friend Boughton. From Ames's youthful widowhood until his sixty-seventh year, his solitude made it seem "as if every winter were the same winter and every spring the same spring." Only upon meeting Lila did he feel that "in all that deep darkness a miracle was preparing."

Throughout the meandering retrospection that constitutes John Ames's letter to his son, the scene of Lila taking shelter in his church recurs until, toward the end of the book, he describes how, during the brief period of their early acquaintance, he felt "as if my soul were being teased out of my body"—an experience that enlarged his understanding "of hope, just to know that such a transformation can occur." Mindful of his age, afraid of making a fool of himself, he nevertheless undertook "a little experiment with hair tonic" and read the Song of Songs. When she came to him seeking baptism, he was struck by the solemn purity of her request. After this unschooled woman began tending his garden and he asked how he might repay her, "she said, 'You ought to marry me.' And I did."

But this proposal, nine years before the novel's present time of 1956, constitutes the back story of *Gilead*, not the subject of its most intense inquiry. The suspense of the narrative, if such a pacific meditation can be said to contain suspense, springs from the eruption of John Ames's distrust when his godson Jack Boughton arrives back in town after twenty years away. I thought of Ames's suspicions about his namesake, his best friend's son, as I went to a FedEx store to photocopy handouts for Don. John Ames worries that he should warn his wife and child, that he should protect them by revealing Jack's sordid past. Especially when he realizes that his godson helped Lila lift and carry his desk, chair, and books down to the ground-floor parlor (to save him from physical exertion), he feels old, mistrustful, and anxious. Later, glimpsing Jack, Lila, and his child seated in his dilapidated church, Ames thinks that they look "like a handsome young family."

When Zak came to pick us up to take us to Windermere Village, I shared Ames's unease about Jack's wrongdoings and his motive for returning to Gilead. But the overriding mystery for me: how does Ames ends up loving Jack as much as his friend Boughton wants him to? By means of what enigmatic process does Ames's hostility toward his ne'er-do-well godson transmute into late-life love?

Those were still my perplexities the day after Zak showed us a condo only two blocks from Kroger's, though you would never know it because the so-called village was on a hill shielded by trees and shrubs. With all the rooms and even the laundry on the ground floor and with a walk-in shower, the place seemed negotiable. The identical cottages looked somewhat similar to those at the Trace; however, this was not a retirement community. There was no "big house" for communal dining, no rehab center, no nursing home. And the brick façades as well as the long windows reminded us of the Inverness. Maybe we could deal with the dark living room by putting in a skylight? We really did have to get out of the Inverness while the getting was good.

"Shit, shit, shit," I heard Don hissing in his ground-floor study. He was angry at dropping papers on the floor, at the weird fonts appearing on the computer screen, at the outdated password no longer connecting him to the Wells Library, at the glasses slipping off his nose or lost on his desk, at being unable to kneel down to reach a lower shelf where he might have stored the Tin Pan

Alley sheet music I needed to return. Both copies of the popular early twentieth-century song "Silver Threads among the Gold" were lodged near the handmade book Judith had given him.

In *Gilead*, Lila asks John Ames a question that he has also asked himself: "Why'd you have to be so damn old?"

"I'm sorry you're getting old," I said, picking up the sheet music.

"I put it off as long as I could," he said.

Judith's book was the best birthday present Don had ever received. *Digging Up the Dog and Other Stories* features a picture of a shovel on the cover. At the top, Judith had centered a banner: "Acclaimed NYT Bestseller #1 Amazon Sales Ranking." On the back cover were (equally fictitious) blurbs, including one from the local paper: "Brilliantly argued, urgently needed, highly comic and deadly serious—precisely what Bloomington has been waiting for." It was a blank book, except for the table of contents: a list of the anecdotes Don had recounted in her hearing.

My favorite was the title story, which the existence of the book inspired Don to type up. In it, he tells about a time—maybe he was seven—when he had been shipped to his grandparents' house, where he was informed that his dog, Fella, had been hit by a car and killed. On the way home, he cried. After his father explained that he had buried Fella in the backyard, Don decided to dig up the dog. With a couple of tries, he uncovered a patch of fur: "That was enough. I scraped the dirt back over the body, and told no one what I had done."

Why the attempted exhumation? He had not doubted that the dog was dead. "Nor do I think that my curiosity was sponsored by some precocious reach for sublimity, a wish to confront death, to see what it looked like. I think that I simply wanted to see what Fella looked like dead." He learned something "about the finality or irrevocability of death": "It would have been possible, I knew, to dig up the body, but not, maybe I learned, to dig up the dog."

Composed with his usual understatement, Don's last sentence illuminates the horror of the Beirut and Paris massacres, and also the significance of all the burying and unburying that goes on in *Gilead* and why its characters' faith in an afterlife that they keep on reimagining feels alien to me. John Ames tells many tales of townspeople of his grandfather's generation digging tunnels on the Underground Railroad and of his father's generation burying and unburying hymnals and shirts, letters and sermons, guns and charred Bibles . . . objects they need to relinquish but cannot bear to destroy. As John Ames's ancestors dig up and tamp down the earth, he burrows into his past. Only toward the end of the novel do Ames's conversations with Jack disinter the reason for Jack's return to Gilead, which in turn unearths the tragic racial history buried in American soil.

After Ames looks at a photograph of Jack with his "colored" wife and his "light-skinned colored" son, Jack reveals that he has returned to town in order to determine whether he could relocate his family to Iowa, a state he sardonically calls "the shining star of radicalism." Ames minimizes the hostility behind the disappearance of Gilead's black population, but the burning of its only black church justifies Jack's irony. Although Jack has lied to his wife's family and disappointed his wife, the fact that the buried history of slavery continues to contaminate the country becomes apparent as he alludes to the anti-miscegenation laws still operative in the 1950s. They have made his cohabitation with people of color impossible or impossibly painful.

Don was standing by the door, clutching a stack of papers; so I carefully took the two sheaves of old sheet music, encased in cellophane wrappers, out of his hands and placed them on the back seat of the car. I would return them to Carrol after Emeriti House and our trip to the courthouse. She had thought their illustrations would be perfect for a study of later-life love. "What's a book without pictures?" she had laughed. It was a cold day, overcast, with spits of rain in the air, the sort of weather Don's mother had called "dravis."

I left Don on the corner across the street from the sizable family house that had been refurbished into Emeriti House, found a reserved space behind it, parked, made it up the steep back stairs, and met him inside. A dozen or so retired faculty were seated in a comfortable living room, including Shehira, who beckoned me to sit by her side. But I wanted to puzzle out *Gilead*'s ending—how did John Ames come to love such a thin-skinned man as Jack? So I waved, mimed apologies, and made my way upstairs to an empty office.

Gilead addresses the mystery of John Ames's late-life love of his unlovable godson through the parable of the prodigal son. Like the young man in Jesus's parable, Jack left his father's house, squandered his inheritance in dissolute living, and was welcomed back by old Boughton with joy as abundant as that of the father who exclaims over the prodigal son's return, "He was lost and is found!" (Luke 15:24). Old Boughton's love does not alter in finding alteration, but rather multiplies in excess of worthiness. However, like the older brother in Jesus's parable, Ames—a dutiful son who never left home—initially feels resentful that undeserving Jack receives his father's rewards. Jesus's parable hints that abundant divine love need not and cannot be deserved or comprehended.

What about human love? As Ames scrutinizes his qualms about Jack, he eventually learns that "Love is holy because it is like grace—the worthiness of its object is never really what matters." He is considering agape, which, unlike eros, does not respond to the merit of its object but rather endows its object with value. The biblical parable conflates sacred with secular realms, as does *Gilead* throughout its pages. John Ames often startles at revelations of a sanctified physical world: "great taut skeins of light suspended" between "a full moon rising just as the sun was going down." At the root of honor, he knows, "is always the sense of the sacredness of the person who is its object." The extravagance of creation means that "Wherever you turn your eyes the world can shine like transfiguration."

Grounded in scripture, Ames's reverence for nature and human nature cannot be conflated with the tradition M. H. Abrams called "natural supernaturalism," but it reminds me of it: literature praising miracles latent in the natural world. Abrams's death, after his long and productive life establishing the Norton anthologies, marked the end of a formidable chapter in scholarship. When he helped Sandra and me with our anthologizing of women writers, he called her "Cookie," maybe because she had been his student. She wanted to create a musical comedy with a chorus line of elderly men singing, "Hello, Cookie," and a chorus line of girls belting back, "Hello, Sir." For many of Abrams's authors, as for Ames, "Existence is the essential thing and the holy thing."

The miracle of Ames's passage from resentment and suspicion to love hovers over the ending of Robinson's novel, for like the prodigal son, Jack has not expressed remorse, contrition, or repentance. Late-life love contributed to the dissipation of Ames's hostility, I decide, as it had to its inauguration. Learning that his godson wants what he had longed for—a wife and a child—softens Ames to forgive Jack his trespasses. He relinquishes resentment and suspicion when he realizes that his jealousy was a groundless and regrettable by-product of his attachment to Lila and their son. Ames has wronged Jack in the present, just as the boy Jack wronged his father and Ames in the past.

Only after a series of mutually bruising conversations does Ames appreciate in Jack "the beauty there is in him." His religion enables Ames to see in undeserving Jack his own undeserving nature, human fallibility, and the impoverishment of our understanding of each other. He channels his grandfather's wisdom: "To him who asks, give" and "Judge not . . ."

Ames doubles his benediction by returning to old Boughton and testifying about a love that constitutes a healing practice, rather than a spontaneous or personal emotion. We never learn what it means to old Boughton that Ames spoke well-worn words from the Hebrew Bible over Jack. "The Lord make His face to shine upon thee and be gracious unto thee: The Lord lift up His countenance upon thee, and give thee peace." These were phrases I had heard at the end of every Saturday morning service I attended as a child at Beth Emeth. Repetition lends them enormous power.

Love in *Gilead* is not an escape from the fallen world but a mode of engagement with it. Later-life love, according to Robinson, abounds in the beneficence of agape, the amiability of philia, and the loyalty of storge. As I start to hear chairs and feet moving around downstairs, as I imagine Ames sitting by the bedside and speaking into the ear of his sleeping friend, I envy the intimacy of an old friendship. Earlier in *Gilead*, Ames had explained his overuse of the word "old," which sets apart something regarded with habitual affection or suggests hapless vulnerability: "I say 'old Boughton,' I say 'this shabby old town,' and I mean that they are very near my heart."

It was time to get the car, pick up Don at the front of Emeriti House, and do our chores. The wind colder now, the sky grayer, the drizzle heavier made me kvetch on the way: we should have applied for a disabled parking permit; we would never be able to find a space close enough to the courthouse in the Beaux Arts building at the center of town. Because of the new, expensive meters, though, we did manage to park in front of King Dough, near a tree hugged by colorful knitting and across from a courthouse entrance without steps.

Huddled in our coats, buffeted by the wind, we traipsed across the street and into the marbled lobby with its high, glassed-in dome over which a copper fish serves as an ornament. Don knew exactly where to find the elevator to the second-floor treasurer's office. Behind a long counter, a staffer looked up and then down at the envelope Don placed before her.

"We can't figure out why our house taxes were returned to us and now we'll have to pay a penalty," I explained.

She looked at the envelope, opened it to see the check, closed it again, and smiled.

"There's no postage," she said, tapping the upper right corner like we lived on some other planet, though it was kind of her, I thought, not to say, "Duh, you forgot to put on a stamp."

Don and I gawked and then avoided looking at each other, as his cane colluded by clattering onto the floor.

"No problem, the date of the check proves it was written before the deadline; we can waive the penalty."

On the way home—and while I stopped at Carrol's to return both copies of "Silver Threads among the Gold"—I kept on thinking of our vulnerability in the world. It was Don who had forgotten to put a stamp on the envelope, but I had forgotten about the taxes altogether. Nor was I sure that I wanted pictures in my new book, even those pleasing engravings of antique lovers on the sheet music: leave sunny imaginations hope. What we look like when we are old is not necessarily what we feel like, and we all look quite different from each other. None of the elderly couples on Carrol's sheet music resemble the partners Jack and his wife might have become in old age.

When Don and I got back home, there were silver threads among the golden grasses mounded on either side of the brick walkway: shiny silver filaments, making patterns like filigree with the gold. Amid the silver and the gold, some blades had turned wheat pale and brittle, thin hairs lifted by the winnowing wind and glistening from the moisture in the darkening air. "Make new friends, but keep the old; / one is silver and the other gold." I may not foresee the heaven that Ames and old Boughton envision, but I share their belief in the grace of the grasses.

Recounting the Ways

BEFOREHAND, I COUNTED on my fingers: the number of suppers to be prepared, the number of settings to be laid, the number of beds to be made, the number of pounds of the bird we needed, which Don managed to lift and place in our shopping cart. On most evenings we would be six—my older daughter Molly, her husband Kieran, his brother Suneil, and Eli, now almost in double digits. Julie was setting off on a road trip, but several friends would attend the feast itself. How many bags of cranberries should we buy for the raw and the cooked sauces Don always prepared and the bread Molly always baked?

With the refrigerator stuffed, I embarked on my late-life cooking preparations and went through half a box of tissues while reading *Lila*, whose conflicted heroine tells me how decidedly John Ames's reticence (in an account meant for the future eyes of their child) had obscured his wife's volatile character as well as their turbulent relationship. For in the sequel to *Gilead* (which is really a prequel), later-life lovers must contend with the after-shocks of trauma. Love that arrives late can come after great pain, as Shakespeare knew. Yet that pain may not arrest or numb but burn or blister a later-life lover, making her wince at the touch of the hand she wants to hold.

Our abundant plenty underscored the privations of Marilynne Robinson's thrown-away character. Written in the third person but from Lila's perspective, the novel illuminates Lila's meeting with John Ames, their marriage, her pregnancy, and maternity through interposed scenes from the decades preceding 1956: her being tossed out as a child, her rescue by a woman named Doll, laboring in the fields, losing Doll, a stint in a St. Louis whore-house and hotel, then hitching rides that land her at a forsaken cabin just outside of Gilead. Even as Robinson moves back and forth between the present and past, she pointedly detaches old age from chronology. Lila was "old" and "had been old a long time," for "all the youth had been worked out of her before it had really even set in."

Lila has lived through violent times. At four or five years of age, she was thrown out on a stoop, where Doll took her up and carried her in the rain to a cabin. There Doll "pinched off little pills of corn bread and put them in the child's mouth, one after another" and then washed her down. Lila thought that "she had been born a second time." Infested with nits, sometimes mute, Lila would keep her deliverance a secret because Doll could go to jail for stealing the child, arriving "like an angel in the wilder-ness." When the little girl is given a name, it becomes clear that this opening scene is a secular baptism, in contrast to the religious baptism Lila would later ask for and receive from John Ames. That she yelled and cursed throughout it suggests that human, even humane, contact hurts.

While I was finding pillows and pillowcases or preparing the meals Eli favored, I pondered the two objects Doll bestows on the child to whom she gives the greatest gift when she scoops her up and wills her to live: a knife and a shawl. After years spent bonded with Doll, working as a migrant with one year off in town for schooling, Lila manages to retain the knife that Doll had whetted until the blade "was sharp as a razor." Like a snake's, the knife's nature is "to do harm if you trifled with it." Lila's need to have it at the ready represents her distrust. It shocks her that John Ames has been using it to pare apples. "All she had was that knife. And dread and loneliness and regret. That was her dowry." Even after the birth of their son, Lila determines to keep the knife, since "he could want it sometime"—which means, she realizes, that she cannot abandon all the bitter thoughts of self-protection that, inherited from Doll, blunt her fears.

The shawl that Doll wrapped around Lila they held onto "till it was worn soft as cobwebs." But during one of their hard times, the leader of their migrant group "dangled it over the fire, and the flames climbed right up it toward his hand." It was "so worn then, threads that stayed together somehow, you could see right through it," and yet they had kept it "for the use they made of it, remembering together. There wasn't much that felt worse than losing that shawl." While the dust bowl scenes of *Lila* remind me of the fiction of John Steinbeck and Harriet Arnow, the shawl reminds me of Cynthia Ozick, who uses the same image to describe the frayed comfort available to a starving child in a concentration camp.

As I cooked and made beds, I realized that I was handling a knife and a blanket that were somehow brought out of Germany: a serrated bread knife and a woolen blanket, which in one corner had the label "Susan Janet David." When Don and I moved into the Inverness, I had a zany fantasy of bearing our son: his first name would be David. Only when the first of the cherished grandchildren arrived did I begin to feel us knitted together into the lives and loves of all four of the girls we share. My mother must have stitched on the nametag when I was sent to Girl Scouts camp for two weeks, an extravagant expenditure for the family.

Like Lila, I had nits as a child, as well as worms, but the impoverishment was not connected to homelessness. Rather, it meant very long hours of parental work. My father laboring in a body and fender shop from six in the morning until six at night, grime beneath his fingernails and under his cuticles, no matter which brush he used to scrub them; my mother sewing gloves all day and after supper, very fine stitches around each of the leather fingers, with calluses on the palms of her hands.

The many bedrooms of the Inverness strike me as vaguely obscene, though I am gladdened by the prospect of seeing the kids and by the news that Suneil's flights from London will land him at the airport around the time my daughter's family should arrive from Boston; they could all drive down together. My son-in-law's brother Suneil is a favorite of mine. A judiciously gentle soul, he must have known something about childhood wounds, I suspect.

That Lila retains the sharpened knife, not the comforting shawl, speaks to the fear, loneliness, and defensiveness that envelop her. Cutting herself off from the "beautiful old man" whose presence brings her a sense of peace, she continually schemes to abandon John Ames, or hurts his feelings, or considers stealing their child and leaving him lonelier than he had ever been before. One can only guess how unnerving this stormy late-life relationship must have been for John Ames, though he is touched by Lila's cultivating the roses on the graves of his long-dead wife and child.

The scene of the Protestant christening, days after Lila proposed marriage to Ames, emphasizes the psychological consequence of Lila's traumatic life: all the edginess triggered by having been unwanted, unnamed, without a family or even a birth date. By the river near the abandoned shack, Lila feels humiliated that she does not understand the words Ames uses, and is determined to leave Gilead on a bus. Ames fastens a locket of his mother's around her neck and asks for reassurances. "I can't see how it's going to work," she says: "What if it turns out I'm crazy?" Lila—mortified by her ignorance and by what John Ames does not know about her past—deems herself unlovable: "I've got shame like a habit, the only thing I feel except when I'm alone." But what she says to him is "I can't marry you. I can't even stand up in front of them people and get baptized." His pain, registered on his "reddened" face, issues in an offer to christen her right there and then, just the two of them, by the flopping catfish she had just caught.

Only after the baptism does Lila confess, "I want you to marry me! I wish I didn't. It's just a misery for me."

"For me, too, as it happens."

"I can't trust you!"

"I guess that's why I can't trust you."

"Oh," she said, "that's a fact. I don't trust nobody. I can't stay nowhere. I can't get a minute of rest."

Despite their subsequent marriage, despite her "creeping into the old man's bed when he never even asked her to," Lila continues to fantasize about leaving Ames or worries that he will abandon her. She even tries to unbaptize herself. In every way possible, she sets out to alienate the old man on whose shoulder she wants to place her weary head. "When you're scalded, touch hurts, it makes no difference if it's kindly meant."

Is it only John Ames's steadfast patience that enables their marriage to prosper or does Lila have resources of her own, I wondered. But the kids had arrived. In the whirlwind of reheating, serving, clearing, and cleaning leading up to and then including the feast, thoughts of Lila had to be stowed away, as they were during the meandering, late-night conversations, always the greatest pleasure of my older daughter's visits.

The apple did not fall far from the tree, I thought when I looked over at Molly during extended discussions of campus politics and institutional practices with her husband and his brother, though in every way she is better and brighter than I, more at home in the world. When a child, she was a gifted actress and singer. In *Really Rosie, Imagine That,* and a succession of musicals, she glowed in the spotlight. If there was friction between us, generally it resulted from headstrong impulses we shared.

About campus politics, there was room for debate. While Eli slept upstairs and a fire blazed in the family room, we considered the protests against college buildings named for Lord Jeffrey Amherst, Woodrow Wilson, and John C. Calhoun. Does the changing of a name redeem history or, as I thought, erase and bowdlerize it? Molly felt it made students of color more comfortable in environments that could be disheartening.

But on the deficits of public versus private institutions, we all agreed. The cheese ball at receptions hosted at Pittsburgh and Indiana contrasted with the sushi and fresh fruit circulated at MIT, where Molly and Kieran had just landed. We laughed at our chagrin back in 1990 when the starter salad at a ceremonial lunch in the Union—Don was receiving an award for service, I was promoted to the rank of distinguished professor—was followed by dessert.

Would the straitened public universities, to which Don and I had dedicated our lives, be able to compete with well-endowed private ones? We planned Eli's daytime activities and our remaining dinners together, Kieran's curries and the English sweets Suneil had brought, before lamenting the miserable job market in the humanities for graduate students in private as well as public schools. We were astonished that Don had received several job offers through the mail—without any campus interviews—when he was finishing up his training at Ohio State back in the fifties.

It was sad, Molly remarked upon leaving, that Fran had not made an appearance. Thinking about the inevitable leftovers, I remembered how famished Fran had been when she would arrive at my house for dinner, as she did frequently back when the girls were very young. Sometimes she would eat her supper and then finish what the kids left on their plates. It seemed to me that she had never had enough of anything: food, attention, affection, praise, privacy, time free from work. Maybe all my Sturm und Drang about the sick grandbaby and then about Don's spring falls had been too upsetting, too confusing for her. Like the mice zapped in stress tests, who respond to painful stimuli by biting other mice, had I snapped? Perhaps she needed to protect herself. Or maybe she was dealing with other vexing issues unrelated to me. In the old days, it was pure joy to cook for her and then joy, too, when she turned the tables and fed me the very best spicy shrimp I have ever in my life been blessed to taste.

Both in *Gilead* and in *Lila*, food is sacramental: a hallowed reward that creates a sense of devotion. When as a boy John Ames went into the wilderness with his father to find his grandfather's grave, the woman who brought them a supper of cornmeal mush seemed "like a second mother." The crumbs of bread Doll fed to little Lila initiate an education into how to get along: "You can eat the roots of things. Cattails. Wild carrot. Nettles are very good if you know how to pick them and cook them. Doll said you just had to know what wouldn't kill you." No wonder, then, that Lila wants to unbaptize herself: "If Doll was going to be lost forever, Lila wanted to be right there with her, holding to the skirt of her dress."

Should I have taken Don's advice and used the Trollope ploy on Fran's letter? With so much history at stake, should I have willfully misinterpret her letter, thanked her for responding, and proposed a meeting? During this holiday season, would she have the companionship of her other close friends or her family? I will write to send her my best wishes for a good new year, I determined, as I took to heart John Ames's view that "it is seldom indeed that any wrong one suffers is not thoroughly foreshadowed by wrongs one has done." Integrity leads him to add, "It has never been clear to me how much this realization helps when it comes to the practical difficulty of controlling anger."

John Ames does not judge but engages Lila's questions about faith, which evolve out of her past deprivations and get to the core of his religion. Two problems persistently nag her. First, she worries that those unbaptized, like Doll, will not attain eternal life but will instead "have to answer" at the Last Judgment "for lives most of them never understood in the first place": "Lila hated the thought of resurrection as much as she had ever hated anything. Better Doll should stay in her grave, if she had one. Better nothing the old men said should be true at all."

Lila also ponders the ancient problem of the suffering of the innocent: "if God really has all that power, why does He let children get treated so bad? Because they are sometimes. That's true." She is thinking of her own past, of another castaway child she tried to help, and of the meaning of a passage in Ezekiel that haunts her: about a baby thrown out—*"No eye pitied thee"*—to whom God says, *"Though thou art in thy blood: live; yea, I said unto thee, Though thou art in thy blood, live."* John Ames interprets the story figuratively, as an allegory about the Lord binding himself in marriage to Jerusalem. Wise about his limited comprehension, he does not presume to answer either of Lila's theologically charged concerns. Instead, he does what I do when someone hurt comes to me: he blathers on.

But Lila by herself has found through her reading a way of understanding her own situation. Like the baby in its blood, she had been told to live. Even though John Ames wishes she would read Matthew, Lila sticks with Ezekiel and Job because their accounts describe apocalyptic events comparable to those she has experienced. She studies biblical texts that reveal the wild ferocity of a natural world she had herself inhabited: "*a storm wind . . . a great cloud, with a fire infolding itself,*" she thinks, "could have been a prairie fire in a drought year."

"*And out of the midst thereof came the likeness of four living creatures*" teases Lila to consider the "likeness" of her own name and nature:

> She had the likeness of a woman, with hands but no face at all, since she never let herself see it. She had the likeness of a life, because she was all alone in it. She lived in the likeness of a house, with walls and a roof and a door that kept nothing in and nothing out. And when Doll took her up and swept her away, she had felt a likeness of wings. She thought, Strange as all this is, there might be something to it.

Puzzling over the most difficult texts in the Western tradition, Lila discovers descriptions evocative of her own experiences, but dazzlingly dissimilar as well. She finds a likeness.

That Robinson's character eases her grief by reading speaks to me of the importance of reading. In stories, we contemplate others like and unlike ourselves, confronting situations we might also face, but differently. As we consider creatures whose background and problems and values differ from our own, we identify and sympathize and see ourselves anew. Empathy for those who are not-us humanizes us. Whether or not it translates into compassionate behavior, it stretches the boundaries of our being. We each of us expand to contain multitudes.

What will happen to us as a people, to our society, if the ancient arts of reading, copying, interpreting, and analyzing continue to be marginalized? That was the worry informing those late-night conversations with Molly, Kieran, and Suneil. Marilynne Robinson, who has spent years of her life "lovingly absorbed in the thoughts and perceptions of—who knows it better than I?—people who do not exist," believes that "fiction may be, whatever else, an exercise in the capacity for imaginative love, or sympathy, or identification."

If she is right, fiction serves as a basis of community, for "community, at least community larger than the immediate family, consists very largely of imaginative love for people we do not know or whom we know very slightly." The novelist Ian McEwan, who credits fiction with providing the possibility of "imagining what it is like to be someone other than yourself," argues that this process is "the basis of all sympathy": "Other people are as alive as you are. Cruelty is a failure of imagination."

Last year, about 43 percent of adult Americans read at least one work of literature. In other words, last year the majority of Americans did not read any imaginative works at all. What an impoverishment, it seems to me. What a loss for those people.

Where have we educators in the humanities gone wrong, I fulminated before wincing at the sound of my hectoring voice in a megaphone.

Lila reads and copies sentences throughout Robinson's novel; however, she finds herself unable to convey, even to the benevolent John Ames, the ghastly circumstances of her experiences. Is this because the discarded Lila did not count as a human being? The philosopher Stanley Cavell, who wrote extensively on love, once explained, "Something counts because it fits or matters." Four- or five-year-old Lila neither fit nor mattered. Because she did not count, Lila cannot recount her past in the way that Don and I and so many other later-life lovers repeatedly do.

Throughout Robinson's novel, of course, Lila silently remembers, but she blurts out only bits and pieces to John Ames, sometimes to warn or tease him. Yet the last sentence of *Lila* holds out hope that her introspective self-recounting may translate into more communicative recounting: "Someday she would tell him what she knew." That certainty has everything to do with faith in future trust that she will fit and matter. But what exactly would she tell Ames? Will she tell him that all the lost children are found? Or that creation is not the beneficent beauty he takes it to be? Late-life love offers security, insight, and pleasure, but no easy resolution.

Counting, it strikes me, is what less traumatized late-life lovers do obsessively, even if for the most part Lila cannot, because she does not have a birth date and because for much of her life days followed days, seasons seasons, without any calendar at her disposal. In the shack at the edge of Gilead, however, she does begin to count off the days to figure out when Sunday will come around and she might see John Ames in his church.

From Elizabeth Barrett Browning, counting the ways, to García Márquez's Florentino Arizo, counting the fifty-one years, nine months, and four days he waited to declare his love, late-life lovers count. We count the years we lived before we met, we count the wide gap in time between our first meeting and our later unions, we count backward to ceremonies of innocence, we divide our pasts, we multiply our memories, we calculate the remainders of our futures, we consider our percentages, we cultivate the roses on the graves of those beloved to our beloveds. After being released from stony silence, Shakespeare's Hermione wants to recount her experience to her daughter. Recounting is what Robinson's John Ames does in the journal composed for his son. Those of us who are old have many different ages within us, all of which must be numbered.

Aging involves counting and recounting, I think as I counted back to my time in Iowa City, some half a century ago. When with John Ames I encountered a recipe for a ghastly "molded salad of orange gelatin with stuffed green olives and shredded cabbage and anchovies," I remembered that Gayatri Spivak and I shivered at the sight of just that sort of gelatinous mess on the smorgasbord of an Amish restaurant. Then she taught me how to make Indian cauliflower. Back in the sixties, when we attended wild and crazy parties where faculty (she was in comparative literature) and graduate students (I was in English) rocked together to Jimi Hendrix and Janis Joplin, I had no idea that Gayatri would become a prominent thinker. We exchanged costumes: she gave me a sari and I lent her a one-piece pants jumper. It was black and, I thought at the time, totally cool.

To show Don, I was poised to go upstairs and bring down an album with pictures of us then, but he was holding out the wishbone I had forgotten to offer Eli.

"Want to make a wish?"

We were standing at the kitchen counter.

"You won," I said in surprise.

"But remember, you can't lose."

Enormous Changes
at the Last Minute

USING EVERY ONE of his remotes, Don had been unable to find the made-for-television movie I wanted him to see, and my assistants could not obtain a DVD in any library. A study of love devoid of popular movies would be doomed to irrelevance. It had been a dreary week and now, in a dreary examination room, I anticipated a dreary trip home, where I would be too faint from hunger to cook dinner.

The frigid cubicle, in which Don and I sat on two plastic chairs, contained a paper-covered gynecological table, a poster of the female belly sliced open to display the four stages of ovarian cancer, a stool, two labeled waste canisters, a blood pressure stand, a sink, and a computer on a ledge of shelves. Earlier that day, the annual mammogram had infuriated me since the document I signed proved that only well-insured patients would receive the better multidimensional imaging. Before and after it, I drank gallons of the sickeningly sweet Gastrografin solution that people under 130 pounds have to imbibe before abdominal CT scans. The trial required recurrent CTs—after thirty or more, my scanxiety disappeared—even though the images were always indeterminate, the radiation could not possibly be good for me, and the second intravenous contrast would undoubtedly harm my kidneys.

The CT itself had taken only seconds. Fully clothed, I lay down on a plank, holding on to a triangular bar above my head. The plank, like a conveyor belt, moved me so deep into the hole of the donut-shaped mechanism that the overhead metal bar (which I clutched with upraised hands) clanged against it. Only my head remained outside the cavernous machine.

"Take a breath and hold" a mechanical female voice said. Did they change it to a male voice for men? I wondered.

Conveyed back out, I heard, "Breathe."

Through the accessed port, the technician injected the second contrast agent. "It will give you an awful taste in your mouth and make you feel like you are peeing your pants," she cautioned, and then the process was repeated.

"Take a breath and hold."

"Breathe."

I waited on the plank for a nurse who could take the needle out of the port. Because the hospital had cut back on staff, the wait was longer than usual. If not this scan, then the next would show a tumor, I thought, or the trial drug would itself cause a secondary cancer. But upon the nurse's arrival, I remembered that Alesha would want the usual blood tests. With the tubing taped onto my chest, I proceeded to Hematology, where I would see Dr. Matei for the very last time.

Blood samples were sent to the lab, the port de-accessed; however, Dr. Matei was running late. The news on my iPhone—killings at a Planned Parenthood clinic, the San Bernardino massacre—deepened my gloom. I had not heard a word from Fran on my birthday and I doubted that the letter I had drafted would convey anything meaningful. On the drive up, Jayne had pointed out Canada geese—still here, she said, because of global warming. My going-away present seemed inappropriate.

In a small leather pouch of my mother's, I had tucked a strand of pearls from my grandmother. It was the only gift I could conceive of commensurate with what Daniela Matei had given me. Back at diagnosis in 2008, when I first met her, she had mentioned a promising drug in the pipeline, but worried it might not be available in time. After my third recurrence, astonishingly, she found a trial and got me in it. Could a string of pearls amply thank her? In fact, it might embarrass her. I slipped the necklace back into my purse when she entered. As always, she raised the room temperature with her ardent intensity and clarity.

"I will miss you," she said. "But we'll stay in touch and you'll be in good hands. I'm giving you to the principal investigator of your trial, a breast cancer specialist; she knows more than anyone about the genetics of your disease. She lectures a good deal and won't see you for six weeks—just think: you'll have a six-week vacation from the hospital! When has that ever happened? You won't have to be here again until 2016! And I'm leaving you in good shape—no evidence of disease!"

"It feels odd using the word 'remission,' what with the daily drugs."

"Say 'remission-on-maintenance' then. You are the only one still alive, and you are on the higher dosage. I'm hearing the NIH will do a study on people like you . . . on the tail of graphs; they call them 'exceptional responders.'"

She was laughing and nervous about moving her family to Chicago and excited about the named chair and, after a hug, out of the room in a flash. We would have to wait for the brown bag of pills Alesha had gone to fetch from the pharmacy, and then for checkout, and then for the valet parking, and then for the emailed blood test results, which would tell me if I could take the pills, and then, after an hour, I could eat.

Jayne offered to drive through the worst of the construction. On the way home, spurred by Dr. Matei's upcoming move, Don told a story of his working at Montgomery Ward and hearing that there was an oxygen machine in the lobby of the Wrigley Building. For a quarter, you could get a whiff that was supposed to be good for hangovers, though maybe this was an urban legend.

The last month of the year stretched before me with the positive prospect of not having to go to the hospital or, not quite as bad, to the Modern Language Association convention. A furlough: it was a good time for movies. Since my favorite late-life love movie was available only on YouTube, I replayed *Love among the Ruins* on my laptop. To me, it represents the best of the romantic comedies through which Don had suffered during the past year.

Even though George Cukor's film won a number of awards, it is generally taken to be a piece of fluff. Perhaps the fact that it was made for television led to its critical dismissal, despite the fine performances of Katharine Hepburn and Sir Laurence Olivier. *Love among the Ruins* launches a witty assault on the bad reputation of older women. Set in Edwardian London, the plot revolves around the wealthy dowager Jessica Medlicott (Hepburn), who engages the services of the eminent barrister Sir Arthur Glanville-Jones (Olivier) to defend her in a breach of promise suit brought by the youthful fiancé she dumped.

In her opulent gowns, ornate hats, and boas, the aging Jessica Medlicott poses and proclaims as if to remind us of the successful acting career she had pursued decades ago. Upon her first meeting with Sir Arthur in his chambers, he tries to allude to his youthful passion when he waited for her by the stage door in Toronto decades ago. "Ottawa?" she asks. "Toronto," he repeats. Baffled that she seems oblivious to a love affair still vivid in his mind, he nevertheless agrees to represent her in the courtroom sparring that turns into a battle of the sexes . . . with him the apparent victor.

The pleasure of this very verbal movie derives from its repartee. During their first sustained conversation, Sir Arthur asks Jessica Medlicott to "consider the boy who loved you," a reference either to the discarded fiancé or to himself in the past. She keeps on insisting that "the worm" Alfred Pratt should not get one farthing of the 50,000 pounds he demands. Trying to make her understand why a jury might side with the impoverished young man, Sir Arthur asks whether she loved her husband or had she bartered her youth for an old man's gold. Her answer—that she grew to love her husband "in time"—begs the question. While Sir Arthur escorts her to a car, they discuss her role in *The Merchant of Venice*, but he believes she has forgotten Portia's most important words: "I pray you know me when we meet again." The wide gap of time, more than forty years, has not dulled his memories but apparently has obliterated hers.

Which infuriates him, as he lets off steam with her solicitor: "I could kill her," he says. "I could tear her to pieces." In particular, he fumes, she had promised to wait one year for him to finish his law degree, declaring that there were only two things she wanted in life: "to be your wife and to die before you." Yet before he returned to her, she married a rich, older man. The irony of the present legal case is not lost on him: she had broken her promise to him, yet now he will defend her against a breach of promise suit.

The antagonism between the dowager and the barrister permeates the remaining courtroom scenes in which Sir Arthur punishes the woman who wrecked his life by presenting her as "a ruin of a woman." After she refuses to take his advice to dress as plainly as possible—she shows up instead in a bright red dress ornamented with flounces of white finery—the defense lawyer gratifies her by emphasizing her appeal : "If this be December, were it not folly to wait for spring?" But Sir Arthur insists that the age disparity proves Pratt guilty of exploitation. A youthful man like Pratt could not possibly have desired such a pitiful has-been; he wanted only her money.

On the stand, Jessica Medlicott refuses to reveal her age— "I was born in the year of my birth"—but the exasperated Sir Arthur goes on to portray her as a deluded old lady: at that point, she erupts in rage and must be dragged out of court. As the jury moves in her favor, *Love among the Ruins* seems to subscribe to the customary view that the genuine attraction of a young man toward an older woman is implausible. She has won the law case, but lost her composure and her pride. Sir Arthur has had his revenge by making her look ridiculous. But the story does not end there: unexpectedly and happily, George Cukor subverts this traditional rap in the movie's conclusion.

First, Jessica Medlicott delights in a verdict that does not surprise her. Her experience on stage enabled her to play the typecast role of the narcissistic has-been, clinging to her youthful charms. By performing the stereotype that Sir Arthur exploited, she empowered him to right the wrong she had done to him decades ago so they could reunite on a more level playing field. Finally, the hoodwinked Sir Arthur appears to apologize for his brutality in court.

As she congratulates him on pleading her case brilliantly and mentions other women in his life—his mother, his aunt—it becomes clear that Jessica Medlicott has remembered all along exactly what transpired in Toronto forty years ago. Admitting that a horror of poverty caused her to jilt him for a wealthy husband, she begins playacting their earlier romance. They are "relics," both agree, but "we've survived." Embarking on a "late start," they exit the courthouse accompanied by a recitation of Robert Browning's "Grow old along with me. . . ."

Shutting down my computer, I gathered all the DVDs that had been recalled by the library. It was not easy to get into that building, because of construction. Neither could I get into the office I shared with other retirees in the English department: the lot attached to Ballantine Hall would be full. But I could pop the movies into a drop-off box near the theater. Maybe because, like Don, I lived at home while attending an urban college, being on a residential campus always delights me. Going there and back, I marveled at the beauty of the wooden bridges, the brick walkways, the arboretum— even the new buildings looked established in their limestone façades—and at all the movies Don had resisted watching: *The Bridges of Madison County, An Affair to Remember, Brief Encounter, The Exotic Marigold Hotel, Last Chance Harvey*. He had seen them before, he claimed, though I didn't remember most of them myself.

In romantic comedies about late-life love, boy does not meet girl so they can overcome obstacles and marry to live happily ever after. Sometimes, as in *Love among the Ruins*, aging men and women recall the boy and girl they had been as they overcome obstacles so they can begin a relationship again. Sometimes, as in *On Golden Pond*, long-married men and women confront the obstacles of unhappy children and physical deterioration as they hope to continue living and loving for a few more years. But a number of later-life romantic comedies end in death. In *The Ghost and Mrs. Muir*, a lonely widow who falls in love with a ghost can unite with him only in death. In *Harold and Maude*, the romance between a ghoulish teenage boy and an antic old woman closes with her funeral.

The tender movie *Love Is Strange* begins with a marriage. After thirty-nine years together, the painter Ben and the schoolteacher George stand at their wedding ceremony, while the officiator asks, "Are you both making this decision of your own free will?" The scene reminds me of the three questions that cracked up Don and me in the jail: were we biologically related, under the influence, or married to anybody else?

In *Love Is Strange*, the public legitimizing of Ben and George's relationship causes the Catholic supervisors of George's school to fire him. Without his salary, the couple can no longer afford their Manhattan apartment. As in the Depression classic *Make Way for Tomorrow*, in *Love Is Strange* Ben and George must split up, crashing in other people's apartments. They continue to talk on the phone and in one sequence attend a concert together, where we see them holding hands, moved by the beautiful music. The last image of Ben—descending the staircase into a subway station— becomes haunting after the final scenes of the movie when the grief of his survivors is made manifest.

"Why limit yourself to romcom?" Jonathan asked via email. "There's a terrific Icelandic movie that just came out . . . late-life love of sheep."

Because Hollywood movies tell me more about American culture than do prize-winning foreign films, I think. Released last year, *Love Is Strange* marks a positive change in the romantic comedy tradition: the inclusion of gay men. Would there be future Hollywood movies about gay women and about heterosexual couples confronting not only the stigmatization of older women but also their resiliency in dealing with it? Why not a movie about the zaftig immigrant Rosie Lieber, the central character of Grace Paley's story "Goodbye and Good Luck"?

Entranced by the promiscuous "Valentino" of the Second Avenue Yiddish theater, Rosie has an off-and-on affair with him until his wife of nearly half a century divorces him for adultery. When he proposes resuming where they left off, Rosie says, "How could you ask me to go with you on trains to stay in strange hotels, among Americans, not your wife? Be ashamed." Of course, an actress would have to capture the cadences of the aging Rosie tri-umphantly exclaiming to her niece, "I'll have a husband, which, as everybody knows, a woman should have at least one before the end of the story."

The prospect of these sorts of movies and the mild weather conspired in my gladness that the baby in New York was thriving: a miracle in which I rejoice very quietly, because I don't want to put the kibosh (whatever that is) on it. Sandra was falling in love again: that, too, seems a wonder. Judith has returned from India, and Don found a brilliant cover for his and Mary's new edition of *Pride and Prejudice*, a charming scene in a book of watercolors: a Regency parlor with one young lady playing the piano and several couples dancing.

I was buoyed, too, by not having to prepare for the MLA con-vention that used to come right after Christmas. Don had a the-ory about its timing: the daddies wanted to flee the horror of the holidays—kiddies home from school, trikes and bikes needing to be assembled—so the professors met on December 27. I always had to spend the first weeks of December preparing for various sessions or talks that Sandra and I presented: on one occasion, when Toni Morrison was speaking simultaneously in another hall, to an almost empty room; on another, to an overflow crowd laughing at a joking parody of the profession inspired by her hus-band, Elliot. On or about the time women entered the profession in force, the date of the MLA convention was changed, but I had already retired.

While I waited through Don's haircut at the barbershop, recalling conventions of the past, I gazed at two faded signs on the wall: "Trespassers Will Be Violated" and "Unattended Children Will Be Given Espresso and a Free Kitten." They emboldened me to ask ancient Herschel if he had time to shave my head. He did not blink when I took off my wig. Instead, he launched into a history of his own terminal diagnosis decades ago, which made him grateful for reaching his seventy-first year. Could he really be my age, I wondered, as Don took one look at me and said, "You got your money's worth." Then he added, "The Nazis shouldn't have shaved collaborators. It made them more attractive."

At the barbershop and later when Don and I purchased a pair of real shoes with laces, I considered two memorials I had organized. Before the panel in honor of Carolyn Heilbrun, Grace Paley marched over to Don, who was suffering from a terrible cold. Coming up to his breastbone, she tapped him on the chest and with each tap instructed him, "Eat soup. Eat soup." While putting together the panel in honor of Barbara Johnson, I remembered striding down the aisle of a huge ballroom to accept a book award she had been too sick to receive herself. How could the most subtle literary interpreter I knew—at the English Institute, she looked like a schoolgirl—be dying so young?

Friendship must be honored, I decided back at home. Even a defunct friendship should be honored, if only with some honest grieving. No, I would not mail the flaccid letter I had written to Fran. In it I had explained that reading about late-life love made me realize that I could not possibly comprehend her intentions or perspective or even her own situation and therefore should not have passed judgment. But in fact, I acknowledged (not in the letter but to myself), she had not broken the friendship; I had.

During Don's falls and surgeries, I must have been off my rocker with anxiety. I should have reached out to her and expressed my needs; she surely would have responded. Why did I wait, like some kind of pathetic damsel-in-distress, for an offer of help? And regardless of how I interpreted her last letter, she had made the effort to communicate. Did it read like a foreign alphabet because of my own stunted soul? I had prioritized my wants over hers. I could not appreciate then—and sometimes I cannot appreciate now—that her spiritual aspirations were as pressing as my physical problems. Is it the case—how can it be the case—that both of us feel abandoned by the other? The unsent letter indubitably conveys my failure and my sorrowful loss, for I had wanted to grow old along with her. Recurrently, the loss widens into an abyss that swallows me, and I am bereft.

"To me, fair friend, you never can be old," Olivier had recited to Hepburn. "Love and Freindship" is the title of the juvenilia that Sandra and I used to represent Jane Austen in the *Norton Anthology of Literature by Women*. "Love and freindship" was how I signed cards to Fran. I will always mourn the absence of someone who gave me the invaluable gift of her unique presence throughout four decades. I cherish my younger and older friends, but she was my prized contemporary, up to and into our seventies, when (I can only surmise) she launched a quiet quest of her own, an inward journey obscure to me but nevertheless compelling and completely unrelated to romance. Neither her story nor our story has yet to register in movies, though surely they might in the future, or so I think as the memories abide.

Growing old in friendship plays a big part in the comedies that Spencer Tracy made with Katharine Hepburn. In the last one, *Guess Who's Coming to Dinner*, he tells the parents of their white daughter's black fiancé that "in the final analysis it doesn't matter what we think. The only thing that matters is what they feel, and how much they feel for each other. And if it's half of what we felt . . . that's everything." He turns toward Hepburn: "Old, yes, burnt out, but I can tell you memories are still there." By acting in her last movies without Spencer Tracy and with her tremors on display, Hepburn went on to bravely address the physical deterioration of aging.

Less poignant than amusing, a sex scene between two characters in *Something's Gotta Give* represents the worn bodies of older lovers. Diane Keaton hands the aging lecher Jack Nicholson a pair of scissors to cut off her turtleneck and then takes his blood pressure before proceeding to make love. The turtleneck captures the anxiety about old flesh that Nora Ephron considers in "I Feel Bad about My Neck," as does the taking of blood pressure. In *It's Complicated*, after Meryl Streep undresses, Alec Baldwin collapses . . . and then must point his finger at Flomax (which eases his urine stream). Nicholson looks haggard and Baldwin overweight, but Keaton and Streep look lovely throughout. Is it just because of my professional prejudice that for the most part literature seems to me superior to film on this subject?

Movie characters—especially the women—tend to appear too rich, too thin, too white, and too attractive. The single exception I can think of is the father in the television series *Transparent*, who explores a late-life gender change as well as late-life sex while looking her age. Does the need to reach a large audience of people ready and willing to go out to the movie theater—which Don and I are not able to do—lead to these faults? In fact, this past year we haven't been to one of the classical concerts in Auer Hall that we used to attend regularly or to the jazz at Bear's Place that we used to attend even more frequently.

Perhaps the tyranny of visual attractiveness renders the visual less valuable in describing the pleasures of late-life love. What late-life lovers do may feel nice and yet not look nice. But it doesn't matter what others think. The only thing that matters is what we feel, I decided as I tried to plan a red, white, and blue supper, but couldn't think of anything blue in season that I could digest. I would settle for a meal of balls—matzoh ball soup, falafel with all the fixings, and maybe I could buy some chocolate truffles or donut holes.

When Zak phoned in the midst of Susannah and Jack's arrival, I had no wish to look at another condo in Windermere Village that had just come onto the market. It was a rainy, gray day and the place sounded too small: only two bedrooms. But, he insisted, it has a den that could become a second study.

Susannah waltzed through the rooms, enthusing about its close-ness to shops, its hardwood floors, and its spacious living room.

"The kitchen is terrible. Cramped," I said.

"You can tear down the dining room wall," she said. "Open it up."

"The bathroom is a pit."

"Yes, you'll have to redo it. That shower is antique fiberglass," she said.

"It's got park-like views and in better weather it will get good light," Julie said.

"It's going to be hell to renovate," Don and I agreed. "And to downsize from 4,000 to less than 2,000 square feet."

But standing with him in the bedroom, I asked if he could imagine living alone in the apartment and he said yes, and of course there were already other people interested in the place; and so Julie and Susannah and Zak persuaded us to embark on enormous changes at the last minute by offering the asking price.

When I pulled into the long driveway of the Inverness, Don and I saw three deer, unflustered by our approaching car, grazing on the peaceful slope of the meadow bordering the circle of beauty. Someone else has lived here before and someone else would live here after, but the landscape will endure. As I thought of the opening of the Robert Browning poem that had captivated George Cukor—"Where the quiet-coloured end of evening smiles / Miles and miles / On the solitary pastures"—Don opened his window and called out to the deer, "You've won, guys. We're leaving."

Chrisnukkah

ON THE MANTLE over the fake fire in the Trace lobby, glittery gold letters spelled out R E J O I C E, but a woman's voice down one hall kept on droning, "No no no . . . no . . ." A skinny Santa Claus hurried through the door with a guitar and disappeared into an adjacent dining hall, as it dawned on me that I had been wrong about Philip Larkin and also about my mother. I was leafing through a sheaf of papers that I had printed out: the most ambitious poems on late-life love by Shakespeare at the start of the tradition and, surprisingly, by Larkin toward the end. What startled yet perplexed me is how paradoxical late-life love poems are. Why should that be, and what does it tell us about late-life love? The answer to these questions may help me sum up in a rousing peroration, since sadly (for me) there is only one more chapter to go.

Shakespeare's justly famous Sonnet 138 sets the mark when its over-the-hill speaker describes how his lady flatters him with deceits about his youthfulness that he pretends to believe:

When my love swears that she is made of truth,
I do believe her, though I know she lies,
That she might think me some untutored youth,
Unlearnèd in the world's false subtleties.
Thus vainly thinking that she thinks me young,
Although she knows my days are past the best,
Simply I credit her false-speaking tongue:
On both sides thus is simple truth suppressed.
But wherefore says she not she is unjust?
And wherefore say not I that I am old?
Oh, love's best habit is in seeming truth,
And age in love loves not to have years told.
    Therefore I lie with her and she with me,
    And in our faults by lies we flattered be.

Shakespeare's surrogate credits the truth of what he knows to be false: his lover's declaration that he is young. Although she realizes that his best days are past, she chooses to suppress the truth and he willingly conspires with her.

The aging speaker wonders about their collusion in deceit: why, he asks, does she refrain from acknowledging his years and why does he not admit that he is old? "Truth" rhymes with "youth," but with aging obfuscation takes over in the service of maintaining "love's best habit." Later-life lovers need to habituate themselves to "seeming truth," for they do not want to remind themselves that their lost prime threatens their passion. In the final couplet, the poet explains that this repression enables late-life-lovers to lie (in bed) together as they refuse to acknowledge the lies (or shams) that bolster them. Collaboratively arrived at frauds secure late-life lovers' troths.

This paradox is strengthened by the ultimate irony of the poem: namely, that the aging poet speaks honestly about his own and his beloved's dishonesty. Shakespeare's worldly speaker will take what he can get; and at his time of life, the getting is good only by keeping up pretenses. Sonnet 138 subverts another line by Shakespeare that reiterates the common, depressing notion that "Youth is hot and bold, age is weak and cold." In Sonnet 138, the aging speaker is neither weak nor cold. Life-affirming, his witty and wily decision to continue lying *to* his mistress so he can continue lying *with* her endows him and the verse with exuberance.

It is hardly surprising to find paradox at work in John Donne's "The Autumnal," I thought, as the voice moaning "no no . . . no" persisted beneath the strums of the guitar. In an email, my friend Ken's partner, an editor of Donne, informed me that critics split in viewing the poem as a tribute to Lady Magdalen Herbert (the poet George Herbert's mother) or an exercise in praise of an older woman as a love object. "Why take an either/or approach?" she reasonably asked. The opening of "The Autumnal" certainly emphasizes the poet's love for an aging woman: "No spring nor summer beauty hath such grace / As I have seen in one autumnal face."

But there is a sinister glitch when Donne begins to describe the lines on this face: "Call not these wrinkles, graves," he declares. The injunction immediately does make the wrinkles seem like graves. And these grave-like wrinkles next become Cupid's trenches and then his tomb. The creased face makes me ponder the link between three words: cracks, crocks, and croaks. Donne insists, "Age must be loveliest at the latest day"; paradoxically, however, "the latest day" invokes carnal "decay." Shockingly, Donne then associates the beauties of autumn with the horrors of a harsh winter that, we know, fall must usher in. He keeps on instructing himself not to name the nightmares of the last season, but he goes ahead and lists the slack skin of the soul's sack, the shaded eyes, and the toothless holes of death's-heads.

"Do you think 'The Autumnal' should be read as a dramatic monologue?" I had asked Don, after he read the poem. "Like the speaker is a lunatic?"

"Didn't he sleep in a coffin?"

At the end of "The Autumnal," Donne's appalled speaker determines to descend "down the hill" with his beloved lady; however, they are progressing toward a physical corrosion that clearly terrifies him. How might the lady have received this expression of his affectionate reverence, I wondered, as the strains of "O Come, All Ye Faithful" started to drown out the "no . . . no."

It is impossible to read poetry when the words of carols intercede. For me, it is also impossible to hear a chorus of old voices—tremulous, thin, mostly soprano—without feeling the same poignancy that children's concerts instill. I attended all the choir performances in which my mother participated. She loved the carols, but insisted that one Chanukah song be included in every Christmas concert program.

Before her decline into senility, my mother had made a heroic adjustment—from her rhythms in Manhattan to the Indiana retirement community that, on her count, sprouted some twelve Christmas trees in its public rooms and not one menorah. She had joined the German table, the writers' circle, the reading club, and the trips to fast-food joints that seemed exotic to her. She appreciated visits from the rabbi, she would never become a "Jew for Jesus," but she attended Sunday services of various denominations because, she informed us, "Jesus was Jewish." Even when we realized she was dying and I gave her little kisses all over her face, she said yes and not no. She giggled at my "smooching" and then curled up in her bed, intent on her sleep and on arriving straight at her own death in the middle of the night. I commemorate my mother on her birthday, whereas I remember my father on his death day.

The ping! of the iPhone interrupted "Frosty the Snowman." That it was a lavish blurb for my cancer book—an advance copy was due to appear in the mailbox—elated but also unnerved me. Once between covers, my books always feel dead and defenseless, no longer growing networks of living thoughts. The *Times* essays—here today, gone tomorrow—would continue to keep me honest, as would this project, I reassured myself. And then there were innumerable emails from Zak and the engineer, who had to be consulted on the Windermere condo, and from the homeowners' association about whether or not the dining room wall was weight bearing.

Back at home, interminably emailing, I marveled at the tree that Judith and Aidan had hauled in and trimmed. Don and I would be alone with it and our buyer's remorse until Mary arrived for a visit at the start of the new year.

"We'll never get the money back for renovations on that kitchen," either he or I would say.

"But we need to make it open or else we'll feel caged," I or he would say.

"Maybe we should take a lower price for the Inverness, let the new owners fix it up," he or I said.

"Zak says it will not sell as is and anyway we owe it to the place," I or he said.

"We won't be able to leave until the spring," we agreed.

"It will be hard leaving," I said.

"I'm glad neither one of us is leaving alone."

"I worry about all the memories we'll leave behind."

"We'll take those with us."

I shifted my position on the blue couch so I could see the musical instruments, the ducks, and the Alice ornaments. I put off my trepidation about boastful Christmas letters—they would arrive as email attachments and were bound to make my family feel like losers—by turning to the longest late-life love poem I had found, William Carlos Williams's "Asphodel, That Greeny Flower." My sympathy for its touching origins jarred with my reservations about the work itself. Williams published it when he was seventy-two, after several strokes had depressed him, as did the blacklisting that kept him from an appointment at the Library of Congress. Partly paralyzed, he wrote it to obtain the forgiveness of his wife of forty years.

The paradox here: Williams expresses his longing to confess his marital failings, but he never does, and yet he concludes by rejoicing in the forgiveness he claims to have received. "Asphodel, That Greeny Flower" records the aged poet's effort to renew his marriage vows after decades of infidelities. In descending triadic lines (for thirty pages), Williams grapples with what he wishes to say yet cannot drag out. He thereby puts on display the evasions and accommodations compounded by the profound need to sustain a long partnership fissured by grudges that have amassed over decades. But the renewal of marital promises after infidelity—and worse than infidelity—reminded me of a more moving rendition of a long marriage fractured by the horrific consequences of history. I closed my William Carlos Williams and opened my Toni Morrison.

The end of Morrison's *Jazz* reads like a prose poem to "old-time love." From the beginning of the novel, we know the enmities of Morrison's aging Manhattan couple. At the start of 1926, Joe Trace shot and killed his teenage lover Dorcas and at the funeral Joe's wife Violet cut the dead girl's face. In the aftermath of slavery and Reconstruction, the figures in Morrison's triangle associate passion with claiming someone as their own, choosing the person they have "picked out and determined to have and hold on to." Certainly, Joe Trace—not a young "rooster" but one of the "old cocks"—chose his teen sweetheart: "I didn't fall in love, I rose in it. I saw you and made up my mind." Morrison explores the intense possessiveness of the dispossessed, even as she debunks the idea that young girls reciprocate old men's desires.

Although aging Joe Trace wants "the one thing everybody loses—young loving," teenage Dorcas swaps her old cock for a young rooster, triggering the shooting and the cutting. All three of Morrison's characters—the killed, the killer, and the slasher—know that choosing means risking, loving means losing. The final scene of *Jazz* imagines the "undercover whispers" of "old-time" spouses in bed, after they have mourned the havoc their violence spawned. Unlike the immovable conjugal bed of Ulysses and Penelope, the bed Joe and Violet chose together they kept together, "nevermind one leg was propped on a 1916 dictionary."

After murder and revenge—and all the depredations that led up to the violence and all the sorrow afterward—Morrison suggests that in later life "ecstasy is more leaf-sigh than bray." Two aging bodies in one bed are "the vehicle, not the point": the vehicle of intimacy. The same could be said of the present moment: it is not the point but the vehicle, for Joe and Violet are lying in bed remembering the past while they murmur under covers "both of them have washed and hung out on the line." Another, more mysterious enigma: reaching out to each other, "they are inward toward the other." The visual plays no role in their enclosure: "They are under the covers because they don't have to look at themselves anymore."

The last page of *Jazz* reviews the more public manifestations of an enduring marriage: fingers touching as a cup is passed or brushing lint from a serge suit. Several conundrums emerge here. First, late-life lovers show their love with "no need to say" it. Second, the flamboyant narrator, who has known love only "in secret," has "longed to show it—to be able to say out loud what they have no need to say." What the storyteller cannot say appears in italics: "*I have loved only you. . . . I want you to love me back. . . . I like your fingers on and on, lifting, turning.*" The unsayable words, printed on the page, publicly acknowledge the narrator's love of her readers as Morrison goes on to dramatize the links between loving, freedom, and reading.

In the novel's final lines, the storyteller urges her reader to "remake me. You are free to do it and I am free to let you because look, look. Look where your hands are. Now." Instructed, I look at my hands holding my copy of *Jazz*, my fingers lifting and turning its pages. The loving narrator, as fallible as the characters, grants me the freedom to remake *Jazz* into a bluesy anthem to injurious but abiding late-life love. Loving Toni Morrison back—she once urged me to take immediate action against a particularly deranged haircut—I try to imagine you, I mean *you* leafing through these pages, but I lack her vision. Your face turns into the visage of first one and then another member of my cancer support group, whom I must join immediately.

There was an important meeting to attend. At our lunches over the past half year or so, we had put on our activist hats. On the day before Christmas Eve, three of us met in the hospital with representatives of the Olcott Center for Cancer Education as well as some nurses and medical administrators. It had been a shower day, which always makes me nervous about the newly applied apparatus. But no accident occurred and the dream of my support group might come true: a registry for newly diagnosed patients who would be paired with and mentored by patients more experienced in dealing with their type of the disease.

On my return to the Inverness, I sniffed with satisfaction: Don was baking. I have always been the savory chef, he the sweet: Christmas cookies, chewy bars, brownies, peach cobblers, pineapple upside-down cakes, muffins—to the delight of whichever visiting grandson was singing "Little Rabbit Foo Foo" or hopping away from Julie's Farmer McGregor. I immediately set to work chopping vegetables so I could join him as he tested, removed from the pan, and tasted the triumph he would almost certainly disparage. Late-life love may heat at a lower temperature, but it bubbles and rises. We were cooking again, as we had back in our dating days, when we would prepare BLTs or a cheese soufflé that we consumed in a picnic on his or my bed. ("You make me feel so young" turned up in the first volume of *Mastering the Art of French Cooking*, maybe because at my house Don had to be careful about hiding notes.)

It seemed gratifying to anticipate laying out a quilt sandwich of topping, batting, and backing. Before and after I sewed during late-night comedy news shows, Don and I would while away the hours by decrying progressive political rifts, signing petitions, mailing contributions, and kibitzing about the world our grand-children might inherit. Happily, the neuropathy that prickles my soles or numbs my toes has not affected my hands. I had found yards of delicate, green-and-white fabric in one of Molly's clos-ets, which meant that the coldest months could be spent with the warm, basted flying geese lying in my lap, ready for the hoop and the tiny running stitches that would bind it together.

Don was sixty-seven when we moved into the Inverness and I will be seventy-one moving out, I thought as I picked up the books I had studied to understand one of Philip Larkin's most famous poems. But we age at different rates and the cancer has taken its toll. Don's response to "An Arundel Tomb" had mysti-fied me. "Safe in their alabaster chambers," he had said; however, Larkin's lovers were hardly safe in their tomb. We know nothing about them or the inside of their ancient sepulcher. Larkin remarks only on the effigies lying on top of it.

Side by side, "The earl and countess lie in stone" with blurred faces. Like Shakespeare, Larkin puns on the word "lie." Stone statues of the husband and wife lie horizontally, but the sculpture itself also lies about their marital intimacy. Although the eye of the observing poet sees with a tender shock that the left-hand gauntlet is empty—the earl's ungloved hand clasps the hand of the countess—Larkin realizes that this detail illuminates not their affection but the commissioned sculptor's wish to prolong the significance of their names. The earl and the countess will never "be stone no more." They will be nothing but the recumbent stone replicas that probably misrepresent their partnership.

The middle of the poem emphasizes the indifferent advance of time as generations of visitors gaze at the medieval figures, not understanding their circumstances. During the passage of season following season, years following years, an endless parade of people come to the cathedral. The earl and the countess recede into an incomprehensible "scrap of history": "Only an attitude remains."

Regardless of the actual nature of the earl and the countess's marriage, the attitude that remains results from their holding hands, stone skin touching stone skin, palm in palm. In pictures of the tomb, he lies on her left, she on his right. Her right hand crosses over her body to hold his right hand. Larkin later faulted himself for getting "the hands the wrong way round," but it makes no difference when we get to the final stanza:

Time has transfigured them into
Untruth. The stone fidelity
They hardly meant has come to be
Their final blazon, and to prove
Our almost-instinct almost true:
What will survive of us is love.

Once again, Larkin the critic later quibbled with Larkin the poet: "Love isn't stronger than death just because two statues hold hands for six hundred years."

The "central paradox" of this poem, according to one scholar: "the historical untruth that the modern visitor perceives *is* the important truth that the figures on the tomb have to show." Despite the onslaughts of centuries and the limits of our understanding, the couple has "Persisted, linked" down through the ages. They may not have embodied their "stone fidelity," but its conveyance has become a testament and tribute not to the poem's romantic maxim—"What will survive of us is love"—but rather to our almost-instinctual need to believe and to act on the "almost true" belief that "What will survive of us is love." Love has not survived, but our wish that it will does.

More modestly than Shakespeare, who boasted about his monumentalizing verse, Larkin hints that the lovers' "final blazon"—the ultimate display of their virtues—is of the sculptor's devising and also of his own. Surely more people read "The Arundel Tomb" than visit the Arundel tomb. Surely many visit the Arundel tomb because they have read "The Arundel Tomb." And Emily Dickinson's poem "Safe in their alabaster chambers" does illuminate Larkin's verse. Dickinson presents the dead in their caskets, oblivious to the ongoing breezes, the babbling bees, and the singing birds. The imperturbable cycles of the seasons mock our fervent wishes. The earl and the countess are not safe inside the chamber of their Arundel tomb; they have crumbled into dusty obscurity. Yet their "stone fidelity" does stay safe in the inviolate chamber of "The Arundel Tomb," which—along with many of the other works I have read this past year—remains immune to the vicissitude of time and shelters the union Don and I hope to continue prolonging a bit longer.

At that moment, on the brink of a new year, a lightbulb went on and I hummed, vibrated, pulsed until I felt marinated, preserved, pickled, cured in a mishmash of rippling realizations. My passionate bond with Don is based, yes, on his humor and on his kindness, intelligence, and reliability, but also on our mutual head-over-heals romance with literature. Wait! Shouldn't that be head-over-heels? Maybe there's an element of truth in every typo. The poems and stories Don and I share have played such a healing role during the past year and, indeed, during our decades together. On so many occasions with him, the mental aerobics of reading have upended me, sent me into exhilarating cartwheels. Without literature, we might have survived all our various upsets, but impoverished of the piquancy it transmits. Not just piquancy, but the word will have to do.

Most poets of late life heed "Time's wingèd chariot hurrying near." Here resides the reason for the paradoxical nature of late-life love poetry, which emphasizes the contradictory nature of desire for couples persistently linked through natural seasons and historical cycles. Awareness of transience can strengthen our human attachments, but human attachments heighten our awareness of transience. "No one in love really believes love will end," Anne Carson once stated in an analysis of a classical text. "They are astonished when they fall in love, they are equally astonished when they fall out of love." Yet lovers living on an implausible cusp know all too well that love will end and not because they have fallen out of love. This tradition—attentive to the brevity of our prospects—imagines not love against death, but love and death. Not W. H. Auden's "We must love one another or die" but his "We must love one another and die."

Anticipatory grief—not morbid, but vigilant—is betrothed to love in late life. I am undoubtedly a nudnik, but my broodings are not unprecedented. Maxine Kumin, in her beautiful poem "The Long Marriage," teaches me the compound German word *Torschlusspanik*: fear of time running out. "Every couple who stays together long enough," Alix Kates Shulman knows, "has intimations that a catastrophe is waiting."

As my dear dead friend Carolyn Heilbrun intuited, "We who grow old can taste the biting edge of passion's anticipated annulment, and savor it as the young cannot." Her remark reminds me of the mellow tints and tart tastes of ripe fruit and of all of Shakespeare's pronouncements about ripeness and readiness. Carolyn, with whom I frequently converse, would have objected to this book's emphasis on personal fulfillment not through courageous work or heady quests or tough-minded politics. I agree with her that women, historically programmed to depend on men, should seek independence. Yet too many aging women are relegated to loneliness, as are too many aging men. The social isolation of the elderly is toxic.

To brace myself against the miseries of moving, I sifted through all the stories and novels, poems and plays, memoirs and films in which later-life lovers cope in a multiplicity of ways with the degeneration of the body, the diminution of the libido, the permutations of eroticism, the prospects of a long past and a short future, the problems of controlling or covetous children and of retirement, the pangs and pleasures of caregiving, the storehouse of memories that have accrued over time or possibly diminished or disappeared, and the repercussions of earlier trauma.

The compendium of couples I have assembled sends a resounding retort to overwhelmingly negative valuations of aging. Not superannuated, the duffers and fogeys, grannies and codgers, fossils and dinosaurs I have found dislodge gloomy premises about old age, for they extol—amid the ordeals of aging—the mutuality and reciprocity, the passion and compassion at the heart of tender relationships in later life. They clamor in a crescendo, voicing variations on an indelible theme sounded by Charlie Smith in his poem "The Meaning of Birds":

> *Look around. Perhaps it isn't too late*
> *to make a fool of yourself again. Perhaps it isn't too late*
> *to flap your arms and cry out, to give*
> *one more cracked rendition of your singular, aspirant song.*

With splendid specificity, all the creative texts I have studied provide alternative models for thinking about aging. Scanty and eccentric though they may be, their tributes to love and friendship tell me that many stories have yet to be recounted. But there *is* a late-life love tradition, and it explores the manifold ways enduring passion sustains older people dedicated to prized partnerships and also to a range of desires: to keep on writing or reading, to go on seeing and savoring beloved places or works of art, to continue nurturing each other or progenitors or descendants, to prolong the kaleidoscope of fractured and reformed memories that accrue as a diminishing future is enhanced by a lengthening past that embellishes the present for those lucky enough to be loving while living in our final years.

Later

DURING THE FIRST third of 2016, I did not think that we would get out of the Inverness. In January, I fell on the driveway, trying to drag the garbage bin up to the road. I can still feel beneath my hands the shock of the icy glaze I had not seen on the asphalt. Throughout that winter and the start of spring, after Carrol and then Ilka died, I hauled myself around on a walker, while Don ominously lost thirty pounds along with the little strength he had accrued. (Julie put purple bling on my walker to distinguish it from Don's.)

Prospects were dismal by the time we got to Passover, when workers began anchoring the walls of the house to stop it from slipping off its foundation. The Inverness, it turns out, had been imperceptibly moving toward the ravine. With the help of physical therapy (for me) and thyroid medication (for Don) and a crew of laborers at the Inverness and also at the condo, we persevered. I began to discern a pattern in aging. It plunges us down precipitous drops, and then (if we are fortunate) we land at a lower plateau, where we stumble and fumble our way through the depleted but gratefully accepted next stage of being.

In that period, when the dumpster Julie predicted did appear and we started bagging and tossing what could not be given to friends or family or donated to charitable organizations, I was startled by the appearance of two new works about later-life love, both of which received rave reviews: Arlene Heyman's short story collection *Scary Old Sex* and Andrew Haigh's movie *45 Years*. Each title underscores themes I had pondered during the previous year.

The first suggests that sex between old people has always been deemed scary: creepy or sinister according to most cultural precepts and daunting or intimidating for those who want to engage in it. The second accentuates the idea that aging lovers become preoccupied with numerical calculations as we count, recount, and commemorate our years apart and together. While Don and I shed boxes of books, stashes of fabric, and sets of crockery, both titles deepened my realization that the older we are in our partnerships, the more past there is to thicken the tissue of the present. Call me an opsimath wannabe.

Especially in the unusually graphic descriptions of "The Loves of Her Life," the first tale in *Scary Old Sex*, Arlene Heyman distinguishes old, premeditated sex from young, spontaneous sex. The story describes the intricate planning that often prefaces lovemaking in later life. Because of acid reflux, sixty-five-year-old Marianne must stay upright for a few hours after any meal. Low levels of estrogen mean she needs various tablets and creams, while Viagra and antidepressants make seventy-year-old Stu feel spacey, and timing becomes important to him as well. Marianne reminds herself to suppress any sounds so that Stu won't ejaculate early, which generally happens unless he masturbates beforehand. "For them, making love was like running a war: plans had to be drawn up, equipment in tiptop condition, troops deployed and coordinated meticulously, there was no room for maverick actions lest the country end up defeated and at each other's throats. . . ."

Then there is the problem of the visual. With every wrinkle exposed on Stu's loose flesh, he resembles a figure in a Lucian Freud painting: sagging breasts and a penis that "looked like a small round neck with an eyeless face barely peeking out above his pouchlike scrotum." Dissatisfied with her own looks as well, Marianne sees bright-red raised spots on a torso reminiscent of her father's, the flesh hanging from her bony ass and thighs, the skin visible beneath her sparse pubic hair.

Arlene Heyman makes me consider how many people get into bed together when an older couple copulates. While Marianne and Stu use K-Y jelly and he performs oral sex, she thinks of her finger-painting granddaughter, her son, and her first husband, who had died unexpectedly. After Stu enters her, she rubs her clitoris and draws on a series of fantasies of herself at earlier stages of her life as she reaches orgasm, trying "very hard not to look pleased" so that Stu would not immediately ejaculate, which of course he does.

There are five people in the couple's bed, not counting her earlier avatars. The heads of older men and women are seemingly crowded with dead and alive people who rarely disappear, even when they ought to. The fact that the noun *clitoris* and variants on the verb *ejaculate* have not appeared before in my consideration of late-life love stories speaks volumes about late-life sex or about the reticence of most writers about late-life sex (including me, myself, and I).

That Marianne's discontent with her second husband reflects a more general discontent she had also conveyed to her first illuminates the final fantasy that closes this story, which reminds us that the primary sexual organ remains firmly positioned between the ears of people of all ages. For oldsters, it can play tricks with the past. At the end of "The Loves of Her Life," Marianne imagines having powerful sex with her thirty-seven-year-old son, who sports the blond hair he sprouted as a baby. Her own body as "taut as a young girl's" responds explosively as "they went on and on." Sex in old age, whether in the head or in the body, can shock us at the perversity of our desires, including the desire to regain the person we remember having been but maybe never were and in any case can never become again. In the senior years, true and false memories go to bed with bodies.

I had ordered a copy of *Scary Old Sex* as soon as it appeared, but I needed to wait until my assistants could obtain a copy of *45 Years*. That took several months, during which Project Divest went into overdrive. What to do with the painting of leeks and radishes, which needs a larger wall than any at the condo? An administrator responsible for artwork exhibited on Indiana University's campuses found a cooking and nutrition program in Kokomo that could give the vibrant canvas a home. The piano went to a young man starting up a school for children. Don donated his collection of three hundred 78 rpm records to a jazz writer who produces a local NPR program. Like the wingback chair, the blue couch was shaggy, but our housekeeper convinced us that she could profit by selling them. When Sandra arrived to introduce us to her new old partner, the Inverness had started emptying out.

Whereas the first part of 2016 was spent hobbled by disability, donating, dumping, shoring up walls at the Inverness, and pulling them down at the condo, the second half was spent unpacking and settling in . . . with Don and me and our friends increasingly fearful about the outcome of the presidential race, despite the optimistic polls.

On July 8, we moved into the Windermere apartment, which was filled with boxes. I worried that our courteous construction workers and movers were harboring deep resentments against the older woman running in a historic election. Don and I struggled to find the strength to unpack clothing, hang paintings, shelve books, and recycle cartons. Along with most of my cast of characters, who helped us survive the chaos of moving, we found it difficult to believe that a candidate spouting racist slogans and flaunting sexist practices was becoming the Republican nominee for president.

We did what we could to invoke the Inverness at the Windermere. The kitchen cabinets are white. Built-in bookshelves in Don's study resemble those in his old study. Julie found a blue couch on sale in a furniture store in town and a La-Z-Boy that looks like the wingback chair. Since the living room windows at the Inverness were bare, we bought shades for the condo that, when lifted, disappear. We used suction cups to affix a clear acrylic window birdfeeder. Warblers arrive, but no chartreuse finches or scarlet cardinals yet. Our bed in its wooden frame sits amid the same photographs of the children and grandchildren as it did in the country: Don is back on my right, me on his left. On Wednesday mornings, the beeping and whooshing and clanking of garbage and recycling trucks awaken me to the thrill that we have landed safely, though in old age we don't tempt the gods by crowing too loudly.

The phone in the condo rang on the bright morning of the closing on the Inverness, two hours before the legal transfer: a frantic call from Zak that the new owners could not get into the house for their final walk-through. Our housekeeper had dead-bolted the front door. I rushed Don into the car and drove for the last time down the highway, through the winding country roads, and finally along the driveway bordering the meadow. I parked next to the elephant trunk of the giant beech. Under a tulip pop-lar, several adults sat picnicking on a blanket with a baby and two toddlers. A man moved quickly toward us to shake hands. "Wel-come to the circle of beauty," I said, handing over a plastic bag with the keys. Standing in the verdant sunshine, I knew it would be my last sight of the place, but the beginning of a beautiful, new relationship for this young family.

There was much commotion about cataract surgeries for both Don and me, and also about the purchase of a sofa bed so that the kids could come to stay. There was great glee, at least on my part, about Don's snagging a disabled parking permit, though I am now the designated driver—his Honda has been sold—when we go to savor Brahms at Auer Hall or Mingus at Bear's Place. Inside the apartment, Don moves around without the cane and has resumed doing the laundry. I find a note in his minute hand-writing, though I don't know when or why he composed it: "The nearness of you." In the late afternoon, oblivious to queries, he sits with his headphones on, listening to his latest passion, Bud Powell, whose biography distresses him. In the evening, with a visitor describing her activism on behalf of the LGBTQIA community on campus, Don adds a new identity category: Lesbian, Gay, Bisexual, Transgender, Queer, Intersex, Asexual, and O for Old. If there are no guests, I concoct a meal of punctuation marks or draft a column while mixing my wine with water.

When our struggles with an Internet provider finally concluded, I could watch *45 Years*, a moving portrait of marriage with Charlotte Rampling playing the sixty-eight-year-old wife and Tom Courtenay the seventy-seven-year-old husband. *45 Years* broods on the unexpected crisis confronting a couple during the days leading up to and then at the party celebrating their forty-fifth wedding anniversary. The genius of the movie hinges on the explosive nature of a past occluded throughout the wide gap of half a century. It suggests that the twined and twinned intimacy treasured by aging couples can be detonated by revelations that sunder them.

The anguish of infidelity in Andrew Haigh's film has nothing to do with sex or adultery and everything to do with emotional obfuscation. When the incommunicative Jeff receives a notice that the remains of a former girlfriend, Katya, have been found preserved in a fissure of the Swiss Alps, he reminds Kate that he had told her about this affair, which occurred before they met. Does the youthful intensity of first love—encapsulated and conserved in memory—eclipse the quotidian pleasures of later-life love? A fissure results in the marriage as Kate struggles with her jealousy of a dead girl. While she prepares for the anniversary party, she begins a series of probing conversations with him—if Katya had lived, yes, Jeff would have married her—and eventually Kate starts sleuthing. A climb up the attic stairs leads to the discovery of color slides that she projects onto a hanging sheet. Blurry, the images present a pregnant Katya.

Old photographs beamed in contemporary settings hint that the present remains a palimpsest: current scenes layered with ghostly traces of earlier scenes. Unbeknownst to Kate, her marriage has been haunted by Jeff's youthful love affair. The shock of seeing a picture of the pregnant Katya renders ominous Kate's childlessness. Had Jeff influenced her against having children because of Katya's and his never-mentioned lost baby? Kate had thought about her marriage that there were two of them, but really there had been three . . . and the promise of a fourth. Katya had the aura of the original, Kate has the replacement value of a copy. As she goes on her daily rounds, Rampling's face registers the sorrow of a loving wife losing faith in the most important relationship of her life.

Upon her arrival at the crowded party, Kate looks at a collage of photographs on a picture board crafted by her best friend, images that she and Jeff had failed to preserve. After toasts, as she and Jeff are dancing, the alarming footage that concludes the movie captures Kate's baffled hurt. Jeff lifts their clasped hands, but she jerks her hand away. The unclasped hands hint at the ongoing pain of irreconcilability, clarifying why I have stowed photographs of Fran inside a desk drawer in my tiny study. The aging

Kate may never achieve the numinous magnetism of the always youthful and lost Katya in Jeff's psyche and now in her own as well. Kate reminds me of James Joyce's character Gabriel Conroy in "The Dead," who judges himself inferior to his wife's first lover, the dead Michael Furey. In her startled distress, she nevertheless proves how passionate she remains. Yanking her hand free, she does not submit to her fate compliantly.

45 Years is a disturbing postscript that I would not have chosen for my conclusion. Yet I had determined to follow the art where it would lead, and somehow it picked me. I finished a draft of this manuscript in circumstances I would also never have chosen: the 2016 election. For someone with my family background, Donald Trump's victory on the anniversary of Kristallnacht resonated ominously with events in Germany during the 1930s. In the story on which *45 Years* is based, David Constantine's "In Another Country," Katya is a Jewish girl trying to escape Bavaria, her parents "very likely dead long before they died of age." Love of country permeates many stories of late-life love. Older people, settled, cannot imagine tearing themselves away from the beloved land of their origins. My paternal grandparents died before they had the opportunity to die of old age in Hamburg.

The movie *45 Years* and the story on which it is based and, for that matter, the political upheaval in November manifest the fragility of long-lasting unions—indeed, the gravity of losing faith in a coalition that constitutes the grounds of an adult existence, whether it be the institution of marriage or the Constitution of the United States: both based on the ideal of "Liberty and Union, now and forever, one and inseparable." But of course my shock at Trump's win cannot be equated with Kate's anguish. They just happened to happen simultaneously.

Still, the political situation unleashed free-floating trepidation. I determined to use my *Times* essays to argue against cuts in health care and cancer research, but the idea of a cockamamie Trump administration seemed terrifying. The vertiginous idiocy of politics propelled me inward, focusing my attention on revising this account, which seeks to emphasize aspirations that remain meaningful to us as individuals. Retreating to the private realm does not relieve my apprehension about the public catastrophe, however. That I am beginning to comprehend the need for detachment makes me feel worse about myself. But detachment may be what we need to cultivate in old age, as we come to terms with divesting ourselves of houses or cars, autonomy or strength, as we reinvest ourselves in what remains.

Only later still did my friend Jonathan lead me to a gem in the late-life love tradition and the conviction that I had barely scratched the surface. With its minute attention to every passing sensation of fervor, jealousy, attraction, delight, and abandon, Guy de Maupassant's 1890 novel *Like Death* seems eminently French if not Proustian in its analysis of the durability and mutability of passion. Maupassant's aging couple comes to believe that "It's the fault of our hearts that have not grown old": "It is only at our age that one loves desperately."

Age cannot wither love, nor custom stale its infinity variety, for Eros does not hate old age, and never did. Nor are older people unsexed; we are sexed differently, or so I came to understand during a fraught confinement that turned into an intensive reading retreat. A punning, broken sentence by Charles Olson sums up my coming-of-age story: "I have had to learn the simplest things / last." Perhaps Elizabeth Bishop put my conclusion best in an admission to her last, younger lover: "The poor heart doesn't seem to grow old at all."

Even if most theorists of love exhibit myopia about late-life love, Roland Barthes makes an important point: "A long chain of equivalences links all the lovers in the world." He finds it "scarcely adequate to say I project myself," for "I cling to the very image" of the lovers found in art. Maybe if Barthes had lived longer, he would have read some of the texts that have linked me with a succession of fictional couples who have proliferated from the times of Ovid and Shakespeare. I cling to the resilience of these aging partners' intimacy. When we integrate old lovers into the "long chain of equivalences link[ing] all the lovers in the world," our ideas of agape, eros, philia, and storge become more capacious, for these types of love, which root us in the world, blend and blur into each other.

While I sit in a postage-stamp-size study overlooking the most grotesque, stubby tree I have ever in my life seen, I consider all the friends who have helped Don and me, realizing how many different sorts of love impel them: Jayne's love of her mother, Jan's love of painting, Shehira's love of her son, George's love of birds, Sandra's love of poetry, opera, and jokes. Jonathan, Alexandra, Judith, Mary, Dyan, and Julie have not yet attained late life, but their loves seem similarly variegated, though their opinions on the tree remain divided.

I had first thought the evergreen outside my study was a hybrid. Short and stocky, it has a fuzzy rounded bottom, but toward the top bristling branches stick out on two sides like the limbs of a Christmas tree or, oddly, antlers on a hat. One day Julie brought over landscapers who explained it was a dwarf Alberta conifer that has started reverting to a Canadian spruce. It was mutating back to its original form. "Not a case of graft incompatibility," they said. "Not two trees, but one that refused engineering. Easy to take down." I'm living with it for now. I admire its ugly tenacity.

In the new kitchen after Thanksgiving, I was rattled by finding the wishbone splintered in the turkey stock.

"Bear, who do you think will go first?"

"My money is on me. You had your chance."

I thought about my voluminous reading over the past two years and came up with the one response that made sense to me.

"Chirp," I said.

Notes

THANKSGIVING

7 The famous lovers are at the respective centers of Homer's *Iliad*, Shakespeare's *Romeo and Juliet*, and Jane Austen's *Pride and Prejudice*. George Eliot's *Middlemarch* was published in 1871–72.

7 Lady Wishfort appears in William Congreve's play *The Way of the World*.

7 The *senex amans* (amorous old man) tradition is discussed by Christopher Martin in *Constituting Old Age in Early Modern English Literature, from Queen Elizabeth to "King Lear"* (University of Massachusetts Press, 2012), p. 103. Georges Minois describes detestable old debauchers in Latin literature: *History of Old Age: From Antiquity to the Renaissance*, translated by Sarah Hanbury Tenison (University of Chicago Press, 1989), pp. 92–95, and discusses detestably desirous old women on pp. 98–100. In the early Middle Ages, Minois argues, "Old people who engaged in debauchery were far more guilty than the young" (p. 123).

7 Plato, *Symposium*, translated by Walter Hamilton (Penguin, 1951), p. 68.

7 On Greek associations concerning love and age, see Thomas M. Falkner, *The Poetics of Old Age in Greek Epic, Lyric, and Tragedy* (University of Oklahoma Press, 1995). His discussion of *The Symposium* begins in chapter 4 (pp. 108–52), which focuses on early Greek poetry. The best book on how Greek philosophy conceptualizes aging is Helen Small's *The Long Life*

(Oxford University Press, 2007). Cicero and Seneca articulate the idea that desire evaporates in people as their capacity to satisfy it diminishes. For Cicero, "the highest praise of old age" consists in the fact that "it does not greatly long for any pleasures." According to Seneca, "One might say that no longer feeling the need for pleasure takes the place of pleasure itself." Both are discussed in Karen Chase, *The Victorians and Old Age* (Oxford University Press, 2009), pp. 210–11.

8 Karen Chase discusses "'senile' sexuality" with respect to the Victorian period in an essay of that title in *Interdisciplinary Perspectives on Aging in Nineteenth-Century Culture*, edited by Katharina Boehm, Anna Farkas, and Anne-Julia Zwierlein (Routledge, 2014), pp. 132–46.

8 "Abhorrent old age": The chorus of Sophocles' *Oedipus at Colonus*, lines 1236–38, is quoted by Stephen Bertman in "The Ashes and the Flame: Passion and Aging in Classical Poetry," in *Old Age in Greek and Latin Literature*, edited by Thomas M. Falkner and Judith de Luce (State University of New York Press, 1989), p. 160.

8 A classicist has informed me that *anus* (old lady) and *anus* (fundament, anus) are Latin homographs—words that are spelled the same but are pronounced differently.

9 The verse by Martial is translated by Palmer Bovie and quoted by Bertman, "The Ashes and the Flame," pp. 165–66.

9 Michel de Montaigne, "On Certain Verses of Virgil," in *The Essays of Montaigne*, translated by Jacob Zeitlin (Alfred A. Knopf, 1934), book 2, pp. 48–106; quotations, p. 104.

10 Isaac Bashevis Singer, introduction to *Old Love* (1979; reprint, Penguin, 1982), p. 7. One obvious exception to Singer's generalization is Daniel Defoe's Moll Flanders.

11 Jenny Diski, *Happily Ever After* (Penguin, 1991), pp. 131, 132.

11 "A *pas de deux* with desire": Diski, *Happily Ever After*, pp. 133, 133–34, 139, 140.

12 "The mad woman in the attic": Diski, *Happily Ever After*, pp. 54, 23, 20.

13 Many books about aging agree with the foundational argument made by Simone de Beauvoir in *La Vieillesse* (translated in Britain as *Old Age* but in America as *The Coming of Age*). According to Beauvoir, to be old is to be "the other," estranged from ourselves and certainly from anyone who views us as old. On Beauvoir's later-life relationships with Claude

Lanzmann and Sylvie Le Bon (later Sylvie Le Bon de Beauvoir), see Bethany Ladimer, *Colette, Beauvoir, and Duras: Age and Women Writers* (University Press of Florida, 1999), pp. 106–28, 139–40. On the later life of Georgia O'Keeffe, see Charlotte Cowles, "Exclusive: Georgia O'Keeffe's Younger Man," *Harper's Bazaar*, 24 Feb. 2016, www.harpersbazaar.com/culture/features/a14033/georgia-okeeffe-0316/. On Frederick Douglass, see John Stauffer, *Giants: The Parallel Lives of Frederick Douglass and Abraham Lincoln* (Twelve, 2008), pp. 313–14.

13 *When Harry Met Sally*, directed by Rob Reiner (Castle Rock, 1989). The number of people over fifty who cohabit with an unmarried partner increased 75 percent from 2007 to 2016: Paula Span quotes the Pew Research Center's findings in "More Older Couples Are 'Shacking Up,'" *New York Times*, 8 May 2017, www.nytimes.com/2017/05/08/health/older-americans-unmarried-couples.html.

13 Eve Pell, *Love, Again: The Wisdom of Unexpected Romance* (Ballantine, 2014), pp. 6, 161. See also the interviews in Connie Goldman, *Late-Life Love: Romances and New Relationships in Later Life* (Fairview Press, 2006).

14 On Our Time, see Helen Fisher, *Anatomy of Love: A Natural History of Mating, Marriage, and Why We Stray* (W. W. Norton, 2016), p. 315. Roger Angell, "This Old Man," in *This Old Man: All in Pieces* (Doubleday, 2015), pp. 280–81, 276, 278.

15 Average life expectancy: See Maggie Scarf, *September Songs: The Good News about Marriage in the Later Years* (Riverhead Books, 2008), p. 25.

15 Joyce Carol Oates, "Deep Reader: Rebecca Mead's 'My Life in *Middlemarch*,'" *New York Times*, 23 Jan. 2014, www.nytimes.com/2014/01/26/books/review/rebecca-meads-my-life-in-middlemarch.html.

15 Harold Bloom, *The Daemon Knows: Literary Greatness and the American Sublime* (Spiegel & Grau, 2015), p. 49.

A SECOND CHANCE

18 Helen Simonson, *Major Pettigrew's Last Stand* (2010; reprint, Random House Trade Paperbacks, 2011).

21 Roland Barthes, *A Lover's Discourse: Fragments*, translated by Richard Howard (1978; reprint, Penguin, 1990), p. 192.

21 "Level above mere pleasant acquaintance": Simonson, *Major Pettigrew's Last Stand*, p. 111.

22 "A welcoming goddess": Simonson, *Major Pettigrew's Last Stand*, p. 155.

23 "A boy could be forgiven": Simonson, *Major Pettigrew's Last Stand*, p. 232.

27 Jane Juska, *A Round-Heeled Woman: My Late-Life Adventures in Sex and Romance* (Villard Books, 2003), p. 12. *Round-heeled* is old-fashioned slang, meaning "promiscuous."

27 *Autumn Tale*, directed by Eric Rohmer (La Sept Cinéma, 1998).

27 On the particular difficulties facing older, widowed, or divorced women, see the chapter "Intimacy beyond the Dreams of Youth," in Betty Friedan, *The Fountain of Age* (Simon & Schuster, 1993), especially pp. 256–71.

29 Dyan Elliott's (unpublished) song is titled "Rampage."

SIGNS OF DECLINE

31 Louis MacNeice, "Bagpipe Music," in *Collected Poems*, edited by E. R. Dodds (Faber and Faber, 1979), pp. 96–97. The actual quotation is "But if you break the bloody glass you won't hold up the weather."

32 On Freud and aging, see Kathleen Woodward, *Aging and Its Discontents: Freud and Other Fictions* (Indiana University Press, 1991), p. 29. She also revises Jacques Lacan's idea of the infant's mirror stage to analyze "the mirror stage of old age," in which the aging person dis-identifies with an image in the mirror that figures disintegration and dependency (see p. 67).

33 "For the sake of these guns": Helen Simonson, *Major Pettigrew's Last Stand* (2010; reprint, Random House Trade Paperbacks, 2011), p. 341.

34 In a chapter titled "Age Anxiety in the Male Midlife Marriage Plot," in *Aging by the Book: The Emergence of Midlife in Victorian Britain* (State University of New York Press, 2009), Kay Heath discusses the two Trollope novels in detail as well as other older and self-doubting fictional male suitors who suffer from insecurity about being inappropriate suitors (see pp. 25–72).

35 *The Lunchbox*, directed by Ritesh Batra (Sikhya Entertainment, 2013).

35 Fay Weldon, *Rhode Island Blues* (Grove/Atlantic, 2000), p. 131.

36 "An indignity and an absurdity": Weldon, *Rhode Island Blues*, pp. 245, 230, 263.

39 Jane Smiley, *At Paradise Gate* (1981; reprint, Scribner Paperback Fiction, 1998), p. 216.

39 Robert Kraus, *Leo the Late Bloomer* (HarperCollins, 1971).

40 "What to make": Robert Frost, "The Oven Bird," in *The Poetry of Robert Frost*, edited by Edward Connery Lathem (Holt, Rinehart and Winston, 1969), p. 120.

FALLING IN LOVE

44 Elizabeth Barrett Browning, *Sonnets from the Portuguese* (1850; reprint, Thomas Y. Crowell, 1936). The sequence can also be read in its entirety on the Web. See the excellent scholarly interpreters of Elizabeth Barrett Browning, especially Helen Cooper, Sandra M. Gilbert, Erik Gray, Angela Leighton, Tricia Lootens, Dorothy Mermin, Mary Sanders Pollock, Glennis Stephenson, and Rhian Williams.

54 Roz Chast, *Can't We Talk about Something More Pleasant?* (Bloomsbury USA, 2014).

55 Anne Bradstreet, "To My Dear and Loving Husband," in *The Norton Anthology of Literature by Women: The Traditions in English*, edited by Sandra M. Gilbert and Susan Gubar, 3rd ed. (W. W. Norton, 2007), 1:153; see also "A Letter to Her Husband, Absent upon Public Employment," p. 153. Katherine Philips, "To Mrs. M.A. at Parting," in *The Norton Anthology of Literature by Women*, 1:171 (ll. 49–50).

57 The lines by Robert Browning begin his 1864 poem "Rabbi Ben Ezra": see *Rabbi Ben Ezra*, edited by William Adams Slade (T. Y. Crowell, 1902), pp. 27–37. The poem can be read in its entirety on the Web.

THE TRACE

60 Philip Larkin, "The Old Fools," in *The Complete Poems*, edited by Archie Burnett (Farrar, Straus and Giroux, 2012), pp. 81–82. See also W. H. Auden, "Old People's Home," in *The Oxford Book of Aging*, edited by Thomas R. Cole and Mary G. Winkler (Oxford University Press, 1994), pp. 334–45.

60 "Sans teeth": Jacques's speech on the last stage of the seven ages of man in

Shakespeare's *As You Like It*, edited by Juliet Dusinberre (Arden Shakespeare, 2006), 2.7.170.

61 Juvenal is translated by Rolfe Humphries and quoted in Stephen Bertman, "The Ashes and the Flame: Passion and Aging in Classical Poetry," in *Old Age in Greek and Latin Literature*, edited by Thomas M. Falkner and Judith de Luce (State University of New York Press, 1989), p. 163.

61 Jane Austen did include a happily married midlife couple, the Crofts, in her last novel, *Persuasion* (1817), which charts an autumnal story of a second-chance romance for its central character. For Philip Larkin, see "Annus Mirabilis," in *The Complete Poems*, p. 90.

62 *The King and I*, directed by Walter Lang (Twentieth Century Fox, 1956); the King was played by Yul Brynner.

66 Isaac Bashevis Singer, "Old Love," in *Passions, and Other Stories* (Farrar, Straus and Giroux, 1975), pp. 24–42; quotations, pp. 31, 33.

67 "Wait till we've stood": Singer, "Old Love," p. 37.

67 "Dear Harry, forgive me": Singer, "Old Love," p. 42.

67 Ludwig van Beethoven, *Fidelio*, performance by the Chicago Symphony Orchestra and Chorus, conducted by Sir Georg Solti, London Records, 1979.

69 A musicologist: Paul Robinson, *Ludwig van Beethoven: "Fidelio"* (Cambridge University Press, 1996), pp. 69, 97.

71 C. S. Lewis, *A Grief Observed* (1961; reprint, HarperSanFrancisco, 1989), p. 25.

71 "Even if we both died": Lewis, *A Grief Observed*, p. 26.

71 "Probably have recurrent pains": Lewis, *A Grief Observed*, pp. 65–66.

PROPS

74 "Shake me up, Judy": Mr. Smallweed's refrain in Charles Dickens's *Bleak House* (1852–53).

75 Dickens's aged flirt Cleopatra: Charles Dickens, *Dombey and Sons* (1848), edited by Andrew Sanders (Penguin Classics, 2002), p. 431.

77 "There is so little one can do": Samuel Beckett, *Happy Days: A Play in Two Acts* (1961; reprint, Grove Press, 1989), pp. 24, 26.

78 "Not head first, stupid": Beckett, *Happy Days*, pp. 27, 25.

78 "We had no toolshed": Beckett, *Happy Days*, pp. 19, 37.

81 "What's the idea?": Beckett, *Happy Days*, p. 44.

82 "To know that in theory": Beckett, *Happy Days*, p. 29.

82 "Always full of cries": Beckett, *Happy Days*, pp. 61, 64.

83 "Eggs" and "Formication": Beckett, *Happy Days*, pp. 32, 66, 68, 55.

83 "Don't look at me like that!": Beckett, *Happy Days*, p. 68.

83 "Every touch of fingers": Beckett, *Happy Days*, pp. 69, 15.

85 Zadie Smith, *On Beauty* (Penguin, 2005), p. 56. "Say goodnight, Gracie": The sign-off (with the response "Goodnight") of the popular comedy team George Burns and Gracie Allen, from their 1950s television show. The later duo Dan Rowan and Dick Martin, famous for *Laugh-in*, did add to the joke by signing off "Say goodnight, Dick." "Goodnight Dick."

86 Old lovers know: The literary critic who argues most stringently against the commonly held idea that "love is invulnerable to the instabilities of narrative or history, and is a beautifully shaped web of lyrical mutuality," is Lauren Berlant in *Desire/Love* (Punctum Books, 2012); quotation, p. 92.

86 "Sucked up" into "the blue": Beckett, *Happy Days*, p. 36.

86 "To have been always": Beckett, *Happy Days*, p. 56.

86 Kathleen Woodward discusses Malone's exercise book in Beckett's 1951 novel *Malone Dies* as a transitional object, associating it with "his last not-me possession," in *Aging and Its Discontents: Freud and Other Fictions* (Indiana University Press, 1991), p. 142.

ALTERATIONS

92 Rebecca Mead, *My Life in "Middlemarch"* (Crown Publishers, 2014), p. 16.

92 Alan Bennett's play *The History Boys* was made into a 2006 movie directed by Nicholas Hytner (Fox Searchlight Pictures); the quoted observation is spoken in act 2 by a literature teacher.

92 Ovid, *Metamorphosis: A New Translation, Contexts, Criticism*, translated and edited by Charles Martin (W. W. Norton, 2010); for the story of Baucis and Philemon, in book 8, see pp. 222–26. Line numbers are given in parentheses in the text.

93 Roland Barthes, *A Lover's Discourse: Fragments*, translated by Richard Howard (1978; reprint, Penguin, 1990), p. 116.

94 The elderly couple appeared in "The Joys of Love: never forgot. A SONG,"

The Gentleman's Magazine, March 1735, p. 153, a poem often attributed to Henry Woodfall; Darby and Joan clubs for seniors proliferated in the United Kingdom in the twentieth century.

96 Jhumpa Lahiri, *In Other Words*, translated by Ann Goldstein (Knopf, 2016), p. 163. Lahiri also discusses Ovid's tales in "Teach Yourself Italian," *New Yorker*, 7 Dec. 2015, pp. 30–36.

97 Eve Kosofsky Sedgwick, "Advanced Degree: School Yourself in Resilience to Beat Depression," *Mamm Magazine*, Sept. 2000, p. 24.

99 A. R. Ammons, "In View of the Fact," in *Bosh and Flapdoodle* (W. W. Norton, 2005), pp. 29–30.

101 "Who would have thought": George Herbert, "The Flower," in *The Complete English Poems*, edited by John Tobin (Penguin Classics, 1991), p. 156.

102 On long partnerships: Richard Hoggart, *First and Last Things* (1999; reprint, Transaction Publications, 2002), p. 172.

102 Molly Haskell, *Love and Other Infectious Diseases: A Memoir* (Morrow, 1990), p. 280.

LOVESICKNESS

106 "Gerontophobia": Gabriel García Márquez, *Love in the Time of Cholera*, translated by Edith Grossman (1988; reprint, Vintage Books, 2003), pp. 37, 26.

107 "Inflamed their feelings": García Márquez, *Love in the Time of Cholera*, pp. 28, 29.

107 of Dr. Urbino's "stallion's stream": García Márquez, *Love in the Time of Cholera*, pp. 30, 40, 238.

108 "The disadvantage of being ten years ahead": García Márquez, *Love in the Time of Cholera*, p. 224.

109 "With the control and the courage": García Márquez, *Love in the Time of Cholera*, p. 47.

110 "For more than half a century": García Márquez, *Love in the Time of Cholera*, pp. 50, 51.

110 "Fifty-one years": García Márquez, *Love in the Time of Cholera*, p. 53.

111 "Frenetic correspondence": García Márquez, *Love in the Time of Cholera*, pp. 71, 83, 102, 129.

111 "He had some twenty-five notebooks": García Márquez, *Love in the Time*

of Cholera, pp. 152, 197. On the game of love, see John Alan Lee, *Colours of Love: An Exploration of the Ways of Loving* (New Press, 1973), especially his discussion of "Ludus," the form of love that becomes a contest challenging the lover's skills (pp. 57–76).

112 "One hundred and seventy-two infallible cures": García Márquez, *Love in the Time of Cholera*, pp. 262, 263, 277, 293.

112 "Intestines suddenly filled": García Márquez, *Love in the Time of Cholera*, pp. 304, 314, 327.

113 "Two icy fingers": García Márquez, *Love in the Time of Cholera*, pp. 329, 335, 338, 339.

113 "Final step": García Márquez, *Love in the Time of Cholera*, p. 340.

113 "They made the tranquil, wholesome love": García Márquez, *Love in the Time of Cholera*, p. 345.

114 "A little cosmos": Roland Barthes, *A Lover's Discourse: Fragments*, translated by Richard Howard (1978; reprint, Penguin, 1990), p. 139.

114 John Betjeman, "Late-Life Lust," in *Collected Poems* (1958; reprint, John Murray, 2006), pp. 171–72.

115 "Calcinated flatlands": García Márquez, *Love in the Time of Cholera*, p. 336.

115 "Clouded by his passion": García Márquez, *Love in the Time of Cholera*, pp. 337, 62, 152.

116 Stendhal, *On Love* (1822), translated by H.B.V. under the direction of C. K. Scott-Moncrieff (Grosset & Dunlap, 1947), p. 16; he also writes, "The moment he falls in love . . . even the wisest man no longer sees anything as it really is" (p. 34). Robert Graves, "Symptoms of Love" in *The Penguin Book of Love Poetry*, edited by Jon Stallworthy (Penguin, 1973), p. 45. Robert Lowell calls love "The whirlwind, this delirium of Eros" in "Wind," in *Notebook* (Faber and Faber, 1970), p. 160. Barthes, *A Lover's Discourse*, pp. 120, 128. Anne Carson discusses the classical poets who associate desire with lack in *Eros the Bittersweet: An Essay* (Princeton University Press, 1986), p. 148.

116 García Márquez, *Love in the Time of Cholera*, p. 293.

117 On setting a "trap" for the reader, see Raymond Leslie Williams, "The Visual Arts, the Poeticization of Space and Writing: An Interview with Gabriel García Márquez," *PMLA* 104 (1989): 136.

119 See not only Thomas Mann's *Death in Venice*, translated by Stanley Apple-

baum (Dover, 1995), but also "The Black Swan," in *Mario and the Magician and Other Stories*, translated by H. T. Lowe-Porter (Vintage, 2000), pp. 299–366. In the second text, the flowering of late-life love is associated with gynecological cancer.

WHAT'S LOVE GOT TO DO WITH IT?

122 Olimpia Zuleta, who "preferred to remain naked": Gabriel García Márquez, *Love in the Time of Cholera*, translated by Edith Grossman (1988; reprint, Vintage Books, 2003), p. 217.

123 "Entrusted by her family": García Márquez, *Love in the Time of Cholera*, pp. 272, 274.

123 "She cut him into pieces": García Márquez, *Love in the Time of Cholera*, pp. 296, 336.

124 "A deluxe servant": García Márquez, *Love in the Time of Cholera*, p. 221.

124 D. H. Lawrence, *Women in Love* (1920), new ed. (Penguin Classics, 2007), p. 352. John Bayley, *Elegy for Iris* (Picador, 1999), p. 44.

125 An "elegant, large-boned mulatta": García Márquez, *Love in the Time of Cholera*, pp. 240, 241, 243.

125 "Panic-stricken love": García Márquez, *Love in the Time of Cholera*, pp. 246, 250.

126 "Black, young, pretty, but a whore": García Márquez, *Love in the Time of Cholera*, p. 182.

129 The meaning of the word *frottage* has been analyzed in Brian Blanchfield's essay "On Frottage," in *Proxies: Essays Near Knowing* (Nightboat Books, 2016), pp. 109–19.

132 Charles Wright, "The Woodpecker Pecks, but the Hole Does Not Appear," in *Scar Tissue* (Farrar, Straus and Giroux, 2006), p. 68.

LATE-LIFE LECHERY

133 Leslie A. Fiedler, *Love and Death in the American Novel*, rev. ed. (1966; reprint, Dalkey Archive Press, 1984).

135 "The delightful imbecility of lust": Philip Roth, *The Dying Animal* (2001; reprint, Vintage International, 2002), p. 15.

135 The sexless matrimonial "cage": Roth, *The Dying Animal*, pp. 24, 51, 69.

136 "Sleek pubic hair": Roth, *The Dying Animal*, pp. 28, 37, 38, 32.

136 "The force of her youth": Roth, *The Dying Animal*, pp. 34, 41, 29, 32.

136 In Chaucer's Merchant's Tale, the gods intervene to reveal the sexual betrayal, but May persuades her husband not to believe his newly restored eyesight. See *The Canterbury Tales*, translated by David Wright, new ed. (Oxford University Press, 2011), pp. 245–73.

136 "The pornography of jealousy": Roth, *The Dying Animal*, pp. 41, 94.

137 "Attachment *is* my enemy": Roth, *The Dying Animal*, pp. 100, 89.

138 "Ruined" by surgery: Roth, *The Dying Animal*, pp. 131, 134, 135, 148.

139 The nameless companion says, "Don't" : Roth, *The Dying Animal*, p. 156.

143 David Foster Wallace, "John Updike, Champion Literary Phallocrat, Drops One: Is This Finally the End for Magnificent Narcissists?," *Observer*, 13 Oct. 1997, http://observer.com/1997/10/john-updike-champion -literary-phallocrat-drops-one-is-this-finally-the-end-for-magnificent-narcissists/.

144 "The worst thing you've ever done": John Updike, *Rabbit at Rest* (Random House, 1990), pp. 497, 396.

144 Harry had "been afraid": Updike, *Rabbit at Rest*, pp. 407, 407–8, 203.

145 Junichiro Tanizaki, *Diary of a Mad Old Man*, translated by Howard Hibbett (1965; reprint, Perigee Book, Putnam's Sons, 1965), p. 5.

SUNSETS

148 Desiderius Erasmus, *The Praise of Folly* (1509), translated with an introduction and commentary by Clarence H. Miller (Yale University Press, 1979), pp. 48–49.

149 On the girl given as a gift by the father to the husband, see Gayle Rubin, "The Traffic in Women: Notes on the 'Political Economy' of Sex" (1975), in *The Second Wave: A Reader in Feminist Theory*, edited by Linda Nicholson (Routledge, 1997), pp. 27–62.

149 Susan Sontag, "The Double Standard of Aging," in *No Longer Young: The Older Woman in America: Proceedings of the 26th Annual Conference on Aging*, edited by Pauline B. Bart et al. (Institute of Gerontology, University of Michigan–Wayne State University, 1975), pp. 31–39.

150 Zora Neale Hurston, *Their Eyes Were Watching God* (1937; reprint, Harper Perennial, 2006), p. 2. Hurston's unusual depiction of Janie Crawford and

Tea Cake makes it clear that the heroine worries about their age difference, though it hardly plays a role in his response.

150 *Sunset Boulevard*, directed by Billy Wilder (Paramount, 1950). The best book on representations of cross-age relationships throughout history is Lois W. Banner, *In Full Flower: Aging Women, Power, and Sexuality* (Knopf, 1992). Her chapter on *Sunset Boulevard* (pp. 30–55) is especially nuanced about the casting of the characters.

151 Erica Jong, *Fear of Dying* (St. Martin's Press, 2015), pp. 26, 151.

151 Sontag, "The Double Standard of Aging," p. 34.

152 *Harold and Maude*, directed by Hal Ashby (Paramount Pictures, 1971).

152 Ursula K. Le Guin, "Dogs, Cats, and Dancers: Thoughts about Beauty," in *The Wave in the Mind: Talks and Essays on the Writer, the Reader, and the Imagination* (Shambhala, 2004), p. 163.

153 "Pink and white": Colette, *"Chéri," and "The Last of Chéri,"* translated by Roger Senhouse with an introduction by Judith Thurman (Farrar, Straus and Giroux, 2001), pp. 8, 21, 24, 83.

153 Mae West, speaking as the character Ruby Carter in *Belle of the Nineties*, directed by Leo McCarey (Paramount Pictures, 1934).

153 Benjamin Franklin, "Old Mistresses Apologue" (25 June 1745), in *The Papers of Benjamin Franklin*, vol. 3, edited by Leonard W. Labaree (Yale University Press, 1961), pp. 27–31; quotation, p. 31.

153 "Walked with difficulty": Colette, *"Chéri," and "The Last of Chéri,"* p. 56.

154 Bodies "joined together": Colette, *"Chéri," and "The Last of Chéri,"* pp. 133, 136, 145, 150, 153.

156 "She was not monstrous": Colette, *"Chéri," and "The Last of Chéri,"* pp. 215, 221, 223.

156 "Unsexed" in old age: Colette, *"Chéri," and "The Last of Chéri,"* p. 228; Michel de Montaigne, "On Certain Verses of Virgil," in *The Essays of Montaigne*, translated by Jacob Zeitlin (Alfred A. Knopf, 1934), book 2, p. 104.

156 "I should have made": Colette, *"Chéri," and "The Last of Chéri,"* p. 152.

157 Doris Lessing, "The Grandmothers," in *The Grandmothers* (2003; reprint, Harper Perennial, 2005), pp. 3–56. In this story, two friends take each other's sons as lovers.

158 Judith Thurman, *Secrets of the Flesh: A Life of Colette* (Knopf, 1999), pp. 307, 285.

158 Doris Lessing, *Love, Again* (Flamingo, 1996), pp. 136, 337.

159 *Clouds of Sils Maria*, directed by Olivier Assayas (CG Cinéma, 2014), with performances by Juliette Binoche, Kristen Stewart, and Chloë Grace Moretz.

159 Jong, *Fear of Dying*, p. 8; Marge Piercy, *He, She and It* (1991; reprint, Ballantine Books, 1993), p. 162.

159 Lessing, *Love, Again*, pp. 33, 338–39. The 1950s lesbian cult classic *The Price of Salt*, by Patricia Highsmith, revolves around a midlife woman and a younger woman, as does its 2015 movie adaptation, *Carol*. Significantly, what threatens the relationship is the contested custody of the older woman's child.

160 Muriel Rukeyser composed a terrific answer to the Sphinx's riddle in "Myth," in *The Collected Poems of Muriel Rukeyser*, edited by Janet E. Kaufman and Anne F. Herzog (University of Pittsburgh Press, 2005), p. 480.

160 Fyodor Tyutchev, "Last Love," translated by Vladimir Nabokov, in *The Penguin Book of Love Poetry*, edited by Jon Stallworthy (Penguin, 1973), pp. 183–84.

CUPIDITY

165 "She grabbed his erection": Louis Begley, *About Schmidt* (1996; reprint, Ballantine Books, 1997), p. 187.

166 "Had become paternal": Louis Begley, *Schmidt Steps Back* (2012; reprint, Ballantine Books, 2013), p. 196.

166 Louis Begley, *Schmidt Delivered* (2000; reprint, Ballantine Books, 2001), p. 249. Phyllis Rose, "An Ordinary Bigot," *New York Times*, 22 Sept. 1996.

166 John Wilmot, Earl of Rochester, "A Song of a Young Lady to Her Ancient Lover," in *The Penguin Book of Love Poetry*, edited by Jon Stallworthy (Penguin, 1973), p. 182.

167 Galway Kinnell, "Oatmeal," in *A New Selected Poetry* (Houghton Mifflin, 2000), pp. 137–38.

171 Sandra M. Gilbert's short story "Shiksa" has not yet been published.

171 Orson Welles is quoted in Keith Uhlich's review of *Make Way for Tomorrow* (dir. Leo McCarey), in *Slant Magazine*, 8 July 2004, www

.slantmagazine.com/film/review/make-way-for-tomorrow. Inspired by *Make Way for Tomorrow*, Yosujiro Ozu's masterpiece *Tokyo Story* (1953) depicts a long-married couple who visit adult children too busy to find time for them.

171 "The temptation to disinherit": Begley, *Schmidt Steps Back*, p. 219.

172 Kent Haruf, *Our Souls at Night* (2015; reprint, Vintage Contemporaries, 2016), pp. 5, 147, 152. The movie—starring Robert Redford and Jane Fonda—appeared in 2017, directed by Ritesh Batra.

172 "I want you to stay away": Haruf, *Our Souls at Night*, p. 164.

173 "Late-onset puppy love": Begley, *Schmidt Steps Back*, pp. 14, 16.

174 "Night in the sack": Begley, *Schmidt Steps Back*, pp. 262, 291, 290.

175 Shirley MacLaine and Christopher Plummer star in *Elsa and Fred*, directed by Michael Radford (Cuatro Plus Films, 2014), a remake of Marcos Carnevale's 2005 Argentine original.

175 He "wasn't sure he had heard": Begley, *Schmidt Steps Back*, p. 218. The Renaissance adage is quoted by Philip D. Collington in "Sans Wife: Sexual Anxiety and the Old Man in Shakespeare," in *Growing Old in Early Modern Europe: Cultural Representations*, edited by Erin Campbell (Ashgate, 2006), p. 202.

WRINKLED IN TIME

178 Vita Sackville-West, *All Passion Spent* (Hogarth Press, 1931), p. 79.

179 *Altersroman*: The German term (age novel) was coined by Linda A. Westervelt by analogy with the term *Bildungsroman* in *Beyond Innocence, or the Altersroman in Modern Fiction* (University of Missouri Press, 1997), p. xii. See also Barbara Frey Waxman, who uses the term *Reifungsroman*, or "novel of ripening": *From the Hearth to the Open Road: A Feminist Study of Aging in Contemporary Literature* (Greenwood Press, 1990), p. 2.

179 "A slight irritability": Sackville-West, *All Passion Spent*, pp. 80, 24.

179 William Shakespeare, *King Lear*, edited by Barbara A. Mowat and Paul Werstine, updated ed. (Simon & Schuster, 2015), 1.4.302–3.

180 "If one is not to please oneself": Sackville-West, *All Passion Spent*, pp. 67, 68.

181 "Those days were gone": Sackville-West, *All Passion Spent*, pp. 117–18.

181 Michel de Montaigne, "On Certain Verses of Virgil," in *The Essays of*

Montaigne, translated by Jacob Zeitlin (Alfred A. Knopf, 1934), book 2, p. 49.

182 "She was eighty-eight": Sackville-West, *All Passion Spent*, pp. 201–2.

182 "So old that they were all": Sackville-West, *All Passion Spent*, pp. 207, 209.

183 "Had exploded a charge": Sackville-West, *All Passion Spent*, pp. 214–15.

183 Carolyn Heilbrun, *The Last Gift of Time: Life beyond Sixty* (W. W. Norton, 1997), p. 112. On friendship, see William Butler Yeats, "After Long Silence," in *The Collected Poems of W. B. Yeats*, edited by Cedric Watts (Wordsworth Editions, 1994), p. 226, and Ezra Pound, "Und Drang," in *Collected Early Poems of Ezra Pound*, edited by Michael John King (New Directions, 1976), pp. 167–74, especially p. 173. Laura Kipnis, *Against Love: A Polemic* (Pantheon Books, 2003), pp. 17, 34.

184 On telic versus atelic activities, see Kieran Setiya, *Mid-Life Crisis* (Princeton University Press, 2017), pp. 133–39.

184 "That little white box": Sackville-West, *All Passion Spent*, p. 223.

187 "Young people compel one": Sackville-West, *All Passion Spent*, p. 98.

188 "Think how much I shall annoy": Sackville-West, *All Passion Spent*, pp. 259, 288.

188 "The unled life": Andrew H. Miller, *On Not Being Someone Else: Tales of Our Unled Lives* (forthcoming).

188 John Keats, *Selected Letters*, edited by Robert Gittings (2002; reprint, Oxford World's Classics, 2009), p. 340.

188 "Eternally vanishing": Keats, *Selected Letters*, pp. 365, 370. Fanny Brawne, "March 27, 1821," in *Letters of Fanny Brawne to Fanny Keats, 1820–1824*, edited by Fred Edgcumbe (Oxford University Press, 1937), p. 26.

GIVE AND TAKE

190 Donald Hall, "The Porcelain Couple," in *Without* (Houghton Mifflin, 1998), p. 14.

194 "I wish you could feel": Donald Hall, "Air Shatters in the Car's Small Room," in *Without*, p. 27.

194 *Amour*, directed by Michael Haneke (Les Films du Losange, 2012).

195 " 'That's it, Perkins,' she said": Donald Hall, *The Best Day, The Worst Day: Life with Jane Kenyon* (Houghton Mifflin, 2005), p. 118; "Without," in *Without*, pp. 46–47, 47.

195 "Vincristine ara-c cytoxan vp-6": Hall, "Without," p. 47. "The days were endlessly the same": Hall, *The Best Day, The Worst Day*, p. 97.

198 "Jane said he looked": Hall, "Air Shatters in the Car's Small Room," p. 22; *Still Alice*, directed by Richard Glatzer and Wash Westmoreland (Lutzus-Brown, 2014), with performances by Julianne Moore and Alec Baldwin.

199 John Bayley, *Elegy for Iris* (Picador, 1999); *Iris*, directed by Richard Eyre (BBC, 2001); Alice Munro, "The Bear Came Over the Mountain," in *Hateship, Friendship, Courtship, Loveship, Marriage* (Knopf, 2001), pp. 275–323; and *Away from Her*, directed by Sarah Polley (Foundry Films, 2006). See also *The Savages*, directed by Tamara Jenkins (Fox Searchlight, 2007), with performances by Laura Linney and Philip Seymour Hoffman; the movie depicts how two siblings deal with a father who is spiraling into dementia.

199 The "omnipresent anxiety": Bayley, *Elegy for Iris*, pp. 38, 53, 39.

200 "Spreads to the one": Bayley, *Elegy for Iris*, pp. 38, 241.

200 Alix Kates Shulman, *To Love What Is: A Marriage Transformed* (Farrar, Straus and Giroux, 2008), p. 102. Hall, *The Best Day, The Worst Day*, p. 35.

201 How can longtime companions: See Kazuo Ishiguro, *The Buried Giant* (2015; reprint, Vintage International, 2016), p. 45: "How will you and your husband prove your love for each other when you can't remember the past you've shared?"

201 Gerard Manley Hopkins, "No worst, there is none," in *The Major Works*, edited by Catherine Phillips, rev. ed. (2002; reprint, Oxford University Press, 2009), p. 167.

202 Iris Murdoch, "The Sublime and the Good," *Chicago Review* 13, no. 2 (1959): 51. Bayley, *Elegy for Iris*, p. 127.

202 "A whole infantile language": Bayley, *Elegy for Iris*, pp. 33, 181, 51.

203 Marion Coutts, *The Iceberg* (Black Cat, 2014), pp. 166, 170, 266.

203 "If Iris could climb inside": Bayley, *Elegy for Iris*, p. 127.

203 Brian Aldiss with Margaret Aldiss, *When the Feast Is Finished: Reflections on Terminal Illness* (Little, Brown, 1999), p. 138.

204 "Inseparable—in a way": Bayley, *Elegy for Iris*, p. 127; Anne Roiphe also refers to her marriage in terms of Baucis and Philemon in *Epilogue: A Memoir* (HarperCollins, 2008), p. 212. Hall, "Letter in Autumn," in *Without*, p. 62.

204 "He felt shame": Donald Hall, "Blues for Polly," in *Without*, p. 34. "Lost

two thirds of a liver": Donald Hall, *Life Work* (Beacon Press, 1993), p. 123.

204 Jane Kenyon, "Otherwise," in *Otherwise: New and Selected Poems* (Graywolf Press, 1996), p. 214.

TEQUILA MOCKINGBIRD

209 "Batty man! Bum bandit!": Bernardine Evaristo, *Mr. Loverman* (Akashic Books, 2014), pp. 119, 130, 133. See also *Beginners*, written and directed by Mike Mills (Olympus Pictures, 2010), a movie about an elderly man coming out of the closet.

209 "To leave here": Evaristo, *Mr. Loverman*, p. 44.

210 "That the female is a female": Evaristo, *Mr. Loverman*, pp. 123–24.

210 "Indestructible ivories": Evaristo, *Mr. Loverman*, pp. 17, 11, 15.

211 "Second thoughts": Evaristo, *Mr. Loverman*, pp. 110, 206, 231.

212 "The good guys are all taken": Evaristo, *Mr. Loverman*, p. 212.

212 "Contemplating how": Evaristo, *Mr. Loverman*, p. 173.

213 "Any time this country starts Nazifying": Evaristo, *Mr. Loverman*, p. 115.

215 "All about philanderers": Evaristo, *Mr. Loverman*, p. 55.

216 Tequila Mockingbirds: For the recipe, see Tim Federle, *Tequila Mockingbird: Cocktails with a Literary Twist*, illustrated by Lauren Mortimer (Running Press, 2013), pp. 45–46. This book is the source of the punny cocktails mentioned later.

217 "Basically, what I have": Evaristo, *Mr. Loverman*, pp. 99, 250.

217 "Barrysexual—correction": Evaristo, *Mr. Loverman*, pp. 277, 270.

WINTERING

223 For my understanding of *The Winter's Tale*, I am indebted to the introduction to the play by Stephen Orgel, whose edition I use (Clarendon Press, 1996).

224 William Shakespeare, Sonnet 73, in *The Oxford Shakespeare: The Complete Sonnets and Poems*, edited by Colin Burrow (Oxford World's Classics, 2002), p. 527.

225 William Shakespeare, *Antony and Cleopatra*, edited by John Wilders (Routledge, 1995).

231 "The pellet with the poison": from *The Court Jester*, directed by Melvin Frank and Norman Panama (Paramount, 1955).

232 "Ole rocking chair": from Hoagy Carmichael's song "Rockin' Chair," composed in 1929.

234 Nicholas Delbanco, *The Years* (Little A, 2015), pp. 16, 87. This novel is a revision and extension of Delbanco's *Spring and Fall* (Grand Central Publishing, 2006).

234 "The school of second chances": Delbanco, *The Years*, pp. 189, 193, 216.

235 Hermia's "passion": Delbanco, *The Years*, pp. 225, 282, 284.

236 On the stresses of youthful and midlife marriages, see Maggie Scarf, *September Songs: The Good News about Marriage in the Later Years* (Riverhead Books, 2008). Scarf discusses the U-shaped curve of marital happiness: research indicates that "a couple's sense of satisfaction and well-being is at its peak during the honeymoon and then begins to erode." For couples who survive the erosion, "a more positive direction predictably occurs" (p. 78).

236 Marianne Moore, "Marriage," in *Complete Poems* (Penguin Classics, 1994), p. 63.

237 "The temporal *layers*": Zadie Smith, *On Beauty* (Penguin, 2005), p. 203.

237 "Two by two": Denise Levertov, "The Ache of Marriage," in *The Norton Anthology of Literature by Women: The Traditions in English*, edited by Sandra M. Gilbert and Susan Gubar, 3rd ed. (W. W. Norton, 2007), 2:863.

SILVER THREADS AMONG THE GOLD

238 Paul Auster's actual sentence is "Just because you wander in the desert, it does not mean there is a promised land"; *The Invention of Solitude* (Sun, 1982), p. 32.

239 Marilynne Robinson, *Gilead* (Farrar, Straus and Giroux, 2004), p. 19.

240 "Unspeakably precious": Robinson, *Gilead*, p. 129.

241 The "begats": Robinson, *Gilead*, p. 75.

241 "Not that I hadn't loved": Robinson, *Gilead*, pp. 55, 44, 55.

242 "As if my soul": Robinson, *Gilead*, pp. 203, 206, 209.

243 "Like a handsome young family": Robinson, *Gilead*, p. 141.

244 "Why'd you have to be": Robinson, *Gilead*, p. 50.

245 His "colored" wife: Robinson, *Gilead*, pp. 219, 220.

246 On the story of the prodigal son, see Peter S. Hawkins, "A Man Had Two Sons," in *Ancient Forgiveness: Classical, Judaic, and Christian*, edited by Charles L. Griswold and David Konstan (Cambridge University Press, 2012), pp. 158–75.

247 "Love is holy": Robinson, *Gilead*, pp. 209, 14, 139, 245.

247 M. H. Abrams, *Natural Supernaturalism: Tradition and Revolution in Romantic Literature* (W. W. Norton, 1971).

248 "Existence is the essential thing": Robinson, *Gilead*, p. 189.

248 "The beauty there is in him": Robinson, *Gilead*, p. 232.

248 "The Lord make His face": Robinson, *Gilead*, p. 241 (quoting Numbers 6:25–26).

249 "I say 'old Boughton'": Robinson, *Gilead*, p. 28.

250 "Make new friends": the beginning of a round sung by Girl Scouts.

RECOUNTING THE WAYS

252 "Old" and "had been old": Marilynne Robinson, *Lila* (Farrar, Straus and Giroux, 2014), p. 19.

252 "Pinched off little pills": Robinson, *Lila*, pp. 6, 12, 30.

253 "Was sharp as a razor": Robinson, *Lila*, pp. 133, 239, 241.

253 "Till it was worn soft": Robinson, *Lila*, pp. 13, 70, 134.

253 Cynthia Ozick, "The Shawl," in *The Norton Anthology of Literature by Women: The Traditions in English*, edited by Sandra M. Gilbert and Susan Gubar, 3rd ed. (W. W. Norton, 2007), 2:931–35.

255 The "beautiful old man": Robinson, *Lila*, pp. 34, 253.

255 "I can't see how": Robinson, *Lila*, pp. 84, 86.

255 "I want you to marry me!": Robinson, *Lila*, p. 89.

256 "Creeping into the old man's bed": Robinson, *Lila*, pp. 103, 253.

258 "Like a second mother": Robinson, *Gilead*, p. 12.

258 "You can eat the roots": Robinson, *Lila*, pp. 27, 21.

259 "It is seldom indeed": Robinson, *Gilead*, p. 194.

259 "Have to answer": Robinson, *Lila*, p. 101.

259 "If God really has": Robinson, *Lila*, pp. 129, 43.

260 She studies biblical texts: Robinson, *Lila*, p. 68. John Edgar Wideman includes a similar scene of redemptive biblical reading in a story about the

second chance of late-life love. See *Two Cities* (Houghton Mifflin, 1999), p. 51.

260 *"And out of the midst"*: Robinson, *Lila*, p. 68.

261 "Lovingly absorbed in the thoughts": Marilynne Robinson, "Imagination and Community," in *When I Was a Child I Read Books* (Farrar, Straus and Giroux, 2012), p. 21.

261 "Imagining what it is like": Ian McEwan, "Only Love and Then Oblivion. Love Was All They Had to Set against Their Murderers," *The Guardian*, 15 Sept. 2001, www.theguardian.com/world/2001/sep/15/ september11.politicsphilosophyandsociety2. "The basis of all sympathy": quoted in Kate Kellaway, "At Home with His Worries," *The Observer*, 15 Sept. 2001, www.theguardian.com/books/2001/sep/16/fiction.ianmcewan.

261 About 43 percent of adult Americans: Tracy Mumford, "Americans Aren't Reading Less—They're Just Reading Less Literature," *MPR News*, 7 Sept. 2016, www.mprnews.org/story/2016/09/07/books-reading-rates -down.

262 Stanley Cavell, *Disowning Knowledge in Six Plays of Shakespeare* (Cambridge University Press, 1987), p. 205.

262 Robinson, *Lila*, p. 261.

263 "Molded salad of orange gelatin": Robinson, *Gilead*, p. 143.

ENORMOUS CHANGES AT THE LAST MINUTE

268 *Love among the Ruins*, directed by George Cukor (ABC Circle Films, 1975).

268 A number of awards: In *George Cukor: A Double Life* (St. Martin's Press, 1991), Patrick McGilligan notes that "Emmys went to the writer (James Costigan) . . . and to both of the stars. . . . Cukor himself won a Best Directing Emmy" (p. 318).

272 *Love Is Strange*, directed by Ira Sachs (Parts and Labor, 2014).

273 The Icelandic movie *Ram*, directed by Grimur Hákonarson (Cohen Media Group, 2015), focuses on the enmity of two neighboring brothers who try to save the last unsickened sheep of their decimated herds. It ends with them holed up in a loving embrace during a ferocious snowstorm.

273 Grace Paley, "Goodbye and Good Luck," in *The Little Disturbances of Man* (Viking Press, 1968), pp. 18, 21, 21–22.

274 A charming scene: *Mrs Hurst Dancing and Other Scenes from Regency Life, 1812–1823*, watercolors by Diana Sperling, text by Gordon Mingay (Gollancz, 1981), plate 33.

276 "To me, fair friend": William Shakespeare, Sonnet 104, in *The Oxford Shakespeare: The Complete Sonnets and Poems*, edited by Colin Burrow (Oxford World's Classics, 2002), p. 589.

277 *Guess Who's Coming to Dinner*, directed by Stanley Kramer (Columbia Pictures, 1967).

277 *Something's Gotta Give*, directed by Nancy Meyers (Columbia Pictures, 2003); Nora Ephron, "I Feel Bad about My Neck," in *I Feel Bad about My Neck: And Other Thoughts on Being a Woman* (2006; reprint, Vintage Books, 2008), pp. 3–8; *It's Complicated*, directed by Nancy Meyers (Universal Pictures, 2009).

279 Robert Browning, "Love among the Ruins," in *Men and Women* (1855; reprint, Ticknor and Fields, 1863), p. 1; online at name.umdl.umich.edu/ABF1203.0001.001.

CHRISNUKKAH

280 William Shakespeare, Sonnet 138, in *The Oxford Shakespeare: The Complete Sonnets and Poems*, edited by Colin Burrow (Oxford World's Classics, 2002), p. 657. On Shakespeare's sonnets about aging, see Christopher Martin, *Constituting Old Age in Early Modern English Literature, from Queen Elizabeth to "King Lear"* (University of Massachusetts Press, 2012), pp. 113–25; also see his excellent discussion (pp. 125–35) of Donne's "The Autumnal," mentioned later in this chapter.

282 "Youth is hot": William Shakespeare, "The Passionate Pilgrim," in *The Oxford Shakespeare*, p. 353.

282 John Donne, "The Autumnal," in *The Complete English Poems*, edited by A. J. Smith (Penguin Classics, 1971), p. 105.

285 William Carlos Williams, "Asphodel, That Greeny Flower," in *Pictures from Brueghel, and Other Poems* (New Directions, 1962), pp. 153–82.

286 Toni Morrison, *Jazz* (1992; reprint, Vintage International, 2003), p. 228. Morrison's fifty-year-old Violet and Joe Trace have outlived their era's life expectancy for nonwhites. See Philip J. Hilts, "Life Expectancy for Blacks in the U.S. Shows Sharp Drop," *New York Times*, 29 Nov. 1990,

www.nytimes.com/1990/11/29/news/life-expectancy-for-blacks-in-us-shows-sharp-drop.html.

286 "Picked out and determined": Morrison, *Jazz*, pp. 95, 133, 135.

286 "The one thing everybody loses": Morrison, *Jazz*, pp. 120, 228.

287 "Ecstasy is more leaf-sigh": Morrison, *Jazz*, p. 228.

287 The last page of *Jazz*: Morrison, *Jazz*, p. 229. In *Toni Morrison: A Biography* (Greenwood Press, 2010), Stephanie Li argues that the narrator of this complicated narrative is the book itself and that Morrison viewed it as a love song to the reader (p. 89).

289 Philip Larkin, "An Arundel Tomb," in *The Complete Poems*, edited by Archie Burnett (Farrar, Straus and Giroux, 2012), pp. 71–72.

290 "The hands the wrong way round": Larkin, *The Complete Poems*, p. 437.

291 "Love isn't stronger": Larkin, *The Complete Poems*, p. 436.

291 The "central paradox": A. T. Tolley, *My Proper Ground: A Study of the Work of Philip Larkin and Its Development* (Carleton University Press, 1991), p. 88.

291 For Shakespeare's boasting, see Sonnet 55, in *The Oxford Shakespeare*, p. 491.

291 Emily Dickinson produced two versions of "Safe in their alabaster chambers" (J. 216 / P. 124), both of which can be found in *The Complete Poems of Emily Dickinson*, edited by Thomas H. Johnson (1960; reprint, Back Bay Books, 1976), p. 100.

292 "Time's wingèd chariot": Andrew Marvell, "To His Coy Mistress," in *Complete Poems*, edited by Elizabeth Story Donno (1972; reprint, Penguin Classics, 2005), p. 51.

293 Anne Carson, *Eros the Bittersweet: An Essay* (Princeton University Press, 1986), p. 124.

293 On W. H. Auden's revision of the final line in "September 1, 1939," see Edward Callan, "Disenchantment with Yeats: From Singer-Master to Ogre," in *W. H. Auden*, edited by Harold Bloom (Chelsea House, 1986), p. 170.

293 Maxine Kumin, "The Long Marriage," in *The Long Marriage: Poems* (W. W. Norton, 2002), p. 85. Alix Kates Shulman, *To Love What Is: A Marriage Transformed* (Farrar, Straus and Giroux, 2008), p. 4.

293 Carolyn Heilbrun, *The Last Gift of Time: Life beyond Sixty* (W. W. Norton, 1997), p. 164.

294 Charlie Smith, "The Meaning of Birds," in *Indistinguishable from the Darkness* (W. W. Norton), pp. 83–84.

LATER

298 "For them, making love": Arlene Heyman, "The Loves of Her Life," in *Scary Old Sex* (Bloomsbury, 2016), p. 4 (ellipses hers).

298 "Looked like a small round neck": Heyman, "The Loves of Her Life," p. 7.

298 Trying "very hard not to look pleased": Heyman, "The Loves of Her Life," p. 13.

298 Recent handbooks by sex educators stand in contrast to the reticence of creative writers. See, for example, Joan Price, *Naked at Our Age: Talking Out Loud about Senior Sex* (Seal, 2011).

299 "Taut as a young girl's": Heyman, "The Loves of Her Life," p. 22.

302 *45 Years*, directed by Andrew Haigh (Artificial Eye, 2015).

304 James Joyce, "The Dead," in *Dubliners* (1920; reprint, Penguin Books, 2014), pp. 151–94.

304 David Constantine, "In Another Country," in *In Another Country: Selected Stories* (Biblioasis, 2015), pp. 9–20; quotation, p. 12.

304 "Liberty and Union": Maureen N. McLane discusses Marianne Moore's use of Daniel Webster's famous speech in her poem "Marriage": see *My Poets* (Farrar, Straus and Giroux, 2012), pp. 100–101.

305 Guy de Maupassant, *Like Death* (1890), translated by Richard Howard (New York Review of Books, 2017), p. 201.

305 Charles Olson, "Maximus, to himself," in *The Maximus Poems*, edited by George F. Butterick (University of California Press, 1983), p. 56. Elizabeth Bishop's letter to Alice Methfessel is quoted by Megan Marshall in "Elizabeth and Alice: The Last Love Affair of Elizabeth Bishop and the Losses behind 'One Art,'" *New Yorker*, 27 Oct. 2016, www.newyorker.com/books/page-turner/elizabeth-bishop-and-alice -methfessel-one-art. The letter was sent in March 1971, "a month before [Bishop's] sixtieth birthday and two weeks past Methfessel's twenty-eighth."

306 Roland Barthes, *A Lover's Discourse: Fragments*, translated by Richard Howard (1978; reprint, Penguin, 1990), p. 131.

Text Credits

"The Aging Lovers," from *Poems of Love and Marriage*, by John Ciardi. Copyright © 1988 Judith Ciardi. Reprinted with permission of the Ciardi Publishing Trust, John L. Ciardi, Trustee.

"In View of the Fact," from *Bosh and Flapdoodle*, by A.R. Ammons. Copyright © 2005. Reprinted by permission of John Ammons c/o Writers' Representatives, LLC.

"Late-Flowering Lust," from *Collected Poems*, by John Betjeman © 1955, 1958, 1962, 1964, 1968, 1970, 1979, 1981, 1982, 2001. Reproduced by permission of John Murray, an imprint of Hodder and Stoughton Ltd. Reproduced by John Murray Press, a division of Hodder and Stoughton Limited.

Excerpt from translation of Fyodor Tyutchev's *Last Love* by Vladimir Nabokov. Copyright © Vladimir Nabokov, used by permission of the Wylie Agency LLC.

Excerpts from "The Porcelain Couple" "Air Shatters in the Car's Small Room" and "Without" from *Without: Poems* by Donald Hall. Copyright © 1998 by Donald Hall. Reprinted by permission of Houghton Mifflin Harcourt Publishing Company. All rights reserved.

Jane Kenyon, excerpt from "Otherwise" from *Collected Poems*. Copyright © 2005 by The Estate of Jane Kenyon. Reprinted with the permission of The Permissions Company, Inc. on behalf of Graywolf Press, Minneapolis, Minnesota, www.graywolfpress.org.

Excerpts from "An Arundel Tomb" from *The Complete Poems of Philip Larkin* by Philip Larkin, edited by Archie Burnett. Copyright © 2012 by The Estate of Philip Larkin. Reprinted by permission of Farrar, Straus and Giroux.

"An Arundel Tomb," from *The Complete Poems of Philip Larkin*, by Philip Larkin, edited by Archie Burnett. Copyright © 2012 by The Estate of Philip Larkin. Reprinted by permission of Faber and Faber Ltd.

"The Meaning of Birds." Copyright © 1990 by Charlie Smith, from *Jump Soul: New and Selected Poems* by Charlie Smith. Used by permission of W. W. Norton and Company, Inc.

Acknowledgments

SANDRA M. GILBERT suggested the title for this book. Her extraordinary influence on my writing goes beyond the boundaries of our collaborative work on many projects. I can never fully express my gratitude to her for encouraging me to pursue the topic in my own idiosyncratic way.

Many colleagues and friends have offered suggestions about texts and contexts. My thanks go to Cynthia Bannon, Bob Bledsoe, Matt Brim, Jim Craig, Ellen Dwyer, Jason Fickle, Jen Fleissner, Constance Furey, Erik Gray, the late Kenneth Gros Louis, Edward Gubar, Kelly Hanson, Bert Harrill, Kenneth Johnston, Eileen Julien, Oscar Kenshur, Sarah Knott, Stephanie Li, Julia Livingston, Ellen MacKay, Herbert J. Marks, Alyce Miller, Janel Mueller, Walton Muyumba, James Naremore, Cornelia Nixon, Alvin Rosenfeld, Scott Sanders, John Schilb, Zak Szymanski, Stephen Watt, and Charlotte Zietlow.

Christoph Irmshur sent me hither and yon with fabulous recommendations. Nancy K. Miller, just a hoot and holler away on email, shared her bleakly hilarious insights into feminism, friendship, and cancer.

Administrators at Indiana University facilitate my work, as do the generous secretaries in the English department. Other individuals enrich my life in too many ways to enumerate, so I resort to listing: Evelyne Brancart, Judith Brown, Shehira Davezac, Nathan Davis, Dyan Elliott, Jonathan Elmer, Mary Favret, Georgette Kagan, Jon Lawrence, George Levine, Andrew H. Miller, Alexandra Morphet, Suneil Setiya, the late Aidan Smith, Jan Sorby, Jayne Spencer, and Rick Valicenti. As for my British cousins—Colin and Helen, Bernard and Georgina—I consider you a source of strength.

My assiduous research assistants—Shannon Boyer and Patrick Kindig—schlepped books and movies from the library, filled in footnotes, negotiated permissions, and queried an early draft. When a manuscript is drafty, it feels dicey to give it to readers. With abiding appreciation, I thank those who gave me the precious gift of their expertise: Judith Brown, John Eakin, Susan Fraiman, Kieran Setiya, and Elizabeth Abel enhanced the manuscript with abundant insights.

Ellen Levine, my agent, has always been a font of wisdom and a pillar of strength. For this book, she was also an inspiration. Jill Bialosky, my editor, became the driving force in my effort to integrate literary interpretation with personal reflection—without subordinating one to the other. Her energetic and forthright advice definitively shaped this book. Jill's assistant, Drew Elizabeth Weitman, astonished me with her savvy responses. It was a great comfort to have my cherished friend and former graduate student Alice Falk spin the safety net that only a brilliant copy-editor can provide. Over the years I have also been buoyed by the support of a traveling salesperson who knocked on my office door in Ballantine Hall decades ago. Since then, Julia Reidhead—now the president of W. W. Norton—has been a treasure for scholars invested in the humanities.

Of course, Don Gray was advising throughout the process of composition. Our gallant sons-in-law—John Lyons, Kieran Setiya, and Jeff Silverbush—provided books, movies, jokes, ideas, and much-needed ballast. We cannot express our devotion to our beloved girls: Julie Gray and Susannah Gray, Marah Gubar and Simone Silverbush. Or our delight in our marvelous grandsons. Jack, Eli, Samuel, and Jonah: long may you prosper. I promise not to be hoodwinked by phone callers claiming to be one of you with an urgent "Grandma, my car just crashed on Sunset Boulevard and I need your credit card numbers." I will try to be circumspect.

31192021591258